CHILDREN'S LITERATURE IN THE CLASSROOM

CHILDREN'S LITERATURE IN THE CLASSROOM

MATTHEW D. ZBARACKI

Sage

1 Oliver's Yard
55 City Road
London EC1Y 1SP

2455 Teller Road
Thousand Oaks
California 91320

Unit No 323-333, Third Floor, F-Block
International Trade Tower
Nehru Place, New Delhi – 110 019

8 Marina View Suite 43-053
Asia Square Tower 1
Singapore 018960

Editor: James Clark
Editorial assistant: Esosa Otabor
Production editor: Victoria Nicholas
Copyeditor: Diana Chambers
Proofreader: Christine Bitten
Indexer: Silvia Benvenuto
Marketing manager: Lorna Patkai
Cover design: Bhairvi Vyas
Typeset by: C&M Digitals (P) Ltd, Chennai, India
Printed in the UK

© Matthew D. Zbaracki 2024

Apart from any fair dealing for the purposes of research, private study, or criticism or review, as permitted under the Copyright, Designs and Patents Act, 1988, this publication may not be reproduced, stored or transmitted in any form, or by any means, without the prior permission in writing of the publisher, or in the case of reprographic reproduction, in accordance with the terms of licences issued by the Copyright Licensing Agency. Enquiries concerning reproduction outside those terms should be sent to the publisher.

Library of Congress Control Number: 2023939309

British Library Cataloguing in Publication data

A catalogue record for this book is available from the British Library

ISBN 978-1-5297-3168-2
ISBN 978-1-5297-3167-5 (pbk)

At Sage we take sustainability seriously. Most of our products are printed in the UK using responsibly sourced papers and boards. When we print overseas we ensure sustainable papers are used as measured by the Paper Chain Project grading system. We undertake an annual audit to monitor our sustainability.

To Jane, thank you!
To Emma, for teaching me determination.
To Oliver, for providing the music.
And to my mom, for starting me on the journey.

In memory of Janet Hickman (FMOA).

CONTENTS

About the author   ix

1. Children's literature   1
2. Beginning books   19
3. Picture books   35
4. Transitional novels   53
5. Poetry   63
6. Non-fiction   75
7. Fantasy   89
8. Realistic fiction   101
9. Historical fiction   117
10. Indigenous literature   129
11. Digital texts   143
12. Humour   153
13. Future leanings   167

Index   177

ABOUT THE AUTHOR

Matthew Zbaracki has lived in Australia since 2008 and is State Head of Victoria in the National School of Education at Australian Catholic University, Victoria. He is formerly of the University of Northern Colorado and Rhode Island College

He is author of the book *Best Books for Boys* (Libraries Unlimited) and co-author of *Language and Literacy* published by Oxford University Press, and *Listen Hear* and *Books and Beyond*, both published by Heinemann. His 2015 book, *Writing Right with Text Types* (Oxford University Press) won an Australian Educational Publishing Award.

CHILDREN'S LITERATURE

WHAT WE WILL LEARN
- What literacy is.
- Early stages of literacy development.
- The role of visual literacy in children's literature.
- What children's literature is and the benefits it provides children.
- The importance of reading aloud to children.
- Strategies for reading aloud.
- How key literary theories relate to children's literature.

Where do we start? Well, it is probably best to start at the beginning, and that is with literacy. So what is literacy? The definition has changed over the years, but in its broadest sense, one of the earliest definitions of literacy was limited to reading and writing (Emmitt et al., 2014). This definition has changed and expanded more now, and, as Emmitt et al. propose, 'literacy is more than reading, writing: it is the use of multiliteracies, including reading and writing, for a range of culturally determined purposes' (p. 15). That may seem both basic and broad, and perhaps you can relate to it when you think of your own school experiences. However, literacy has changed and developed recently, and now it is more commonly defined as Reading, Writing, Speaking, Listening *and* Viewing. Winch et al. (2010) discuss this change and, again, connecting back to the ideas and definition discussed above, 'while the term "literacy" still expresses the basic idea of making meaning through and from text (whatever form that text takes and whatever ways it is engaged with), the popularity of the term "multiliteracies" demonstrates recognition of the burgeoning text modes' (p. 465). This supports the idea that

there is much change in the definition and field of literacy. Why the change, you may be asking yourself? Well, before we go there, let us start with what is commonly referred to as the literacy process for younger children.

Table 1.1 A child's initial journey to literacy

Listening	From birth, and even before, babies and young children are constantly listening. They listen to their parents' voices, to stories and to songs. Children listen to and absorb everything around them.
Viewing	Babies start by using their eyes and view the world around them. Think about how you have seen a baby looking at and with their eyes, and how they stare at faces, objects (mobiles above cots/cribs) with limited colours, so why not continue this focus (pun intended)?
Speaking	The constant listening that a baby does encourages them to experiment and this is where speech begins. At around 1 year of age, a child will change their babbling into single first words, and then they are off and start putting words together and becoming more fluent speakers.
Writing	Young children learn the alphabet and, using those letters, they put them together, most commonly forming the letters of their own name, before creating basic small words.
Reading	At the same time as they learn letters and form their name, young children are beginning the reading process. Notice that the word 'process' is used here because children do not magically learn to read; it is a process that is quite involved. From learning letter names to small words, and building on those skills, learning to read takes time and practice.

The table above shows the developmental process of a child as they learn those key aspects of literacy. It becomes clear that early literacy experiences are crucial for a child to become literate. In fact, well-known Australian children's author, Mem Fox (2005), has written extensively on this idea and extols the importance of a child having a thousand stories read to them before they start school. She highlights how, if a young child is read three stories a day, this thousand-book goal could be met in one year alone. There has been much research (Trelease, 2013) about how important it is to read to young children, and this will be discussed later in this chapter.

VIEWING

First, though, the more modern definition of literacy must be discussed. You will recall that the new definition includes the concept of *viewing*. Let us revisit that idea further. Why do you think viewing is now included in literacy?

How often do you view things in your life? From looking at your mobile phone for texts, or social media posts, or videos, or even directions, we view those things and so much more. For example, think about when you watch a newscast. How many things are happening on the screen at one time? It could be a newscaster telling the main story. At the same time there is a video playing of the news event, while at the same time on the bottom of the screen the 'scroll' rolls across the screen telling viewers more about what is happening, or what might be coming up. In a newscast alone, viewers are bombarded with information from a number of different places.

Think about how this can almost lead to information overload. Wilhelm (2004), however, also discusses the importance of visual literacy at length:

> students read visual texts in many arenas: cartoons, television shows and movies, websites, other multimedia texts, and so on. So it makes sense to use visuals in the classroom to link school reading with these other cultural literacies. (p. 16)

Children of all ages are exposed to visuals throughout their everyday lives, and, as Wilhelm has discussed, it is critical that we value these experiences both in and out of school.

Image 1.1 A double-page spread from Bob Graham's *Vanilla Ice Cream* (Copyright © 2014 Blackbird Design Pty Ltd from VANILLA ICE CREAM. Written & Illustrated by Bob Graham. Reproduced by permission of Walker Books Ltd, London, SE11 5HJ, www.walker.co.uk)

Picture books themselves are examples of visual literacy. Children must differentiate text and image in order to create meaning from the book. This is an example of visual literacy. Visual literacy plays a crucial role in literacy in general. Children are not the only ones who must navigate texts with multiple visual images and then comprehend them. One example of this is with the Bob Graham book, *Vanilla Ice Cream*. This story about a sparrow who travels the world and helps a young girl with her first taste of vanilla ice cream is a wonderful example of the images helping tell the story, and at times being the only vehicle to do so, with the various wordless pages.

Take a look at Image 1.1. Notice in this double-page spread that the sparrow is a key part of the story in the left page, and on the right-hand page the four sequence boxes still include the sparrow, but the viewer (reader) must navigate the four images in order to understand the role the sparrow continues to play. This is a perfect example of what a young reader must do in order to comprehend a picture book. Again, it is clear that viewing truly is a necessary component of literacy. Now it is important to briefly delve into the other literacy components as well.

LISTENING

According to Opitz and Zbaracki (2004), listening 'is an active process that includes the attention of meaning to the spoken message' (p. 2). They also state more simply that 'listening has not occurred unless comprehension has occurred' (p. 2). While we all believe that listening is important, it is actually a literacy component that is rarely taught formally to children. While children might often hear the words 'you need to listen', they are rarely formally taught how to do so. When one examines how large our listening vocabularies are, we realise the great importance this literacy component has.

SPEAKING (ORAL LANGUAGE)

Winch et al. (2010) discuss how oral language is the combined processes of listening and talking. They also note that 'development in oral language involves learning how to use language for a growing number of purposes in an increasing range of situations' (p. 51). Children practise a lot of their initial language through speaking and experimenting with vocabulary and grammar, which assists in their early oral language development. This is the opportunity where they can put the words they have heard into use and experiment with new vocabulary. Children's literature that has repetitive text in it models for children the effective use of language. Think about books such as *We're Going on a Bear Hunt* or *Where is the Green Sheep?* Both books use repetitive text ('We're going on a bear hunt, we're going to catch a big one. We're not scared . . . ' or 'Where is the green sheep, here is the green sheep . . . ', etc.) to not only engage the reader and involve them in the reading, but to help teach and develop vocabulary and language skills.

READING

Reading is probably the most well-known element of the five literacy components and it connects directly to the other four aspects. When examining these five ideas, it is clear how they are interconnected. It is crucial to understand, as discussed earlier, that reading is a process and not one person has a specific experience where they simply learned how to read. As Winch et al. (2020) write: 'reading is the process of constructing meaning from text, whether written or graphic, paper-based or digital' (p. 4). Throughout the reading process, children learn from a number of different sources – for example, listening to books that are read to them, learning new genres and stories from books they read, and even telling stories to their family and friends. While reading may be the most common element of literacy, it is one that connects across the others and shows how important it is to develop all aspects of literacy.

WRITING

At the beginning of the chapter it was discussed how young children began by writing their names and then learning new words. However, the writing process is a key one in which children learn to write for different audiences and purposes. They also learn different text types and genres for writing, and children's literature helps with learning and modelling not only the writing process, but also how texts can be written and used for different audience and purposes. Zbaracki (2015) notes: 'writing can at times be a daunting process, but this does not need to be the case. Writing can also be a fun and enjoyable experience where children and adults can experiment while entertaining and informing audiences' (p. 15). Children's literature is one of the best ways to help children understand the power of writing and provide model texts to teach them the skills and strategies needed to be an effective writer.

So what does this all mean? Well, to begin with, it accentuates how important the role of children's literature is in a child's literacy journey. Realistically, children's literature is a way to develop initial literacy in children. Using all the things a baby hears from before birth and onwards, as well as Mem Fox's advice based on research for the number of stories a child needs to be read before they start school, as well as the complexity of visuals in our society, we begin to see how important this journey is and how children's literature is a vital part of the process.

For the sake of this book, children's literature is defined as books for children from birth to age 12. After age 12, there is a transition to young adult literature as the concepts, topics and themes in the books become more complex. A common sequence for children's literature is seen in the table below.

Table 1.2 Children's literature developmental sequence

Beginning books	A primary example of this category are board books.	Birth to age 2
Picture books	The most well-known example of children's literature.	2–8 years
Transitional novels	These books are meant for children as they transition from picture books to longer novels.	7–8
Novels	The traditional novel that is written for children with appropriate content and vocabulary.	9–12
Young adult literature	More complex literature that addresses more involved life issues for older ages.	12 years and above

Hopefully, you are beginning to see the important role that children's literature plays both at home and in schools as well. Children's literature is a tool that not only supports children in their literacy journey, but can also help them see the world in new and different ways. Winch et al. (2010) write: 'children's books, from board books for pre-schoolers to sophisticated texts for young adults, are a vital part of a lifelong participation and life-enriching engagement in literature' (p. 466). It is essential to help children become actively involved in this process to truly engage and enjoy the plethora of wonderful books, authors and genres available to them within children's literature. This book presents a wide range of genres including beginning books, picture books, transitional novels, poetry, non-fiction, fantasy, humour, realistic fiction, historical fiction, indigenous, digital and humorous. As McDonald (2018) recommends, 'students need to taste a diverse literary smorgasbord' (p. 11), and these different genres help make a very delicious meal of literature. Daley (2019) continues this theme and its impact, noting, 'encouraging young people to read widely and enjoy a balanced literary diet can add immeasurably to their enjoyment of recreational reading' (p. 112).

The importance of reading widely through different genres is not limited to having a balance of genres and encouraging lifelong readers; it also helps to familiarise children with specific text types, vocabulary, information, narrative styles, and much more. Specifically, when children read non-fiction texts, they learn how the structure is factual, will include visuals to help provide information and will have specific formats (table of contents, glossary, index, etc.). Helping students understand a variety of structures not only assists them with reading, but it also connects to their writing, again finding that link to literacy, and children's literature helps them with this.

Not only are there motivational and literacy reasons for the benefit of children's literature, there are also social and emotional reasons as well. For example, early children's literature was written for children to learn how to behave, socialise and even acculturate themselves to contemporary society (Winch et al., 2010). This will be discussed further in the picture book chapter. Contemporary children's literature can help children learn about current issues in contemporary times, educate about historical times and events, create fantasy worlds with complex issues and ideas or just entertain with a good story. In a sense, this helps children learn what Winch (2010) term 'cultural literacy, or a knowledge and appreciation of this world of others and valuing difference' (p. 479). Children's literature allows children to live life vicariously through the characters in the books they read. They can learn to navigate family issues, friendships, bullying, learn about new cultures and countries, or even about specific historical events and what happened during those times.

READING ALOUD

With the importance of reading aloud to children introduced earlier, this section will delve deeper into this concept. Mem Fox is well loved in Australia and her advice is important, but it was actually Jim Trelease who has written extensively about this in his book, *The Read-Aloud Handbook*, now in its seventh edition as it was first published in 1982. As has already been established, it is essential that children are read to at a young age and that caregivers are able to provide children with a plethora of experiences with text. As Trelease (2013) writes: 'As you read to a child, you're pouring into the child's ears (and brain) all the sounds, syllables, endings, and blendings that will make up the words she will someday be asked to read and understand' (p. 15). The image on page 8 highlights this, showing baby Emma being read to three days after she was born, with her older brother, Oliver, listening as well. The picture alone connects with what both Daley (2019) and Fox (2005) support about how parents should start reading aloud to their child from the day they are born. Kiefer et al. (2004) discuss the impact that reading aloud to children has on their motivation to read: 'Hearing books read aloud is a powerful motivation for the child to begin to learn to read' (p. 10). Returning to the picture on the next page, not only does the reading experience provide both children with necessary text and language experiences, it also validates reading and in turn sets the two children up for literacy success when they start school. As Mem Fox (2005) warns us, 'children who have not been regularly talked to, sung to or *read aloud to* from birth find life at school much more burdensome than they otherwise might' (p. 13, emphasis mine).

BUST A MYTH

Reading aloud: children do not need to hear the same book more than once.

Think about how many times you have watched your favourite movie or television show again and again. Children are no different from adults, and repeated readings of the same book allow them to hear the flow of language and vocabulary, and to connect with characters and stories they enjoy. Repeated readings with young children should be celebrated and enjoyed for as long as they enjoy the book.

Image 1.2 Oliver and Emma sharing a read-aloud experience together from an early age

Reading aloud can raise a few challenges for teachers and parents alike. With this in mind, the chart below presents you with a top-ten approach of ideas to consider when you plan a read-aloud experience for your classroom or children. Hopefully, these suggestions will support you as you learn, practise and begin to read aloud to your students.

Table 1.3 Top ten tips for reading aloud

Book selection: appropriate for the age of the child.

Make sure the book tells a good story.

Always read the *entire* book through before reading it aloud.

Use voices to help read with expression.

Look for the flow of language in the book.

Identify places for interaction to maintain engagement/participation.

Ensure that the illustrations work *with* the text.

Think about how you will hold the book.

Practise reading the book out loud multiple times.

Have genuine enthusiasm/enjoyment as you read the story.

BOOK SELECTION

The first place to start when planning a read aloud is to choose a book that is appropriate for the audience. This means that you need to consider the age of the child(ren) and the content as well. So, when choosing a book to read aloud, it must be one that will engage and interest the listeners. For example, young readers will enjoy stories with less text, but engaging pictures, while older readers will be able to listen to longer stories with more text, but again engaging pictures are a must in picture books. A book like *This is Not My Hat* is a good title for children around the age level of prep students, as the story about a little fish who has stolen a hat from a bigger fish contradict what the images are showing. The big fish knows who has taken his hat and is on the chase, while the little fish thinks he will be able to get away with the theft. A couple of wordless pages at the end of the book allow readers to infer what they think has happened in the end. Book selection for read alouds may be easier with picture books, but one key idea for novels is to choose a book that has a main character that is one year older than the child(ren) you are reading to. Book selection, though, is one of the cornerstones of a good read aloud.

MAKE SURE THE BOOK TELLS A GOOD STORY

This point connects directly with book selection. Not only does the book need to be appropriate for the audience, it needs to tell a good story. If the story is not enjoyable, then children will lose interest very quickly and the read-aloud moment is lost. Those moments are key building blocks for a child's literacy journey. Think about the well-loved Australian picture book *Koala Lou* by Mem Fox. The beautiful story about a young koala who feels neglected when her siblings are born strives to hear how much she is loved by her mother again. Although she tries to please her mother by winning the Bush Olympics, Koala Lou learns the beautiful connection of love between a parent and child, and learns that her mother has and always will love her. A newer title *Duck and Penguin are NOT Friends* (Julia Woolf) is an entertaining story about two girls who are good friends, but their toy stuffed animals, duck and penguin, are not. Readers will enjoy seeing the pictures and realising they do not always match what the text says, especially the interactions between duck and penguin. Both of these titles engage the reader/listener because they tell a good story. That is paramount to the success of a read aloud.

ALWAYS READ THE *ENTIRE* BOOK THROUGH BEFORE READING IT ALOUD

This is an important idea and sometimes the reason why is quite clear. If you have not read the entire book, you will not know what the content of the book is. This is important so that you are able to prepare for what issues may arise with your students if there are any sensitive topics. For example, *Girl from the Sea*, by Margaret Wild, seems like a traditional picture book. However, when exploring the story and illustrations more deeply, there is a lot going on within the book. Who is the girl in the story who seems to have a coloured shadow in the illustrations? What is her relationship to the family walking and playing by the sea? In order to address the questions or ideas that children may have while hearing and seeing the story, it is important that you as the reader know the entire book first. The language in the book is something else to be considered. By reading the book through first, you are able to be prepared to address any language you feel is inappropriate or that you do not want children to be exposed to. Regardless of the reason, it is important that teachers and parents are familiar with the book before they read it aloud to a class or their child.

USE VOICES TO HELP READ WITH EXPRESSION

This is probably one of the most enjoyable aspects of reading aloud. It is where you can make the story come alive for the child. As Mem Fox writes, 'The more expressively we read, the more fantastic the experience will be' (p. 36). Be open to finding people that you can listen to read aloud and get ideas from them. Go to the local library or classroom and listen to a story time, and take some ideas and voices from them. Think about the voices you may hear in your head as you read the book to yourself and practise with those voices. This author once read a book and thought, 'Yeah, that's an okay book', but when he heard a colleague read the book with a specific accent thought, 'Wow! That's a perfect voice, it makes the book come *alive*' and from that day forward has used the same voice whenever reading the book aloud. *Baz and Benz* by Heidi McKinnon is a great book to look at for voices. The story has two characters and their speech is differentiated between a blue font and a green font. This helps provide practice when telling the difference between characters. *Don't Call Me Bear!* by Aaron Blabey is another title that allows an easy way to use different voices. When the main character is angry, it is easy to use a loud exasperated voice. When koala is providing detailed information about koalas, you could use a more scientific formal voice. These are good ways to start to hear different voices in your head for different characters in the books you find. When there are multiple characters and so, multiple voices, one trick to keep track of the voices is to think about the position of your mouth when you read certain characters. Remember what Mem Fox (2005) advises: 'There's no right way of reading aloud, other than to try and be as expressive as possible' (p. 36).

LOOK FOR THE FLOW OF LANGUAGE IN THE BOOK

The language and vocabulary in a book play a crucial role in the story and how it is read. Mem Fox can tell you exactly how many words are in her book *Koala Lou* (585, after 49 drafts) and each of those words are crucial in the success of the story and how it flows. Mem understood that each word played an essential role in the flow of the story. Pay attention to the rhythm of the words and if there are repeated sections that can engage children. Books like *A Hippy-Hoppy Toad* (Archer and Wilsdorf, 2018) do this well with the opening lines:

> In the middle of a puddle
>
> in the middle of a road
>
> on a teeter-totter twig
>
> sat a teeny-tiny toad.

Whether it be a catchy rhyme or repeated text, the flow of language is what gets the reader of the text excited to read and share the story with others.

IDENTIFY PLACES FOR INTERACTIONS TO MAINTAIN ENGAGEMENT/ PARTICIPATION

Children, no matter their age, enjoy being involved in a read aloud. It is important to see where and how you can involve a child in the book. Daley (2019) writes: 'Engaging all of your child's senses in book-based experiences is crucial in maintaining their attention and creating a sense of playfulness' (p. 10). With younger children, this may be with a repeated phrase such as 'Where is the Green Sheep?' from Mem Fox's book with the same title, or it may be an action. Many of Jan Thomas's books can be used for this purpose – specifically, *Can You Make a Scary Face?* (Thomas, 2009) as an example. For older readers and longer books, it is important to find a place where you can break up the story and provide interaction, asking for a prediction or a question. It is critical, though, that your stopping point does not disrupt the flow of the story. Regardless of what you choose, it is important that you are aware of the age of your audience or length of the book and plan accordingly for ways to actively engage your listeners.

ENSURE THE ILLUSTRATIONS WORK WITH THE TEXT

The role of illustrations in books will be talked about extensively in the picture book chapter, and it also plays an important role with reading aloud. The images are ones that will enhance the book, but it is also important that they do not distract, overwhelm or disengage the listener. Finding a book that has illustrations that are an integral part of the text can add to the enjoyment and love of the book. *My Friend Fred* by Francis Watts (2019) is a perfect example of a book where the audience must pay close attention to the illustrations in order to find the hints that reveal who the friend is. Leigh Hobbs's Mr Chicken series also does this with the illustrations revealing how the different characters actually feel about their interactions with Mr Chicken on his different adventures. Illustrations are a key part of a picture book, which you will learn more about in the picture books chapter, so it is important to find books where the illustrations work with the book and make the story more engaging and enjoyable.

THINK ABOUT HOW YOU WILL HOLD THE BOOK

Parents have an advantage when it comes to reading a book to children because the experience allows them to be side by side, together, during the read aloud. Teachers, however, need to decide how they will hold the book during a read aloud. This is a key idea that connects the reader with the audience and impacts the read-aloud experience and can also be a very personal choice. Some choose to hold the book facing the audience so the children can see the pictures while the book is being read. This can lead to complications as you are reading across your body and facing the book, not your audience as you read. I much prefer to read the pages to the children first, and then show the illustrations. 'Why?', you may ask. The main reason is because I want the child to create their own visuals in their mind before they see the text. A key reading comprehension strategy is visualisation; by showing the pictures second, it allows the child to create their own image in their head first. As Wilhelm (2004) notes: 'reading aloud to students is a great way to help them build their image-making abilities' (p. 58). Waiting to show the illustrations also strongly encourages listening comprehension so students are not simply looking at the illustrations and not paying attention to what you are reading. Remember, though, how the book is held is up to each individual person.

PRACTISE READING THE BOOK OUT LOUD MULTIPLE TIMES

This idea may seem pretty basic, but it is no less important. Think about how we encourage people to practise a speech before they give one in front of an audience, or how performers in a play or musical rehearse their lines again and again. This is the same idea for read alouds. By practising challenging words and pages, it ensures the flow and enjoyment of a book. One of my all-time favourite books is *The Web Files* by Margie Palatini (2001) and it has some tricky alliteration/tongue twisters in it. It is through much practice (and at this point hundreds of read alouds) that I can successfully navigate the page that has the following text:

> The squad room. My partner and I were still trying to *quack* the case, but we didn't have any idea whom to I.D.

'Rats!' said Bill.

'That's it!' I shouted. There was only one suspect who was sneaky enough, wily enough, and tricky enough to *pick a peck of perfect purple almost-pickled peppers, take a tub of tasty tart tomatoes, and lift a load of luscious leafy lettuce.* (Palatini, 2001, italics mine)

HAVE GENUINE ENTHUSIASM/ENJOYMENT AS YOU READ THE STORY

Children will pick up on the excitement a teacher or adult has when reading a book. That excitement is contagious and a key element of a read aloud. By finding a book that is appropriate, tells a good story and can engage children, you are well on your way to a good read aloud. By making sure you are motivated and excited, this will carry over to your students. Allow your 'inner' performer to come out and make reading an exciting time for your students. Making stories such as *Ten Little Fingers and Ten Little Toes* or *Ducks Away*, both by Mem Fox, come alive with your voice, expressions and intonations is essential for a successful read-aloud experience. Be open to discovering ways to bring to life memorable characters such as Rodney in Michael Gerard Bauer's *Rodney Loses It* and help present their true feelings and emotions while reading aloud, and ensure you are able to actively engage your listeners.

These top ten tips for reading aloud to children will hopefully assist you in helping young children experience literature and literacy as well as grow their literacy skills. By engaging children in books and modelling good reading, it helps motivate them to be readers. Whether it is a parent or a teacher, it is essential that children see the adults in their lives as readers. This helps motivate them to read and explore new books, authors, genres, and so much more. Always remember that 'Hearing books read aloud is a powerful motivation for the child to begin to learn to read' (Kiefer et al., 2004: 10).

THEORIES AND CHILDREN'S LITERATURE

Theories: the word alone can send a shudder up the spine of even the most devout readers. Why are theories included in this book, you may ask. McGillis (2015) queries this as well, writing:

> Should the teaching of children's literature necessarily involve the teaching of theory? Is there such a thing as a theory of children's literature? Or is theory something that exists independently of children's literature, like a flag or an ointment that we wave or apply when we begin to discuss children's books?

Table 1.4 Key literary theories found within children's literature

Theory	Description	Examples from children's literature	Connections between books and theory
Critical theory	This theory reflects a type of philosophy that aims to critique society, social structures and systems of power. Within literature, you will be able to see how structures and systems of power in society are explored and examined.	*Last Stop on Market Street* and *Milo Imagines the World* (both by Matt de la Peña); *Wolfred* (Nick Bland).	*Last Stop on Market Street* breaks down social and power structures within society as the story follows a young boy and his grandmother as they travel on the bus to volunteer at a soup kitchen. The people they meet both on the bus and at the soup kitchen help address the societal elements of critical theory.
Postmodernism	In this theory, readers are invited to navigate non-linear structures and attend to the various symbolic representations, literary codes and conventions in order to make sense of the complexities inherent in these texts. One off-shoot of this theory is that it will playfully eschew definitive meaning and even parody that quest.	*The Stinky Cheese Man and Other Fairly Stupid Tales* (Jon Scieszka); *Black and White* (David Macaulay).	Both these titles are the groundbreaking innovators of postmodernism in picture books. The books do not follow a linear structure, but instead follow a completely different structure in which the stories could be intertwined or even stand alone. Both books are well worth finding.
Post-structuralism	In this theory, both truth and meaning are dynamic rather than stable, meaning we all pull different meanings from the same text, or, to use the old expression, 'you can never dive into the same river twice'. Within this theory it is important to remember how different readers will construct different meanings with the same text in each different reading.	*Mirror* (Jeannie Baker); *My Two Blankets* (Irena Kobald).	*Mirror* is a wonderful wordless picture book in which two stories mirror each other. Readers must construct their own meanings as they comprehend the stories being told, and find both similarities and differences between the stories.

Theory	Description	Examples from children's literature	Connections between books and theory
Post-colonial theory	When exploring this theory, think about the traditional concept of 'colonisation' and how it has been found in the world of foreign control over people, cultures and countries. Now take the idea one step further and think about how children might be 'colonised'. Because adults write and create the books, they determine how the children within the stories behave or are expected to behave. It is important to think about how books might even challenge this in some of the characters we meet in the stories.	*No! Never!* (Libby Hathorn); *Why Can't I be a Dinosaur?* (Kylie Westaway).	How do we expect children to behave? Both of these stories have a young child who wants to have their own way and expresses this quite clearly. However, they also learn that there is a time and place for certain responses and the children learn what expectations and behaviour are. Both books highlight how children's literature can incorporate colonisation of children into the books.
Gender theory	Within this theory, it is important to remember that gender is a sociocultural construct. For this theory, the books that include gender roles will encourage shattering gender stereotypes, challenge gender norms and illustrate characters who may not fit into 'traditional'gender roles. When exploring this theory, it is important to examine books that both challenge and shatter stereotypes, as well as maintain the stereotype so that children are able to see and understand all aspects within this theory.	*Julian is a Mermaid, Julian at the Wedding* (both by Jessica Love); *The Runaway Hug* (Nick Bland).	The Julian books are ones that break down gender stereotypes as the main character celebrates (and is celebrated) who he is and is free to express this with no judgement from others. *The Runaway Hug* maintains the traditional gender roles as readers see the father trying to watch a sporting event on the television while the mother is doing the laundry. It is important for readers to see and understand both the stereotypes and the books that shatter those stereotypes as well.

Regardless of where you fall on the theory spectrum, it is something that is important to acknowledge and understand, as it helps readers delve into books more deeply as well as expand our knowledge and understanding not only of the books, but also the world around us. We must all remember not to get caught up in theories, so we lose the purpose of children's literature to tell a good story while still being able to entertain and educate young readers, viewers and listeners.

The previous table serves as an infograph of information about different theories, and includes specific titles from children's literature that connect well with the theory.

Now that you have an awareness of some key literary theories found within children's literature, it is important to further this and explore the idea of a 'canon' within this field. This is typically known as the classic books or stories that have survived the test of time and are still relevant and read today. While children's literature may not have an extensive canon, perhaps it is better to term this the 'modern canon' of children's literature. We remember such titles as Maurice Sendak's *Where the Wild Things Are*, Eric Carle's *The Very Hungry Caterpillar*, Mem Fox's *Koala Lou* and *Possum Magic*, Graeme Base's *Animalia*, Dr Seuss's *The Cat in the Hat* and Margaret Wise Brown's *Goodnight Moon* which fit into this modern canon. Why is a modern canon needed, you may ask. Nodelman and Reimer (2003) answer this:

> The category of 'the canon' has been used in the past to authorize some texts and exclude others. But the concept of a canon can continue to be useful, if only because it allows us to think about the implications of the idea that some books are better than others. (p. 247)

The book you are reading now contains evaluation criteria for the different genres included. Because of this, some books can be determined to be stronger than others. Remember, however, that these determinations are subjective. Just because we like a book and can justify why we like it using the criteria, does not mean that everyone will agree. The criteria found throughout this book is meant to be a guide as you read and discover new titles and authors.

CONCLUSION

Returning to the start of the chapter, we have learned about the components of literacy and how young children learn language as well as the key components of literacy. It is important that children are assisted throughout their literacy and language journey, and children's literature is one key aspect that has significant benefits for children. The section about reading aloud presented ten tips to help you as you plan read alouds to children or students in your own classrooms. Being aware of the importance of literacy and its role in a child's life is crucial. As Kiefer et al. (2004) write: 'A love of reading and a taste for literature are the finest gifts we can give to our children, for we will have started them on the path of a lifetime of pleasure with books' (p. 6). And all of this is why you hold this book in your hands right now. You understand the importance and critical need for children's literature and its place in the classroom and in children's lives. It is hoped that through the pages of this book you are able to discover new authors, illustrators and titles that will entertain and educate you about children's literature. As you finish this book, the goal is for you to have evaluation criteria and skills that help you recognise the aspects of quality children's literature. This will make your selection process easier when you are looking for books in the future and provide you with the opportunity to explore and better learn the values of children's literature further, as well as understand its crucial role in a child's literacy journey.

WANT TO KNOW MORE?

Lysaker, J. and Hopper, E. (2015). 'A kindergartner's emergent strategy use during wordless picture book reading'. *The Reading Teacher*, 68(8): 649–57. Available at: https://doi.org/10.1002/trtr.1352

Vallotton, C.D., Gardner-Neblett, N., Kim, L., Harewood, T. and Duke, N.K. (2023). 'Ready for read-alouds: 10 practices for book-sharing with infants and toddlers'. *The Reading Teacher*, 76(4): 459–69. Available at: https://doi.org/10.1002/trtr.2176

REFERENCES

Daley, M. (2019) *Raising Readers: How to Nurture a Child's Love of Books*. Brisbane: University of Queensland Press.

Emmitt, M., Zbaracki, M., Komesaroff, L. and Pollock, J. (2014) *Language and Learning: An Introduction for Teaching* (6th edn). Oxford: Oxford University Press.

Fox, M. (2005) *Reading Magic: How Your Child can Learn to Read Before School and Other Read-aloud Miracles* (new edn). Tuggerah, NSW: Pan Macmillan Australia.

Kiefer, B.Z., Hepler, S.I., Hickman, J. and Huck, C.S. (2004) *Charlotte Huck's Children's Literature* (8th edn). Maidenhead: McGraw-Hill.

McDonald, L. (2018) *A Literature Companion for Teachers* (2nd edn). Newtown, NSW: Primary English Teaching Association Australia

McGillis, R. (2015) 'Looking in the Mirror: Pedagogy, Theory, and Children's Literature'. In C. Butler (ed.) *Teaching Children's Fiction*. London: Palgrave Macmillan.

Nodelman, P. and Reimer, M. (2003) *The pleasures of children's literature* (3rd edn). Boston, MA: Allyn and Bacon.

Opitz, M.F. and Zbaracki, M.D. (2004) *Listen Hear!: 25 Effective Listening Comprehension Strategies*. Portsmouth, NH: Heinemann.

Trelease, J. (2013) *The Read-Aloud Handbook* (7th edn). New York: Penguin Books.

Wilhelm, J. (2004) *Reading IS Seeing*. New York: Scholastic.

Winch, G. (2020) *Literacy: Reading, Writing and Children's Literature* (6th edn). Oxford: Oxford University Press.

Winch, G., Ross Johnston, R., March, P., Ljungdahl, L. and Holliday, M. (2010) *Literacy: Reading, Writing and Children's Literature* (4th edn). Oxford: Oxford University Press.

Zbaracki, M. (2015) *Writing Right with Text Types*. Oxford: Oxford University Press.

2

BEGINNING BOOKS

> **WHAT WE WILL LEARN**
> - What beginning books are.
> - The different types of beginning books.
> - What makes quality alphabet and counting books.
> - What a concept book is.
> - How to evaluate beginning books.

Where does it all begin? Well, from what we learned in Chapter 1, it all begins with reading aloud to very young readers and beginning books. Beginning books are what start off a child's reading journey. Charlotte Huck and Doris Young (1961) wrote years ago about the idea of lap books and those types of books have changed and developed through the years. The board book is probably the most common type of beginning book that provides an early book experience for very young children. These books are durable in construction with thicker cardboard pages that will withstand a child's teeth as well as being thrown out of a crib (cot) when a child has finished 'reading' them. For example, when Oliver was a young toddler, he was given a number of books to read in the morning as he was in his cot/crib. He had a much-loved book called *Goodnight Gorilla* by Peggy Rathman in board book format. As discussed above, board books are meant to be very durable. However, this particular copy was read, and reread, and reread again and again, thus leading to its demise as the binding broke and it fell apart and had to be replaced. This story is shared for more than the reason to explain how well worn a board book can become, but to showcase the power a book can have and how children enjoy 'reading' and 'rereading' these books again and again. The story

highlights the idea that beginning books are a child's first experience with books, whether they are being read to by adults in their lives, or they are exploring them on their own. Through these early literature experiences, children learn concepts about print (Clay, 1993) and how books work and that they have meaning, and they learn how to 'read' them on their own. It is important to provide very young children with the opportunity to have these text and reading experiences.

In Chapter 1, the importance of young children having numerous experiences with literature was established. As Kiefer et al. (2007) note: 'the young child who has the opportunity to hear and enjoy many stories is also beginning to read' (p. 142). With the large number of books published each year also discussed in Chapter 1, it is important to establish that beginning books are those that help a child learn such things as the alphabet, numbers, colours, shapes, animals, and other concepts. It can be quite challenging to determine what a quality beginning book is, as there are so many to choose from. The easiest way to establish this is to identify key categories. The two main categories consist of alphabet books and counting books.

There are a number of common features found in beginning books: to begin with, they are usually *small* in size, so young hands are easily able to hold and interact with the book. As mentioned before, they are *durable*, which is usually in 'board book' format. To entice and invite young readers, these books are *colourful*. Look at the books by American author and illustrator Todd Parr, with titles such as *The Feelings Books, Dos and Don'ts*, and this author's favourite Todd Parr title, *Underwear Dos and Don'ts*. This bright and colourful style is also found in many books by Australian illustrator Ambelin Kwaymullina with how she highlights the main objects in her illustrations with yellow (see titles such as *Billie and the Blue Bike, Bush Dance* and *Joey Counts to Ten*).

Overall, a good beginning book will include these three features:

- **Inviting:** they invite a child into the book/story in order for them to enjoy the story and come back to the book again.
- **Engaging:** the book will engage them, whether through repetitive text, interactive features (lift the flaps) or just an engaging storyline.
- **Repetition:** the book will include repetition through repeated sentences, phrases or words, which incorporates the first two features inviting them into the book and engaging them as well.

BUST A MYTH

All beginning books in board book format are good for young readers.

It is important to remember that there has been a lot of commercialisation, especially in the field of children's literature. This means that some books that are in board book format do not provide a quality literacy experience for young children and can be quite a weak book to share with children. It is important to use the evaluation criteria to determine the quality of board books.

Early beginning books for young babies are very durable books and usually in black and white, with one picture on each page. This is done intentionally as it supports a baby's eyes in focusing on one image only. Also, the use of black and white is done because a baby is unable to distinguish colours until they are around five months old. While some parents may believe that their baby is unable to comprehend what is happening when they read to their infants, this again supports Mem Fox's point that children need as many reading experiences as possible. This helps the child when they begin school: 'Boys and girls who enter school having had many learning experiences with books are well prepared to acquire literacy, and these children are more likely to remain active readers well into late primary (elementary) and middle school' (Kiefer et al., 2007, p. 142).

Table 2.1 Beginning book age guide

Birth to 6 months	Very basic black-and-white illustrations with one picture on each page. Reading is more talking to the child about what is seen on the page and in the illustration. These experiences are more about letting the child hear the caregiver's voice.	Books such as *Mesmerised*, *Baby's Very First Black and White Book: Faces*, and *First Baby Days; Night, Night*, are all books that fit this category. They each have black-and-white images to draw the baby's eyes to the pages. These books are meant to be a chance for the parent to talk with the baby about what is seen on each page. The back cover of *Mesmerised* states: 'during the first few months of life, high-contrast, black and white images are much easier for baby to see. The fun, simple graphic in *Mesmerised* will not only enhance your baby's vision, but will keep your baby stimulated and engaged during these early stages of development.'
6 months to 12 months	There will be more colour in the illustrations now and may have a couple of objects to talk about with the child, and this will start the one-to-one correspondence between word and image.	As stated, these books will have a bit more colour on the pages, but still limited to one or two images on a page. Jeannette Rowe's books *Zoo* and *Pets* are examples of these books. They have one image on each page and the animals included are easily recognisable.
12 months to 18 months	There may be shorter stories coming into play at this point and more active/engaging stories, illustrations or play within the book. Books will bring in more tactile experiences.	At this point there may be small stories that are being told in these books. There may also be a theme behind the book. There will definitely be a tactile experience for the child as found in the popular That's Not My . . . series. For example, in *That's Not My Koala* the young child can feel the textures of different animals parts, such as the koala's nose, belly or paws. *Never Touch a Crocodile* is another example of a book that allows for a tactile experience.

(Continued)

Table 2.1 (Continued)

18 months to 24 months	These books will have more engagement as well, through song, rhyme, movement.	In these books the engagement level will remain high. These books will have the tactile experience, and may include a lift the flap element. The books may also have a song or action for children to complete. Well known songs like Five Little Monkeys are examples of these beginning books. These types of beginning books are the first link for children to explore the idea of *learning to talk, and then learning to read*. Well known classic, *We're Going on a Bear Hunt* (Rosen, 1989) has an Australian twist with Laine Mitchell and Louis Shea's *We're Going on a Croc Hunt*. By using Australian animals and habitats the well known classic has a new approach that continues to keep the classic song in play. This connects well with what Winch et al. write: 'Babies and toddlers often first respond to the sounds of music and *singing*' (2006, p. 147).

Toy books are another type of beginning book, although they are not necessarily a concept book. Instead, toy books are interactive and engaging, providing a tactile experience for young children. Kiefer et al. (2007) describe these books as having 'a kind of "built-in participation" as part of their design' (p. 124). The first example of this type of book was *Pat the Bunny* by Dorothy Kunhardt, published in 1940. While viewed as a classic, it also inspired a whole new 'genre' of books that actively engage children in reading and provide participation experiences for them. *Dear Zoo* by Rod Campbell is an extremely popular example of a toy book in which a child writes to the zoo for a pet and the zoo sends different packages back to the child. Each page has lift-up flaps in which the child discovers a different animal the zoo has sent. Another popular example is the That's Not My . . . series by Fiona Watt (mentioned in the table above – *That's Not My Train, That's Not My Wombat, That's Not My Lion*), where the child is able to feel the different textures, and touch and feel the book, actively engaging in the book. Other books do the same thing with eyes that roll around or with holes on the pages. There are also toy books for older readers which are predominately pop-up books. A wonderful example of a pop-up book author/illustrator is Robert Sabuda. His artistic creations include such titles as *Alice's Adventures in Wonderland, The Twelve Days of Christmas* and *The Wizard of Oz*, featuring an actual pop-up tornado! These books are definitely more for older readers as the pop-ups can be quite delicate. Pop-up books can be a fun (and interactive) way to present classic stories, as Sabuda does, and inspire creativity among children of all ages.

Press Here by Hervé Tullet is a brilliant engaging title that will have young children directly interacting with the book. This is the ultimate participation book as it asks children to press the buttons in the book, shake the book and move the book around to control what happens on the next page. Children will believe that the directions they are following are actually controlling what happens in and to the book. This is an amusing and engaging title for young and old alike. His newest title *Tap, Tap, Tap: Dance, Dance, Dance* is another wonderful example of an interactive book that will have young children engaging in the title again and again.

ALPHABET BOOKS

Alphabet books, however, are probably the main types of beginning books, as they begin the process of teaching young children the alphabet. There are some key criteria that alphabet books should contain.

1. Clear presentation: whatever objects are presented should be done so clearly and they should be easily identifiable.
2. One or two objects on a page: this depends on age. For very young children, there should be one-to-one correspondence between the picture on the page and the letter/word. For an older child, there will be more images for each letter and there may be other concepts in the book as well.
3. Avoid the use of objects that are known by several names. Similar to the first point, the objects should be clear and easily identified as one thing, and not objects that can be referred to with multiple terms.

A wonderful example of a basic alphabet book that meets this criteria is *Alpha Pups!* (Beer, 2018). Notice how in this board book format, the pages contain one object on a page that is easily identifiable. While the dogs included may not always be the most well known, each letter is represented accurately and is the beginning of each word. The Baby series by Francis Lincoln Children's Books (*Baby Loves Calm; Baby Loves Earth*) has a number of ABC books that have one word for each letter, although the vocabulary is a bit more complex for young babies.

Alphabet books can be quite complex, however. You may remember Graeme Base's classic alphabet book *Animalia*. The book has a plethora of objects on each page that represent the letter *and* it has a mystery to solve as well. This shows how alphabet books can be more complex for those children who know the alphabet already. *Alphabetical Tashi: A Story Told in ABC* is an example of a more complex alphabet book that has more developed vocabulary and contains a narrative, which shows that it is more than the traditional point-and-name format commonly found in alphabet books.

Sometimes it can be a challenge to identify what makes a good alphabet book. May I introduce you to 'The Zbaracki Test'? Alphabet books can be very creative, but there are challenges, too. For example, look at these letters in alphabet books: Q, X and, of course, Z. How are they used? Are the words understandable and relatable? With the letter Q there are many commonly used words – for example, Queen or Quilt. A good alphabet book will go well beyond the obvious and include new vocabulary but not uncommon words either. A good alphabet book finds a solid balance with the chosen words. The letter X is, of course, a great challenge. The most common choice in alphabet books is the word Xylophone, but what other words are there, you may ask? This is where a good alphabet book is creative and finds a word that goes beyond the usual. However, this can cause issues as well. For example, what happens if it is an alphabet book about animals and every word chosen has the first letter that matches for each page – for example, A = Armadillo, B = Baboon, C = Cat, but when you get to X and it equals Ox – it does not match the pattern of using the initial letter in the word? Instead of using the first letter, it is using the ending letter and the pattern is off, which is confusing to young children just learning the alphabet. A published ABC book about feelings used the letter X to include Xx – 'I love you'. Again, the pattern that was established in the book from the letter A was the initial letter to represent the word – e.g., A = angry, B = Bashful, etc. When the reader arrives at the letter X, this is completely different from the established pattern, as well as the fact that Xx does not directly connect to 'I love you'. Coming back to the issue mentioned earlier about new vocabulary, but not completely uncommon words, there is a published animal ABC book that includes the word 'uakari' for the letter U. You may have had to look that word up; if so, you can see the importance of making sure that the word chosen is a common name that is easily known.

Another issue with alphabet books is that objects chosen are not ones that could be identified as other objects starting with a different letter. For example, a book that uses a rabbit for the letter R can be confusing to young children who could say 'look at the cute . . . bunny or hare', which would lead to confusion. Another example of this is if a book had a picture of an alligator for the letter A. Again, confusion would come because in Australia it would most likely be referred to as a crocodile, and some might even say 'dragon', again leading to letter confusion.

Some alphabet books will use a tracker for each page that highlights each letter that is being addressed on the specific page. This supports a reader as they are looking and learning the alphabet. There is an abundance of alphabet books to discover and they range in appropriateness for different ages. Some will be for very young children who are just learning the alphabet. In this instance, it is crucial that there is only one letter and object to avoid confusion. With older children for whom the alphabet is already established, there may be more objects on the page, or the objects included may expand a child's vocabulary. *An A to Z Story of Australian Animals* by Sally Morgan is an example of such a text. With animals such as Bilby, Dingo, Quokka and Zebra Finch, there is a mix of known and new animals to learn, and it is definitely an alphabet book that would pass the Zbaracki Test. *Dreaming of Australia*

A to Z could be paired with *An A to Z Story of Australian Animals*, as both are excellent titles that take children through Australian culture and animals to present the alphabet. They definitely also both pass the 'Zbaracki Test' by the way they use the beginning letter pattern throughout the book and include objects with the difficult letters of Q and X.

A very creative alphabet book is *The Alphabet of Peculiar Creatures.* This book will expose children to some animals they know and many new ones, too. Each page presents the animal, as well as including a pronunciation guide for the animal's name and some factual information. It will definitely interest animal-loving children and is a good title for children who already have the alphabet established.

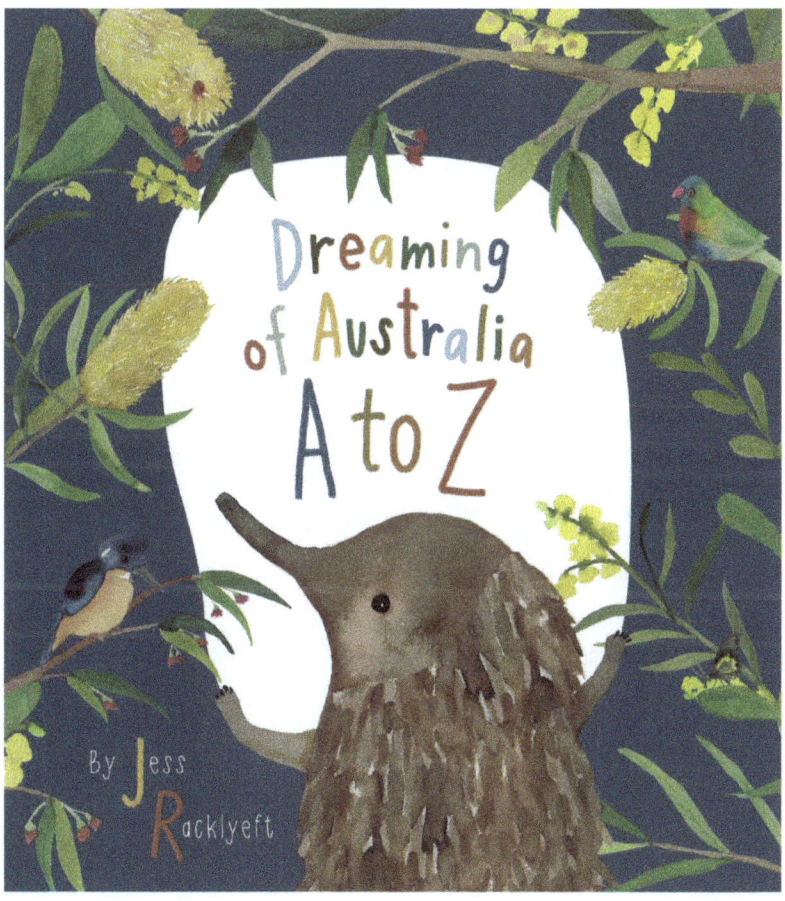

Image 2.1 Racklyeft: *Dreaming of Australia A to Z* (with permission from Windy Hollow Books)

Table 2.2 Evaluation criteria: beginning books

ABC books	Counting books
Clear representation of objects.	Accuracy is crucial.
For younger children only 1 or 2 objects per page/letter.	Objects to be counted are easily recognisable.
Objects are clearly known by a young child (or does it pass the 'Zbaracki Test'?).	Common objects that are easily known to children that match with the book (i.e., animals that young children would know).
Illustrations are not cluttered or 'too busy'.	Illustrations are not cluttered or 'too busy'.
Objects that are not known by multiple names (i.e., rabbit/bunny, alligator/crocodile).	Objects are placed into groups or sets that are easily differentiated.
Clearly identifiable purpose for the ABC book that is understandable for the main audience.	Number concepts are easy to understand and there are no competing concepts in the book.
Clear illustrations that connect with the style of the book.	The concepts being introduced/taught are appropriate for the age level of the book.
Words connected to each letter are appropriate and match the pattern (i.e., beginning letters: A = Apple, B = Ball, X = Xylophone, not Ox).	

Some strong alphabet books to be aware of:

Alphablock is a very thick alphabet book that is in board-book format and very interactive and engaging. The book has one easily identifiable object per page and is easy to enjoy. The format of the book is similar to a pop-up book so children are able to see the letter in a 3-D format.

The Oi Frog! series is a fun alphabet book series that has frog writing his own alphabet book and has fun variations of words starting with the initial letter and having a fun rhyme scheme.

There are some alphabet books that are designed for older readers with more complex storylines, format or content. For example, *Anisa's Alphabet* is an amazing book that confronts the challenging topic of refugees. The rhyming text and powerful images showcase the difficulties that refugees face.

M is for Mutiny! History by Alphabet is another title for older readers. The book presents the history of Australia through the alphabet and also presents some complex ideas, as well through the pages (A is for Acknowledgement of Country, K is for Kangaroo, R is for Rum Rebellion). The concepts are more challenging and each page provides further information about them. *A is for Australia* by Frane Lessac is an alphabet book presenting different places in Australia and the double-page spreads present further information about those places. It is

Image 2.2 Mike Dumbleton: *Anisa's Alphabet* (with permission from MidnightSun Publishing)

a good example of a multilevel text in which readers can pick or choose sections to read, or they can read the entire book, as the multilevels of text do not take away from the overall meaning found within the book.

Not Yet, Zebra and *Allergic Alpaca* are both books that are designed for older readers who already have the alphabet established. They are fun books that will reinforce the alphabet in a fun way. *Allergic Alpaca* is a very creative book that avoids the pitfalls of the Zbaracki Test and allows children to have fun with a very expressive alpaca.

COUNTING BOOKS

Counting books are the second most common beginning books. This category is one that teaches young children how to count and identify numbers. Again, there are key criteria to address when exploring counting books:

1. *Accuracy is essential.* Whatever number is given, the illustrations must clearly match the number. For example, if the number is four and the illustration depicts four lion cubs, those lion cubs must be clearly established without additional lions (adults) on the page, or the child would be counting more than the four that are on the page.
2. *Common objects.* The objects depicted in the illustrations must be clearly identifiable and understood. The book should include objects that young children would easily be able to identify and relate to (animals such as ducks, dogs or frogs).
3. *Concepts in counting are easy to determine or understand.* Does the book count up to 10 or 20? Is the book counting up to 10 and back down again? For younger readers, the concept must be basic and easy to follow (counting to ten); for older readers, it can be more complex (counting the total number of objects throughout the book or learning how to double numbers).

Let's Count Australian Animals by Ochre Lawson is a very simplistic counting book using common Australian animals as the objects to be counted. The animals are easily identified and counted. The book counts up to ten and then includes a picture of all the animals together in the end.

A Parade of Animals by Roger Priddy is a tactile counting book that encourages young children to engage with the pages. This book is good for very young children experiencing books and counting with an adult in their lives, as they can touch and feel the book while learning numbers. *Koala: A Book of Counting* by Patricia Hegarty is another tactile counting book. The book has a wonderful rhyming verse that allows children to count koalas from one to ten. There are cut-out finger holes where the koala's ears are allowing the tactile experience, and again, the basic counting allows children to learn and engage with the text.

Counting Our Country by Jill Daniels is a solid example of a beginning board book that teaches the concept of counting. There is one-to-one correspondence between the image and the text (number) on the page. The fact that is uses Australian animals and also provides the Indigenous, Ritharrnju language from the Northern Territory makes the book even stronger.

Little Koala Lost by Blaze Kwaymullina tells the story of a koala trying to find his family. As he goes around the forest asking different animals for help, he is being greeted by animals that will help the young reader count up to ten.

Well-known Australian author Mem Fox's *Ducks Away!* will delight young children as they follow a fun story about a family of ducks and also learn to count to five. The illustrations are lively. The book could easily be paired with Derek Anderson's *Little Quack* published in the United States.

Joey Counts to Ten by Sally Morgan is a wonderful example of a very early counting book. The objects on each page are common Australian animals. Each is highlighted in a yellow or orange silhouette so they are easily identifiable. The numeral is on each page and a story is being told in the book as well. It would be a good book to use to help children learn how to count. *Let's Count Australian Animals* by Ochre Lawson is another title that will help young children learn to count to ten using native Australian animals in the illustrations. *One Keen Koala* by well-known author Margaret Wild and well-loved illustrator Bruce Whatley is a school-based counting book told in rhyme with counting up to twelve.

One Banana, Two Bananas by Adam and Charlotte Guillain is a fun adventure with bananas as they count up to eight, and then an additional two bananas join the adventure. The word play and creativity throughout the story will engage young readers on the adventure and add to the counting as well.

Chicken Break! A Counting Book by Cate Berry is a fun adventure about ten chickens whose main goal is to fly the coop (or escape), but when they are all on the loose, they get tired and one by one return back to the farm. The book does a nice job of counting up and then back down.

Ten Sleepy Sheep is a wonderful Australian counting book by Renée Treml that could be read to children at night as they prepare to go to sleep. The book counts down from ten using common Australian animals. The soothing colour palate continues the calming theme through the book, and works well for a quiet time or bedtime book.

One Blue Shoe by Jane Godwin is an enjoyable book that teaches both counting and number concepts. The book starts off with a child looking for their missing shoe and counting different items along the way. In the middle, there are specific pages that invite the child to count the different objects on the pages counting up to the number ten. In the end, the child finds their missing shoe, while learning the concepts of counting and numbers along the way.

Ten Clumsy Emus is a fun board book that will have children laughing as they learn to count. The emus get into some fun exploits and the long necks can slightly complicate the counting, but with adult guidance children will enjoy counting up to ten with the emus.

As children get older and learn their numbers, counting books become more complex. For example, *One Fox: A Counting Book Thriller* counts up to ten, but there is a twist in the story that will delight younger readers as well. *Can You Find 12 Busy Bees?* also counts up to 12 and will have readers looking for all the animals on each page up to 12. The illustrations by Patrick Shirvington are amazingly detailed.

For even older readers, there is *Found in Sydney: A Counting Adventure* and a companion book, *Found in Melbourne*. These picture books take readers through the iconic sights in the cities of Sydney and Melbourne while counting up to 12. It also addresses larger numbers – 100, 1,000 and even 1 million. The titles do a nice job of showcasing the beauty of both cities.

Another good title for older readers is *When Numbers Met Letters*. This story was published in the US and is about a classroom clash between the letters and numbers in the room. Chaos and puns ensue as they compete for who is better – letters or numbers. When the Roman Numerals intervene, order is finally able to be restored in the classroom.

CONCEPT BOOKS

As discussed earlier in the chapter, concept books play a critical role in helping young children learn about new concepts and ideas, and expand their learning. Galda and Cullinan (2006) confirm, 'concept books contribute to a child's expanding knowledge and language by providing numerous examples of an idea. Some books present shape, colour, size, or sound, through many illustrations' (p. 59). This section will explore different examples of concepts such as shapes, colours and opposites to help educate younger readers.

Shapes and Colours by John Canty is a basic shape and colour book that would be a good book for young children to read with an adult in their lives. The book presents a number of different outlines of shapes in a specific colour – for example, red. The next page has the exact image within the shape. For example, with red, there is a fire truck, tomato, balloon and strawberry, to name a few. Children will be able to identify well-known objects through the outline, but they will also explore and learn new objects as well.

This is a Book of Shapes by Kenneth Kraegel is a humorous take on board books and shapes. The book introduces three shapes and then contains a humorous image not at all related to the learning of shapes. Then the pattern is re-established with three new shapes. The back and forth between learning and humour will have young children enjoying whatever comes next. *A Trapezoid is Not a Dinosaur!* by Suzanne Morris, is an entertaining adventure for older readers that presents a number of different shapes in a humorous story. Trapezoid is confused as a dinosaur for a local play about space. During the story, he meets a number of other shapes; the word play in the book adds to the humour and the learning of new concepts, and all the shapes learn the importance of having a trapezoid in space travel.

Jurassic Pug Knows Shapes by Katie Abey is a fun way to teach shapes from basic objects that children will see around them. Jurassic Pug is a pug dog dressed up as a dinosaur. He encounters different shapes around him and presents them to children – for example, a bicycle tyre is a circle, a door is a rectangle. Children will delight in the silly character of Jurassic Pug, while also learning about shapes that surround them in their worlds.

Watch This!: A Book about Making Shapes by Jane Godwin and Beci Orpin is a creative way to teach shapes to young children. The book uses photographs of children in different shapes. For example, three children are photographed in a triangle and two children are photographed making a big square. This is a good way for young children to see what shapes they can make both by themselves or with their friends.

Aussie Animal Opposites by Elizabeth Lea is a concept book that teaches both opposites and Australian animals. Each page has one Australian animal and two words to describe it. For example, one page has a 'young yabbie' and the opposite is an 'old owl'; the opposites and Australian animals work well to teach concepts, and the letter alliteration helps as well.

Sometimes the new concept can be a story that comes from a child's perspective. Chris Raschka's *New Shoes* does exactly that. All the images are from a child's perspective as they look at their worn-out shoes and then take a trip to the shoe stop to find a new pair of shoes. Raschka's well-known illustration style is clear in this book.

A newer title by Raschka that is worth reading with young children is *Mama Baby*. This is an engaging title that would be an excellent read aloud between mother and child as they talk and play together. Both of these books would work well with very young children.

COLOURS

Crab: A Snappy Book of Colours written by Patricia Hegarty (who also wrote *Koala: A Book of Counting*, discussed earlier) is a fun story about a little crab who snaps his way past a number of different friends in the ocean while learning a few colours along the way. Similar to *Koala*, the book has cut-out pages in the shape of the claws that young children can touch and explore while reading.

Roo Knows Blue by author Renée Treml presents a lesson in colours as a kangaroo is hopping around seeing different friends and learning some colours. The text presents a song and some repetition, which will engage young readers into the story as well.

Colouroos by Anna McGregor is a colourful tale of different coloured kangaroos (red, blue, yellow) that hop around Australia and meet up, and when they do, secondary colours are created. This is a good example of a story with a concept of colours taught throughout it as well.

Green on Green by Dianne White is a beautiful story told about the colours seen throughout the year. The book is from the US perspective, so the vocabulary and what is seen in specific months is influenced by that perspective. However, the appreciation for the colours seen throughout the year present a good outlook and way to see the world around us.

This Book is Gray by Lindsay Ward presents a fun story about a character named Gray who is simply trying to tell his story, until all his friends of different colours (literally) become involved. Their input overwhelms Gray, but he also learns that colour can be a good thing, and even liven up a good story. The interplay between characters is humorous, but also provides an opportunity to explore colours further.

CONCLUSION

In this chapter, we have discovered the important role that beginning books play in the reading development of young children. Concept books include the well-known alphabet and counting books, but there are also books that teach concepts such as colours, shapes and opposites. There are many key features to look for in these types of books, and finding quality beginning books can assist young readers in learning new concepts and helping them on their literacy journey. Regardless of the concept book that is being used, all these types of books provide children with important learning experiences with books that will further develop their language and literacy skills.

ADDITIONAL TITLES TO EXPLORE

Calm Down, Zebra – Lou Kuenzler

The Colouring Competition – Heath McKenzie (older readers)

Rainbow Bear – Stephen Michael King

Bush Bedtime – Lorette Broekstra

Bush Birthday – Lorette Broekstra

Meerkat Splash – Aura Parker

Summer Song – Kevin Henkes (part of the seasons series, including *In the Middle of Fall, Winter is Here, When Spring Comes*)

WANT TO KNOW MORE?

Jalongo, M.R. (2004) *Young Children and Picture Books* (2nd edn). Washington, DC: National Association for the Education of Young Children.

Jalongo's book reinforces the ways that picture books can support literacy development in children, as well as the importance of reading aloud to children.

Kümmerling-Meibauer, B. and Meibauer, J. (2005) 'First pictures, early concepts: Early concept books'. *The Lion and the Unicorn*, 29(3): 324–47. Available at: https://doi.org/10.1353/uni.2005.0039

This connects the different points raised in this chapter with early concept books and how they can be used with young children.

Vallotton, C., Gardner-Neblett, N., Kim, L., Harewood, T. and Duke, N. (2023) 'Ready for read-alouds: 10 practices for book sharing with infants and toddlers'. *The Reading Teacher*, 76(4): 459–69. Available at: https://doi.org/10.1002/trtr.2176

This article reinforces the importance of reading to children, specifically young children, connecting with the intended audience of beginning books.

REFERENCES

Clay, M. (1993) *An Observation Survey*. London: Heinemann.

Galda, L. and Cullinan, B. (2006) *Literature and the Child* (6th edn). Belmont, CA: Wadsworth.

Huck, C. and Young, D. (1961) *Children's Literature in the Elementary School*. Austin, TX: Holt, Rinehart & Winston.

Kiefer, B.Z., Hepler, S.I., Hickman, J. and Huck, C.S. (2007) *Charlotte Huck's Children's Literature* (9th edn). New York: McGraw-Hill.

Winch, G., Ross Johnston, R., March, P., Ljungdahl, L. and Holliday, M. (2006) *Literacy: Reading, Writing and Children's Literature* (3rd edn). Oxford: Oxford University Press.

3

PICTURE BOOKS

WHAT WE WILL LEARN

- All about picture books.
- Why it is important to use picture books with children
- The features of a quality picture book.
- How to evaluate picture books.
- The different issues presented in picture books.

Continuing the natural progression of readers and learning to read, picture books continue the natural development of helping young children learn to read and to continue to develop their literacy skills. It is important to remember that picture books are meant for readers of all ages. One of the best features of picture books is that they are excellent to read aloud. This reinforces what was discussed in Chapter 1 and the importance of reading aloud to children of all ages. This chapter will present different types and features found in picture books, highlighting how they can be used with many readers. However, to start the discussion, it is important to define what a picture book is.

So, what is a picture book? They come in so many different shapes, sizes, formats and content. The best definition would be a book that incorporates text and illustrations together in order to tell a story. Galda and Cullinan (2006) define this well: 'When text and illustrations are masterfully combined, their interaction, often referred to as *unity*, creates a unique work of art—the picture book' (p. 29). However, this unique design is well established in children's literature and is quite possibly the most well-known and loved book format found within the field. When exploring what makes a quality picture book, Charlotte Huck and

Doris Young (1961) wrote years ago in the first edition of their trailblazing children's literature textbook describing the interplay between text and images, 'Both media must bear the burden of narration. There must be a unity between the two that must be indivisible' (pp. 89–90). It is also important to note that not all picture books have words. There are a plethora of wordless picture books that tell complex stories through images alone. The most common form of a picture book contains 32 pages. It is also important to remember in the creation of a picture book an author and illustrator will rarely work together. Illustrator Tania McCartney notes this in an article in the *Magpies* children's literature journal '…most of the time, the illustrator and/or designer work independently, the author might give feedback once the layouts are complete'. Jane Godwin, another Australian illustrator concurs, 'some authors and illustrators create a work without ever meeting each other…'. Almost everyone remembers a favourite picture book from their childhood. These memories could be because of the book itself, the way we related to the character, or even just the memory of having the book read to us by a loving parent or adult. One of the most memorable series of picture books were the Little Golden Books. This series of books made famous by the golden strip down the spine helped make picture books more accessible and affordable for families and also introduced the world to many famous authors and illustrators. Margaret Wise Brown, author of *Goodnight Moon*, was a Little Golden Book author, and Garth Williams, illustrator of *Charlotte's Web* and *Stuart Little*, also illustrated a number of Little Golden Books.

How the endpages of a picture book are used varies across titles. For example, Mo Willems starts his well-loved pigeon series (*Don't Let the Pigeon Drive the Bus!*) with the endpages already beginning the story and ends the book, again using the endpages. Endpages, or endpapers, are the pages on the inside cover of the book and while they may seem like innocent little pages that have no relevance, they actually play a crucial role in setting the scene for the story or relating back to the content in some subtle way. Examine Leigh Hobbs's Mr Chicken series. The endpages for *Mr Chicken Goes to Paris* are actually a key part of the story. The front endpages show Mr Chicken as he prepares for his trip, with common phrases to know in the French language, his passport and a postcard telling his friend to expect him. The endpages at the end of the book show different French people reading the paper or watching television, and they see Mr Chicken and the adventures he has had.

Sometimes the use of endpages is more subtle. Take a look at Lucy Estela and Matt Ottley's book *Suri's Wall*. The endpages are a collage of textured paper and represent the wall from the front cover that Suri is touching as she walks along it. This can also be seen in the recently published *To the Bridge*. When looking at the front endpages, you can see the boy on his horse and the illustrations are rather dark. However, on the back endpages, it is brighter.

Sometimes you can see that things change with endpages, and this is quite clear between the front and back endpages in the book *My Real Friend*. At the front of the book you see the main character by himself in the bottom right-hand corner of the pages as he walks to school. At the end of the book, you see him walking with his new friend in the same spot. The reader can also notice subtle differences between the two endpages.

Who are picture books meant for, though? Years ago, when teaching a children's literature class at a university in Colorado in the United States, I had a student named 'Will' who felt

Image 3.1 *Mr Chicken goes to Paris* (with permission from Allen and Unwin)

that picture books were only meant for prep (kindergarten) children. When asked why this was, he replied, 'because they are easy to read and there's not much to them'. Needless to say, I spent the entire semester teaching him otherwise. As Norton (2007) asserts, 'the term Picture Books covers a wide variety of children's books, ranging from Mother Goose books and toy books for very young children to picture storybooks with plots that satisfy more experienced, older children' (p. 162). Galda and Cullinan (2006) take this idea even further, noting, 'Students of all ages read picture books. Preschoolers, as well students in primary, intermediate, and advanced grades read picture books appropriate to their interests' (p. 32). The semester was eye opening for 'Will' and through the weeks he learned that picture books actually cover a diverse range of topics and an audience that is equally as diverse and wide. This chapter will carry that message even further and showcase a wide variety of titles and how they address a diverse number of areas.

BUST A MYTH

Just because the intended audience is for children or young adults does not mean it cannot tell a great story!

The main focus of any book, regardless of the audience, is to tell a good story. Remember, no matter what the genre or audience, a good story, especially in children's literature has creative licence to be more creative, innovative and engaging in the format and approach.

ANIMALS VERSUS HUMANS

One very common feature of picture books is the use of animal characters. Think about *The Very Cranky Bear* (Nick Bland), *Pig the Pug* (Aaron Blabey), *Josephine Wants to Dance* (Jackie French), *Koala Lou* (Mem Fox), *Who Sank the Boat?* (Pamela Allen), *This is Not My Hat* (Jon Klassen), *Lilly's Purple Plastic Purse* (Kevin Henkes) or the *Oi Dog!* series of books by Kes Gray. Why do you think the author/illustrator used animals instead of humans in the stories? Mainly because using animals as characters makes the issues, topics and thus the story, universal. The use of animals takes away the issue of ethnicity and sometimes gender as well, and it makes the story more focused on the realistic issue addressed in the book. Whether it is making new friends, feeling alone in the world, getting in trouble at school or just wanting to be your own person (or kangaroo or dog), an animal main character makes the idea more relatable and exciting for the child reader. This allows the younger reader to enjoy the story and make connections or relate it to their own lives. So, when we review *Koala Lou*, it could be any child who is feeling unloved by their parents because of another sibling and that they must prove themselves worthy of their parent's love, but in this case a koala was the main character.

More recently, *Bat vs Poss* tells a story about using all animal characters to address a common childhood issue. The creative use of illustrations and emotion will have children wondering if the animals in the story will be able to get along in the end. The use of animals helps children learn that it is not only humans who deal with various issues, and their inclusion provides a non-threatening way to teach life lessons. Further examples of this are found later in this chapter addressing realistic issues in books.

LESSONS IN PICTURE BOOKS

Reflect on all the picture books you remember reading. How many of these books had lessons that the character(s) learned by the end of the story? One of the key elements of picture books is their ability to teach a lesson or for children to learn something after they read them. It could be about sharing, caring, friendship, sibling rivalries or just getting along with others, to name but a few. How these lessons are delivered is important in the best picture books. At their conception, children's books were very preachy and didactic; the message was there and it came across very strong, to the point that a sledgehammer could have been used. Back in 1710, in describing children's books, it was written that the 'purpose of such books was to foster the health of the child's soul' (Huck and Young, 1961, p. 56). Look at some of the titles as examples: *The Book of Courtesye; Youth's Behavior; The Pilgrim's Progress; Spiritual Milk for Boston Babes, in either England; A Token for Children: Being an exact account of the conversion, holy, and exemplary lives and joyful deaths of several young children*; at least *The History of Little Goody Two-Shoes* was

Image 3.2   *Goody Two-Shoes*

published by John Newbery (remember the Newbery Medal?) who published stories *for* children to actually enjoy. Newbery's most famous work was *A Little Pretty Pocket-book, Intended for the Instruction and Amusement of Little Master Tommy, and Pretty Miss Polly*. These books provided the much needed shift from the formation of children with the books they read to the enjoyment of reading stories.

   The main point here is that quality children's literature can both teach a lesson and entertain a child. It need not sacrifice an entertaining and engaging story in order to teach a lesson. Keeping those historical titles in mind, remember that while a picture book can contain a message and teach a lesson, it should not be didactic and preachy in the process. The lesson can be a subtle one for children to learn through the story or their love for the character(s). Keep this idea in mind as you read and evaluate various picture books.

REALISTIC ISSUES

A good picture book is one that all children can relate to. Picture books can deal with real-life experiences – for example, starting school (*Starting School* by Jane Godwin) or moving to a new house (*Clancy & Millie and the Very Fine House* by Libby Gleeson), or even making new friends, as seen in *My Real Friend* mentioned earlier. Even childhood fears are real-life issues that all children face. Anna Walker's book *Lottie & Walter* exemplifies this, showing a young girl who has a fear of water and swimming. It is through her imaginary friend Walter that she learns that the water is not that scary at all. One could pair Walker's book with *No Swimming for Nelly* (Gorbachev), which also deals with a young child's fear of the water and swimming. Also, *Be Brave, Little Penguin* by Giles Andreae is a UK title that addresses the same fear of swimming but from a penguin's perspective. All three of these books show how realistic issues such as learning to swim or fear of water are actually universal ones that can be addressed in multiple ways.

The first day of school can be a very scary time, and Jane Godwin's book *Starting School* is a perfect book to ease a child's tension with that idea. Published a little earlier, Kevin Henkes's *Wemberly Worried* is an excellent book that addresses two issues – a child who worries a lot about everything, and probably her biggest worry is about starting school. A newer title, *Ready Rabbit?* by Fiona Roberton, is very similar to *Wemberly Worried* about an anxious main character who may worry too much. The connections between the two are clear, but the main difference is that rabbit is more worried about going to a party. The pages are clear examples of Huck's point about how the illustrations and text must work together to tell the story. One key example of this is when Little Rabbit sees his friend Hugo, a turtle at the party, and the reader sees the party from Hugo's perspective from his shell.

In *Wemberly Worried*, when Wemberly meets a new friend who is just like her, she tells her teacher not to worry. These two books exemplify the point earlier that animal characters help represent real-life issues in a non-threatening but still accessible manner.

Davina Bell has published a number of books that also address realistic issues of growing up. *The Underwater Fancy-Dress Parade* describes how Alfie feels too shy to attend a fancy-dress party, so he has a party of his own. *Maya & Cat* by Caroline Magerl deals with friendship and the inclusion of animals helps address the universal issue in a more relatable way.

New siblings also raise a challenge for young children and *My Brother the Duck* by Pat Zietlow Miller is a creative story that addresses the issue in a fun and more innovative way as Stella follows the scientific process to determine whether her brother is indeed a duck. There is humour throughout her journey as she begins to come to terms with her new sibling.

SOCIAL ISSUES

Sometimes picture books can address real-life social issues that children face in their life. While this will be covered in more depth in Chapter 8 on realistic fiction, it is important to introduce how books can cover such social issues as refugees, natural disasters and even a global pandemic.

REFUGEE BOOKS

Anisa's Alphabet (discussed in the previous chapter) is an amazing picture book that tells the story of a young girl, Anisa, as she begins her journey to a safer place. As found in many alphabet books, there is limited text as the book introduces each letter of the alphabet while still telling the story of Anisa's journey. *My Two Blankets* by Irena Kobald tells the story of a young girl named Cartwheel who leaves her home behind to find a safer life. Blankets are a metaphor for how she has language and other parts of her culture from her homeland, but when she meets a new friend in her new country, she begins to have a new blanket with words and images. This book would combine well with *My Beautiful Birds* by Suzanne Del Rizzo.

A Different Pond by Bao Phi tells the story about a young boy who wakes early to go fishing with his father. Through this adventure, the boy reflects on the challenges his family face in their refugee journey. This book would pair well with 2022 Caldecott-winning title *Watercress* by Andrea Wang in which a young girl tells of her family's outing which is interrupted when her parents discover watercress on the side of the road and make the entire family pick it. When they go home and cook the watercress for dinner, the girl is even more upset, until she learns about her parents' journey to their new homeland and what they left behind.

Windows by Patrick Guest is a wonderful title that addresses the challenges the world faced, and specifically Victoria, Australia, with lockdowns during a global pandemic. The book shares how when people were in lockdown, they saw the world from their windows. It is a subtle way to introduce and present the difficulties of lockdown, but describes how the human spirit worked through it to stay connected.

Jackie French and Bruce Whatley's books, *Fire, Drought, Flood* and *Cyclone*, are all about the real-life events that Australians have faced repeatedly. The unique illustration style of Whatley makes the books powerful reads.

Boy by Phil Cummings tells the story of a young boy who is deaf and doesn't hear all the battles in the forest around him. In the end, it is Boy who helps resolve the differences because of his ability to 'hear' all sides of the story.

FANTASY AND FAIRY TALES

Fairy tales and folk tales are some of the earliest stories that young children learn. These stories, however, were not originally meant for children. The Grimm Brothers' stories are well known for being collected years ago, in the early 1800s. They were originally stories from servants and peasants who were asked what stories they remembered. When exploring some of the stories they collected, one might find that their name is fitting, as the stories they tell are quite grim. For example, *The Juniper Tree* is one title that shows how dark they can be. Disney has rather watered down these stories in its film versions, but they are still present in children's literature and a part of many children's schema for folk tales and fairy tales.

There are numerous new versions, parodies and interpretations of these well-known classic tales. *Three Billy Goats Gruff* is a classic story that many children may not have heard and Nick Bland gives us his spin on the story. His illustrative style is present in the book, but it is very well placed to be a read-aloud classic as children hear and can repeat, 'Who is that tromping on my bridge?'.

A number of years ago, Aussie Gems published a series of Australian-themed folk and fairy tales. With titles like *Goldilocks and the Three Koalas, The Lamington Man* and *The Three Little Bush Pigs*, readers will delight in the old classics with a 'new' Australian twist to them. These types of stories, when read after children know the original version, will make variations more enjoyable. Jon Scieszka and Lane Smith's now classic *The True Story of the Three Little Pigs* and *The Stinky Cheese Man and Other Fairly Stupid Tales* are what inspired the numerous variations and use of different perspectives to tell the classic story. A very good example of this is *Wolfie: An Unlikely Hero* by Deborah Abela. The book is a fun twist in a similar vein to Scieszka's work. It will leave the reader questioning whether they should believe or trust Wolfie as he presents his version of the story they know so well. *Fairy Tale Pets* by Tracey Corderoy is a fun title that has the main character Bob 'pet sitting' for various fairytale characters. It is a humorous story that will have children shouting out the different characters they recognise. The Aussie book *Good Question: A Tale Told Backwards* by Sue Whiting is another creative story that introduces a number of various characters that readers will have fun identifying.

From New Zealand comes a fun version of *She'll Be Coming Round the Mountain* by The Topp Twins and, combined with the delightful illustrations by Jenny Cooper, this book will have children of all ages yelling out a good 'Yeehaw!'. There is also the entertaining *Goldilocks and the Three Dinosaurs* by Mo Willems which has a moral at the end that will have children laughing. This book would be a good opportunity to introduce Aesop's Fables and teach the concept of morals that come at the end of books. Known as one of the classic genres in children's literature, there are a plethora of titles for children to find and enjoy.

WORDLESS PICTURE BOOKS

Wordless picture books are also included in the category of picture books and play a crucial role in literacy. They provide children with the opportunity to create their own story, based solely on the illustrations. This idea of visual decoding is a critical component of visual literacy. Winch et al. write: 'In contemporary picturebooks, pictures are not just a prop to language but a language (visual language) in their own right' (2010: 473). While this may appear to be simple, it is actually quite complex. Jeannie Baker is the master of wordless picture books in Australia. Her groundbreaking title, *Mirror*, deserves the many accolades it has received (CBCA Picture Book of the Year, joint winner, 2011; Indie Book Award, 2011). The book involves two stories told simultaneously. One side tells a story about a boy in Australia with his family and the other side is a story about a boy from Morocco. The overarching idea is that the stories 'mirror' each other as the reader can compare and contrast the two stories with the common factor of a woven rug that is exported and imported.

Baker's newer title, *Circle*, follows the journey of two birds as they migrate. Well-known modern classics *Belonging* and *Window* are books that children can use to explore different perspectives and views from windows, houses and homes around the world. The environmental themes found in Baker's books are well worth providing to children as they tell their own stories based on the illustrations alone.

Shaun Tan's well-known title *The Arrival* also shows how complex even a wordless picture book can be. One must also look to David Wiesner's work for even more quality wordless picture books. For example, *Flotsam* is an intricate story about a boy who finds a camera washed up on the beach that contains pictures within pictures, within pictures, reminiscent of the movie *Inception*.

Many will say that wordless picture books are beneficial to second-language learners because they can practise language skills and vocabulary with the books. This is true, but not the sole reason to explore and use them with children. The untapped creativity that can be found within these books supports their use with children.

The Flying Light by Yuanhao Yang is an amazing new wordless picture book title whose format looks similar to *The Arrival* with its use of sequence boxes and smaller frames telling a much larger story. The illustrations are intricate and amazing, and well worth a read with children of all ages. *Leaf* by Stephen Michael King tells the tale of a leaf as it floats down from the tree and starts on its own adventure after leaving the tree. The use of curved and action lines helps the reader/viewer interpret the story.

Children of many ages will enjoy Barbara Lehman's many wordless books: *The Red Book* (Caldecott Honor Book), *Museum Trip* and *The Secret Box* are all books that tell intricate stories with images that will amuse, entertain and challenge the readers. Molly Idle's Flora books (*Flora and the Flamingo, Flora and the Penguin, Flora and the Peacocks, Flora and the Chicks*) all tell the story of Flora as she meets her feathered friends, and the images show Flora and the birds copying each other. Such subtle illustrations are also present in the book *Where's Walrus?*, when walrus escapes from the zoo and 'hides' from the zookeeper throughout the town. JiHyeon Lee's book *Pool* is a fun story of a day at the pool, and how a child finds a friend in a crowded city pool and they navigate everyone else.

For younger children, Caldecott Honor winning, *A Ball for Daisy* and *Daisy Gets Lost*, both by Chris Raschka, provide young children with the opportunity to tell their own stories of Daisy, a dog that loses her beloved first ball, and then the continued adventures of Daisy as she gets lost and her search for home.

The Treehouse by Marije Tolman is a UK title that features a number of animals that find a common 'home' in a treehouse. They share many adventures and fun, as well as challenges.

The detailed illustrations are entertaining and children will enjoy sharing their own representations of the story.

Everyone should take a walk with *Footpath Flowers* by UK author JonArno Lawson. This is a beautiful book that follows a young girl and what she sees and picks up as she walks with her father through the town. The message of the importance of small things carries throughout the book and is one that we should all remember.

PICTURE BOOKS FOR OLDER READERS

Remember what Will said years ago? This section is designed to continue to show Will that picture books can be used for all ages, even throughout university, and support what Norton, Galda and Cullinan stated. Sometimes it may be the content or delivery of the material, but in the end, picture books can be a comfortable way to present challenging material.

Shaun Tan has a number of books that are aimed at older readers. Well known for *The Lost Thing*, the unique illustrations and story will intrigue readers as to what the lost thing might actually be and introduce them to a number of other books by the same author. *Cicada* is a new book by Tan that will also be interesting and intriguing for older readers, as it explores the life of an insect that works in an office and is unappreciated by everyone around him. Other books to explore by Tan are *Tales From Outer Suburbia*, *The Red Tree* and, of course, the well-known wordless picture book/graphic novel, *The Arrival*.

Zeno Sworder's *My Strange Shrinking Parents* is a powerful story about how parents' love for their children helps them to grow, quite literally. The metaphors in this book will challenge older readers to learn how their own family helps them grow and the sacrifices that are made for them. The illustrations and text work well together to show how the parents shrink while the child grows.

Madame Badobedah by Sophie Dahl is a recent title that is definitely designed for older readers. The book is about a young girl who lives in a hotel, or rather a bed and breakfast accommodation, and finds adventure in every room. When a new guest arrives, she creates her own backstory about the guest. However, she gets to know one particular guest, Madame Badobedah, more and more as the story develops. With longer text and short 'chapters', children will enjoy going on adventures with the main character, Mabel.

One Step at a Time by Jane Jolly is a picture book that is for older readers, as it addresses the issues of landmines and their impact on the landscape after a war. When a young boy in Thailand discovers that his elephant has been injured by a landmine explosion, he is determined to help the elephant as best as he can. The solution leads to a heartwarming ending, but the content provides teachers with many avenues to explore deeper learning.

Remember the refugee titles discussed earlier? *The Island* and *The Mediterranean* both by Armin Greder delve into the issue of refugees. *The Island* shares this idea in what can be a confronting manner with how new people from unknown places are treated. The sequel, *The Mediterranean*, continues that story and allows the reader to inference what may have happened to the stranger from the first book. This pair of books would lead to good discussion with older readers about refugees, the challenges they face and ideas for the future. *The Journey* by Francesca Senna is a UK title that addresses the issue of refugees and forced migration. The story of a family as they migrate to a new country is sad but very much realistic. The title could be paired with other titles for older readers such as Shaun Tan's *The Arrival* or *Anisa's Alphabet* mentioned earlier. *Room on our Rock* by Jol and Kate Temple is a wonderful title and complex picture book, because it can be told forwards or backwards, with different meanings depending on how it is read. The book also addresses the complexities of how we treat others, and presents the subtle difference of how things can be perceived and how this can have an impact not only on the story, but on how others feel.

Girl on Wire by Lucy Estela tells the story of the issues that girls may face dealing with such concepts as self-esteem and anxiety. The text is limited, but the content and idea are more advanced, describing the tightrope that children may feel they are walking. This is a very inspirational book.

One Photo by Ross Watkins presents the difficult story of a family dealing with a father who has Alzheimer's disease and how he (and the family) deal with the challenges this condition presents to the family. In the end, the father presents a beautiful gift to his family that will give the readers a better understanding of the impact that this difficult disease can cause.

The All New Must Have Orange 430 by Michael Speechley addresses the issue of fads, when children want the latest toy. But when Harvey sees the 'all new must have Orange 430', he falls for the marketing trap, and then learns the truth of what he has purchased. He seeks a way to return it, but in the end finds out that he's not the only one who fell for the marketing ploy. This book would connect very well with *The Lost Thing* by Shaun Tan. Older primary school readers will understand the predicament and the outcome.

Margaret Wild is at her best yet again with her books, *The Feather* and *Girl From the Sea*. In *The Feather*, Freya Blackwood's illustration style shines through in presenting a dystopian world where two children find a beautiful feather. They are unsure of what to do with it, and when the villagers decide to encase it, the children see that this has a detrimental effect upon the feather. This forces their hand to decide whether they should free such a wonderful thing. The book has excellent discussion points that older readers could delve into – for example, what is the feather, what does it represent and why do people want to display it? These questions and more are worth exploring with older readers. In *The Girl from the Sea*, the illustrations by Jane Tanner again complement and extend the text. Readers will examine the illustrations to try to understand the relationship between the family in the story and the girl who is present in the illustrations. The multiple interpretations that can be made from the book highlight how the intended audience is older readers, even though the text in the book is quite limited.

EVALUATION CRITERIA

We've explored a number of picture books that showcase multiple genres within the category, but how can picture books be evaluated? The next section will address categories and ideas to be aware of when evaluating picture books.

Table 3.1 Evaluation criteria: picture books

Format	Illustrations	Content	Language	Overall evaluation
Does the size of the book and format of the book match the style of the book?	Do the illustrations extend and enhance the written text?	Is the book appropriate for the age level?	Does the language/story of book flow smoothly?	Is the structure and format of the book/illustrations innovative?
Do the cover page and endpapers directly connect to the book, or add to the theme of book?	Does the illustrator have a specific style and medium in each of their books?	Is the intended audience children or is it meant for adults?	Is the language in the book authentic to children?	Are the illustrations/style similar to other authors/illustrators?
Is the type design consistent with the overall theme of the book?	Do the illustrations reflect the mood of the story?	What is the purpose of the book, or how could the book be used with children?	Is the language appropriate for the intended audience?	What do reviewers think of the illustrations/story?
	What do you notice about the colour, vibrancy, and texture of the illustrations?	Are the characters well established – do you feel connected to them?	Does the text extend and enhance the illustrations?	Does the illustrator talk about their work anywhere?
	How do the use of line, shape, and colour influence the layout/design of the book?	Does the book avoid race, gender, diversity stereotypes?		Will the book make a significant contribution to children's literature?

FORMAT

As discussed earlier, picture books come in different shapes and sizes, and sometimes readers can see obvious size differences – for example, Bob Graham's book *Vanilla Ice Cream* has a taller format than usual, and Shaun Tan's titles *Cicada* and *Eric* have a smaller square shape.

Sometimes authors and illustrators use a change of direction to read a book. To read the story of *We're Stuck!* by Sue deGennaro, the book must be held sideways (long way) in order to see all the floors of the apartment building where young turtle lives. *Shake the Tree!* by Sylvia Borando is a UK title that requires the reader to tilt the book sideways in order to interact with it and to shake the tree to tell the story.

This is a Moose by Richard T. Morris makes the reader turn the book to the side to fully see Dr Giraffe introduced to the readers. *Bear Came Along* is another title by the same author that completely breaks down the traditional picture book format.

Endpapers (endpages) mentioned earlier in this chapter are a key format style that authors and illustrators use to set the tone of a story and provide sometimes subtle information about the book.

TYPE/FONT . . .

CBCA winning picture book *I NEED a Parrot* by Chris McKimmie breaks down the many format components of picture books with a change in font size and style throughout the book, as well as a use of images that sometimes take up the entire page or other times are a small part of the double-page spread and very much represent a child's own drawing style.

Drew Daywalt's *The Day the Crayons Quit* and sequel *The Day the Crayons Came Home* use actual handwriting as the font for the story that is told through letters written by each of the crayons to their owner, Duncan; in the sequel, they write postcards to Duncan.

ILLUSTRATIONS

As has been discussed throughout this chapter, the illustrations in a picture book play a very critical part in the success of a picture book. Sometimes it can be about how they reflect the mood of the story or book. Take a moment to remember and revisit *Koala Lou* and *Possum Magic* illustrated by Pamela Lofts. When you look at these books, you notice that they have softer shades of colour throughout them, which matches the mood and tone of the book.

Sometimes we see a specific illustrator style – for example, look at how in her earlier work Alison Lester used ovals within her books. Bruce Whatley has a specific style as well, but this also varies. His distinctive style is found in most of his books, and this is when he illustrates with his right hand; when he illustrates with his left hand, it is vastly different. Take a look at the Diary of a Wombat Series and compare them to the Natural Disaster Series (*Flood, Drought, Fire*, etc.). The styles are distinct but definitely interesting, and it helps us see how different those styles can be.

One can also look at the vibrancy of illustrations. Explore the title *My Beautiful Birds* by Suzanne Del Rizzo. Very strong brush strokes of acrylic paint are combined with polymer clay, found within the illustrations as we follow the story of a young refugee boy who had to leave his birds behind as he journeys to a new home, and they make the illustrations look like paintings.

Bat vs Poss by Alexa Moses has illustrations that match the nighttime setting of the book and also changing perspectives with bird's-eye views to highlight what is happening as Bat battles Possum.

Ann James's illustrations in Margaret Wild's book *Goodbye House, Hello House* uses black-and-white drawings of the main character brought forward on the coloured background, which is an innovative approach. This book could be paired with *The Hello, Goodbye Window* written by Norton Juster, which is very brightly illustrated by Chris Raschka.

Hello Lighthouse by Sophie Blackall (Caldecott Winner and CBCA shortlisted book) would fit well here. Its absolutely gorgeous illustrations use the porthole windows to see what happens both inside and outside the lighthouse, as would her newer title *Farmhouse*.

Three by Stephen Michael King and *Cyril and Pat* by Emily Gravett both use dotted lines to follow the character as they run through the park. *One Runaway Rabbit* by David Metzenthen includes this both within the book and in the endpages at the back of the book. *My Friend Fred* by Frances Watts keeps the reader guessing and they must pay close attention to the details in the illustrations for clues. *By the Billabong* by Maura Finn and *Ella and the Ocean* by Lian Tanner both contain illustrations that connect perfectly with the Australian landscape. In *By the Billabong* a child takes a walk by the billabong and encounters a number of Australian animals along the way. In *Ella and the Ocean* Ella is curious about what the ocean looks like and asks each member of her family. Her family lives on a drought-stricken farm and are too busy trying to survive in order to answer Ella's question. The illustrations capture the red landscape well and will have Australians easily able to connect to the story. *Thank you, Omu!* by Oge Mora has gorgeous collage-style illustrations. The story teaches about sharing, as many people bring food to Omu after she shares her homemade stew with them. The book easily connects to the classic story *Stone Soup*.

CONTENT

With the great number of picture books published every year, it can sometimes be confusing who the intended audience is. Is it always for children, or are some picture books aimed at older and even adult readers? For example, a very fun picture book, *Adventures of Cow*, invites the question, 'Who is the intended audience?'. The book shares cow's adventure trying to get home, the illustrations show photographs of a toy cow on a farm with animals that do not match what is being presented in the illustrations. While it might be confusing to children, adults will enjoy the humour with the contradiction in the photographs. For example, the text says, 'and swam into a herd of scary frogs', but the illustration is a photograph of the toy cow with a bunch of real cows. Another book that highlights the idea of intended audience is *Halloween* by well known comedian, Jerry Seinfeld. One of the issues with a celebrity author is that the book is pitched at those who will purchase it – adults. And based on the fact that the book is based on Seinfeld's comedy act, it reminisces about Halloween experiences, and is intended more for adults than for children.

Do you connect with the characters? Earlier in the chapter, many popular characters were discussed and what makes them interesting or engaging. One of the biggest reasons for this is that we connect with characters in different ways. This author's favourite character in children's literature is Lilly, from *Lilly's Purple Plastic Purse*. Why is this character one that I connect with? Because I love her spirit and attitude. Plus, the red cowboy boots with a star on them perfectly capture her personality. We all have different characters we connect with, and Koala Lou, Pig the Pug, the cranky bear, or many others may connect with different readers. Perhaps a newer character Tilly, from the book *Tilly* by Jane Godwin, will connect with children as they relate to how the main character has special things in her life and searches for a special place for them in the house. Young children will relate to a character who dresses up as something else. *I am Actually a Penguin* by Sean Taylor is an entertaining tale about a girl who has lots of things she dresses up as, but when her penguin outfit arrives, she actually believes that she is one, much to the annoyance of her family, until they finally convince her that she may need to change.

The book could easily be paired with *When Billy was a Dog*, as Billy imagines he is a dog, similar to the girl who believed she was actually a penguin.

LANGUAGE

FLOW OF LANGUAGE

There is a natural flow to picture books, and this should be found in the text and the words chosen. Mem Fox will be the first to tell you the exact number of words found in her book *Possum Magic* (512pp.). This is important because she understands the significance of each and every word used and how they influence the flow of language of the story. Fox notes: 'Rhythm needs to be in the marrow of your bones if you're thinking of writing a picture book. And I don't mean rhymes, necessarily. I mean the perfect placement of syllables anywhere: in a prose sentence or in verse' (memfox.com).

Picture books will have this in different ways – for example, Nick Bland's *The Very Cranky Bear* starts with 'In the Jingle Jangle Jungle, on a cold and rainy day' – the catchy flow of the language engages young readers. Emily Gravett's rhyming text in *Cyril and Pat* plays with language in a fun way that also avoids rhyming with the word 'rat', thus teasing young readers who would yell out that word in order to complete the rhyme. *Extraordinary!* by Penny Harrison has beautiful lyrical language that flows exquisitely throughout the story and encourages the reader to find beauty in the ordinary:

> But what of the ordinary, everyday thing?
>
> The soft, quiet moment that makes the world sing?
>
> This is the time you must listen and look.
>
> For it's found in the branches, the puddle, the nook.

This could be discussed at great length, but this is the opportunity for you to be aware of this idea and to find books that have a natural flow of language and celebrate how words are used to tell a story.

When looking at books from an innovative standpoint, there a number of different ideas that appear. One of those could be found in the illustration style, and *Noodle Bear* by Mark Gravas is a fun title in which a bear loves noodles, and the illustration style matches the flow or design of noodles. When the bear's stash runs out, his forest friends recommend the normal foods they enjoy. None of those interest him and he is off to the city to go on his favourite game show,

Noodle Knockout. This is a fun adventure and children will enjoy following Noodle Bear as he follows his dreams, but still finds he is wanting more.

Sometimes innovation can be found in the content and the following two books match this very well.

Fly by Jess McGeachin is a realistic fiction title that addresses loss of a parent in a very subtle way. When Lucy finds a bird with a broken wing, she tries to help it fly again by making her own plane. The adventure helps bring her closer to her father, because after all it is just the two of them, as the book states. This could be paired with Anna Walker's book *Hello! Jimmy*, although the circumstances are different for why his parents are no longer together.

The Fabulous Friend Machine by Nick Bland takes on the real-life issue of technology with chickens as the main characters. While the characters and story may be fictional, the topic itself is timely and real, and is a lesson on the dangers of technology and mobile phones.

However, probably the most important aspect of the evaluation criteria for a picture book is, 'Do children like it?'. Be aware of a child's response to the books you read to them or that they choose on their own. It is important to recognise the key features that make a book appealing to children. Also, it is necessary to understand that not every book that children like will be enjoyed by adults. Keep in mind the flip side of that, too. Just because an adult likes a book, does not mean that a child will. Regardless, it is critical that the main audience of picture books – children – are remembered when evaluating and talking about them.

CONCLUSION

So, what is the takeaway from all this? There are many ideas to highlight and remember. First, picture books can be used with readers of all ages; they are not limited to a narrow age range. There are complexities, including the content, illustrations, message, theme, and much more in picture books, but it is crucial to remember that the words and illustrations must work both in unison and independently to fluidly enhance and advance the story. There are four key components to keep in mind when evaluating picture books: format, illustrations, content and language. Each component has multiple aspects to evaluate. There is a lot of information to address, but remember that picture books are most likely a child's first entry point into books and reading, so it is vital that these experiences are positive ones that provide a child with an opportunity to be lifelong readers.

ADDITIONAL TITLES

Charlie's Whale – Libby Gleeson

To Greenland! – Pip Smith

Timeless – Kelly Canby

Old Fellow – **Christopher Cheng**

Move that Mountain – **Kate and Jol Temple**

WANT TO KNOW MORE?

Bintz, W. (2022) '"I don't like peas!" Using picturebooks to think differently & critically about curriculum, teaching, learning, and technology'. *The Reading Teacher*, 76(6): 673–81. Available at: https://doi.org/10.1002/trtr.2172.

This article provides teachers with the opportunity to think more critically and deeply about picture books and how they can be used in the classroom.

Iordanaki, L. (2021) 'Older children's responses to wordless picturebooks: making connections'. *Children's Literature in Education*, 52(4): 493–510. Available at: https://doi.org/10.1007/s10583-020-09424-7

This article connects two ideas addressed in this chapter: wordless picture books and older readers.

Tan, S. (2002) 'Picture books: Who are they for?' [Blog]. Available at: www.shauntan.net/esssay-picture-books-who-for

Well-known Australian children's author and illustrator Shaun Tan's words provide his insight into what picture books are and who they are designed for. This is a good read to discover an author and illustrator's insights into picture books.

REFERENCES

Galda, L. and Cullinan, B. (2006) *Literature and the Child* (6th edn). New York: Wadsworth.

Huck, C. and Young, D. (1961) *Children's Literature in the Elementary School*. New York: Holt, Rinehart & Winston.

Norton, D. (2007) *Through the Eyes of a Child* (7th edn). New York: Pearson.

Winch, G., Ross Johnston, R., March, P., Ljungdahl, L. and Holliday, M. (2010). *Literacy: Reading, Writing and Children's Literature* (4th edn). Oxford: Oxford University Press.

TRANSITIONAL NOVELS

WHAT WE WILL LEARN
- What a transitional novel is.
- The role that transitional novels play in the development of early (transitional) readers.
- The key components of transitional novels.
- The importance that series books play on emerging readers.

So far through this book we have talked about the importance of literacy and the important part it plays in children's lives. We began with reading to young children and exposing them to literature and the importance this plays in their literacy journey. We have also discussed picture books and the role they play in growing children's literacy skills. With these early experiences with literature, it is natural for children to begin to read with picture books and then more advanced literature as well. Transitional novels, sometimes called beginning or early chapter books, play an integral part in the continuing development of young readers, yet there is a plethora of children's literature textbooks that leave them out. This raises one key question: 'Why is this the case?'. When children first learn to read, they are intrinsically motivated and in turn have a natural desire to read more and more. They are personally motivated to move beyond picture books and go on to novels (chapter books), and at times that can be a big jump. However, it is crucial to encourage that leap and find the books that can help establish the building blocks to become lifelong readers.

The move from picture books to novels can sometimes be a daunting shift, so it is important to find a solid bridge to assist in this process. Szymusiak and Sibberson (2001) describe

this specifically: 'series books and early chapter books are a great bridge for children at the transitional stage of reading' (p. 37). Roser et al. (2004) also support this notion, stating how transitional novels 'are intended to ease the picture book to chapter book transition, filling a niche for young or developing readers who are not yet ready to attempt more complex chapter books' (p. 308). Teachers, parents and adults in general should recognise that a bridge can be created, which can be a great benefit to them, but again, perhaps it is worth revisiting the earlier question, 'Why is there not a greater focus on these types of books?'. Graves and Liang (2004) write: 'transitional books are especially important because they provide a body of literature for children at a critical make-or-break time in their literacy development, a time when they are likely to have an ever-increasing number of interests competing for their time and attention'. Such a critical juncture deserves attention, and teachers must be aware of the traits and characteristics that will interest and motivate their students.

It is important to remember that when children learn to read, it is a complex process that takes time and there are different steps taken along the way. As mentioned earlier, one could imagine a bridge that children cross from picture books to novels. The first section of the bridge are the easy readers that simply introduce high-frequency words to young readers. Dr. Seuss was famous for these with such titles as *The Cat in the Hat* and *Green Eggs and Ham*. It was Dr. Seuss who started this new 'genre' which is currently defined as decodable texts (Kiefer et al., 2004). Mo Willems has a fun series with Elephant and Piggie as the main characters telling fun stories of meeting new people, being scared or making something together with your friend, and much more. Willems is able to use appealing and humorous characters (Elephant and Piggie) and match them with a decodable story (text) that will have young children devouring the books and then realising they are able to read independently. Well-known Australian children's author Sally Rippen, also mentioned later in this chapter, has a series of books called School of Monsters in which the text is easy to read but emphasises words that rhyme – for example, 'his shoulders are huge and his arms are quite long. He's terribly big and he's terribly strong'. The main focus for these types of books is to successfully read the words on the page, increase vocabulary (and high-frequency words) and build confidence in very young readers. The illustrations in these books are used more as a support of what is on the page, which reinforces for the early reader what is happening in the text and assists them in being able to understand exactly what they are reading. These very early readers then extend the 'bridge' idea by growing young readers through the introduction of more vocabulary, characters, plot and stories to further extend the learning to read experience.

BUST A MYTH

Transitional novels are simple short novels with limited value.

Nothing could be further from the truth. Transitional novels play an essential role in a child's reading journey. They provide young readers with the chance to practise and develop their reading skills and work towards reading longer books. The books serve as a transition from picture books to traditional novels, while growing a young reader's confidence.

Transitional readers or early readers (the children themselves) discussed above are an important readership that deserve further examination. Cianciolo (1989) defined transitional readers as 'eight to eleven year olds who can read fairly independently and are mature enough for fairly lengthy stories but need to sharpen and extend their reading comprehension and critical thinking skills' (p. 72). Expanding this idea a bit further and including the literature aimed at these readers, Fiore (1987) wrote how 'transitional readers like the predictability of knowing the continuing cast of characters that a series has to offer' (p. 40) (in McNair and Brooks, 2012). This means that the characters in the series are already established for the young readers and thus they can jump right into the story and enjoy the books. Because most transitional novels are found within a series, it is important to study them further.

It is essential to remember that series books play a key role in the development of readers. If you take a moment right now to reflect on the series you read as a child, the list would most likely be quite long and contain books you remember fondly. The value of series books is that they build confidence in readers. Opitz et al. (2006) write:

> Series books have unique instructional and recreational features. These features may encourage significant self-initiated reading practice that can improve a reader's competence, confidence and comfort. Key is that predictability of the formulaic features of each text. This makes it easier for readers to negotiate the language structure and content of each book. (p. 83)

They also comment that 'Series books can be a significant way to promote reading that is done away from the teacher, both in the classroom as well as beyond the classroom' (p. 89). As mentioned earlier in this chapter, beginning readers are excited that they are learning to read, and with these main ideas in mind, it is crucial for teachers to embrace and promote series books, especially with early readers, both in and out of the classroom. These books are the ones that serve as a stepping stone for early readers and are an essential part of a child's reading journey.

So what are the common characteristics of transitional novels? According to Caravette (2011), these books have 3–6 chapters, and each chapter has its own beginning, middle and end. The books themselves are roughly 45–60 pages long and have more complex sentences and richer vocabulary than the traditional 'readers', or basals, that many of us may remember (and most likely, not that fondly). As Kiefer et al. (2004) warn how the early primers can turn readers off from reading: 'They might use repetitive phrases or questions, but they have deadly dull plots and the unnatural language of primers' (p. 154). Adults must tread carefully with early readers to ensure that the motivation to read grows. McNair and Brooks (2012) write: 'Transitional books usually have a number of common characteristics, such as a table of contents, larger font sizes, brief chapters with some illustrations interspersed throughout, and around 100 pages of text.' As stated earlier, it is quite common for transitional novels to come in a series, so that the transitional readers do not need to spend time learning new characters, settings or other such features. McGill-Franzen and Ward (2015) confirm the common structure found in this genre:

the very redundancy and formulaic patterns of series books provide support to novice readers at every stage of literacy development—those readers who are developing automaticity in word recognition, those who are building a robust vocabulary, and those who are developing understanding and interpretation of text. (p. 57)

There are some key ideas in that quote. One of them is about the 'formulaic pattern' in series books. This pattern helps early readers develop confidence and understanding of story and text structures. While it may dull experienced readers, for early and transitional readers, it is necessary. With these ideas in mind, it is essential to match readers with the correct texts, and early readers need many of the structures and features that transitional novels offer in order to ensure successful reading experiences.

KEY TRANSITIONAL NOVELS

Aussie Bites and *Aussie Nibbles* were some of the first Australian transitional novels that inspired a trend, especially within Australia. These series include a number of the key elements addressed in describing this genre and are aimed at two different types of readers – both the earlier readers mentioned above and the younger readers just beginning to start on the smaller novels. The books are also relatable to Australian early readers with the topics, content and Australian culture. For example, some earlier *Aussie Bites* books included stories by well-known Australian children's authors and illustrators such as Garth Nix, Stephen Michael King, Jane Godwin and even Danny Katz, to name a few. This popular series, brought back as *Aussie Nibbles*, shares stories of children surviving swimming lessons, time with a babysitter, birthday parties, as well as fantasy adventures of becoming an astronaut or a mermaid. The various stories found within these books will interest and engage early readers. as well as build their confidence as readers.

Australian children's author Sally Rippin has a couple of well-known and loved series specifically geared towards both genders. Billie B. Brown is Rippin's well known series of stories about a girl named Billie B. Brown, who is strong, smart and brimming with confidence. Young readers will relate to the various issues that Billie B. Brown encounters, such as making new friends, watching scary movies and wanting a new pet. They will also enjoy the ability to read the words themselves and build on their independence in reading while having the illustrations support what they are reading. Sally Rippin's Hey Jack! series connects directly to the Billie B. Brown series and tells stories about Billie's best friend Jack. The series follows the familiar structure found in the Billie B. Brown books, but is aimed at boys. Jack deals with issues such as navigating bad moods, his family, worrying about a multitude of issues and finding someone to play with at school when your best friend is away. Rippin is able to capture the problems that children face and write in a format that young readers will not only relate to, but become excited by, with their independent reading allowing them to take pride in their ability to read shorter novels.

D-Bot Squad is a newer series by well-known collaborators Louise Park and Susannah McFarlane, writing under the pseudonym Mac Park. Dinosaurs return and run loose around the world, leaving it up to the D-Bot Squad to capture them and save the world. Readers will be introduced to a different dinosaur in each book as the D-Bot Squad tries to apprehend them. Early readers will enjoy the fast-paced adventures, but also the ability to read the story on their own with vocabulary that is not too challenging, as well as illustrations that support what they are reading in the text.

British author Allan Ahlberg presents *The Gaskitt Stories*, four books about a family with a dad who wears all his clothes at once, a mother who is a taxi driver, a twin boy and girl, and a television-watching cat named Horace. The books present different adventures from capturing a bank robber, winning prizes in the post, to Horace the cat going on an unexpected adventure. The familiar vocabulary and humorous stories will have young readers enjoying all four books in the series, again building their reading skills and confidence.

Bink and Gollie, created by Newbery Award winning children's author Kate DiCamillo and Alison McGhee is a wonderful short series of books for early readers that showcases a beautiful friendship between the two main characters, Bink and Gollie. The books contain three separate stories within each short chapter and contains such adventures as visiting a state fair, learning what friends enjoy, trying to set a world record, or just sitting around enjoying some pancakes. Bink and Gollie have those adventures, and more, as well as learning the value of having a trusted friend by your side. The format of the book helps early readers gain confidence within the transitional novel format.

Well-known Australian children's author Libby Gleeson has an early reader/transitional novel, The Cleo Stories. The book has two stories in it that early readers will be able to enjoy as they are introduced to a young girl named Cleo and her different adventures. In the first book, she wants a new necklace, but her parents let her know that it would be a gift for a special occasion. Cleo is impatient and finds a new way to have a necklace. The next story in the book, 'The Present', tells how Cleo wants to create and give a special birthday present to her mum. Again, she finds a creative idea for the gift. Young readers will enjoy the illustrations throughout the book that support the reader and will remind them of the picture books they are familiar with. Zac Power is another transitional series about a 12-year-old spy and the adventures he faces. This is a more advanced series because there are more words on the page, as well as more complex vocabulary. However, it matches many of the components of transitional novels – specifically, the shorter length (under 100 pages), as well as the action-packed plots and stories that leave readers wanting to devour more and more of the titles. From capturing an evil mad scientist, protecting top-secret information, to foiling the attempts of computer hackers, Zac Power is quite a busy young spy, who also tries to lead a normal life as a twelve-year-old. The transitional novel features found in this series will again build the confidence of its readers.

A series that has images playing a strong role within the books is the UK series The Goozillas. In these books, a young boy named Max falls into his favourite app called World of Slime. Within the world, Max meets all the Goozillas, but also finds another troupe of characters in the Sicklies (super-sweet characters) who want to leave the hum-drum life of sweetness and live within the World of Slime and the slime volcano. Each book presents another challenge for Max to save everyone from destroying the World of Slime. The books contain full colour illustrations throughout the pages which will be inviting to the readers and which will also provide support for the text they are reading, thus increasing comprehension.

Another series that also contains full colour illustrations throughout the books from the UK is Teacup House: *Meet the Twitches*. A young girl named Stevie is upset because she and her mother are moving to a cottage in the country which will allow her to be closer to her dad. However, Stevie is torn because she loves her room, her apartment building, her school and her friends. When her grandmother gives her a gift of a teacup house with rabbit residents, Stevie discovers a whole new world which could make the move a bit more bearable. Transitional readers will enjoy the fantasy world that is created, as well as the illustrations that support both the text and the reader.

Children will recognise Nick Sharratt's illustrations from the books he has illustrated for Julia Donaldson. The Cat and the King series introduces young readers to the title characters and presents funny and exciting tales about each as they navigate their surroundings. The two characters need to find a new home after their old castle was destroyed by an 'unfortunate incident' with a dragon. Because of this, the king must find a job in order for him and the cat to live. With that task accomplished, life seems rather routine, until the dragon comes back and wreaks havoc once more. The comfortable illustration style and engaging story will excite readers as they devour this title.

Jasper and Scruff is a series of books about a smart kitty and a rambunctious dog. Jasper is a very ambitious cat with the ultimate goal of joining a very select club called the Sophisticats. Jasper creates a plan to make this happen. However, on his way he meets Scruff and from that moment forward his life is turned upside down. He learns the value of friendship and also that perhaps his dream of becoming a Sophisticat is not such a good idea. The illustrations throughout the book will assist young readers who will also enjoy the fun stories and humorous characters. The limited text on each page will also prevent younger readers from becoming overwhelmed.

A final transitional novel series from the UK is the humorous Uncle Gobb books by Michael Rosen. In this series, a young boy named Malcolm explains how his Uncle Gobb came to live with him and his mum. Uncle Gobb is a unique individual and Malcolm's perspective of life with Uncle Gobb is entertaining and will have readers devouring the pages of the books. The illustrations and font changes throughout the book add to the story and how it is told, and allow for further enjoyment by readers.

Transitional literature can even come in the form of non-fiction. Big Picture Press from the UK has a series of non-fiction books for transitional readers. The series has a book called *Meet the Ancient Greeks*, which includes key information about the Ancient Greeks in an entertaining and educational format that follows the structure of non-fiction books, with a table of contents, labelled diagrams and even a timeline. This is a good format to use for transitional readers who are fans of non-fiction books. Other books in the series include *Meet the Ancient Egyptians* and *Meet the Ancient Romans*.

It is worth noting that there are many that value this genre, so much so, that they recognise it with a children's literature award. For example, the king of the 'learn to read books', Dr. Seuss, mentioned earlier, has an American Library Association Award (ALA) named after him. The Theodor Seuss Geisel Award is given 'to the author(s) and illustrator(s) of the most distinguished contribution to the body of American children's literature, known as beginning reader books published in the United States during the preceding year' (www.ala.org/awards-grants/awards/12/all_years). King & Kayla and the Missing Dog Treats (a series) is a Theodor Seuss Geisel Award winner about Kayla's dog, King, that is accused of eating freshly baked dog treats. King uses his canine sleuthing skills to solve the mystery. The text and vocabulary are easily decodable and the illustrations provide support and further information for early readers.

The Gryphon Award is a book award for the best English language work whose audience is Kindergarten (Prep) to grade 4 and is awarded by the Bulletin of the Center for Children's Books from the University of Illinois. The award is for 'The title chosen that best exemplifies those qualities that successfully bridge the gap in difficulty between books for reading aloud to children and books for practiced readers' (https://bccb.ischool.illinois.edu/gryphon-award/gryphon-award-archive/). A few examples to note would be *See the Cat: Three Stories About a Dog* (also a Theodor Seuss Geisel Award Winner), which contains exactly what the title states (three fun stories about a dog). However, the stories contain humour and connect to one another, culminating in an unexpected but humorous ending, all while including vocabulary that early readers can work with. *Weekends with Max and His Dad* is another Gryphon Award winner that captures many elements of transitional novels. It presents a contemporary story of a boy named Max coping with his parent's divorce. The realistic issues found in the book are ones that children will be able to relate to. The text is readable, but also contains illustrations that provide support for the reader.

CHARACTERISTICS OF TRANSITIONAL NOVELS

So what do quality transitional novels look like? It is important to explore the criteria that make these books good. For starters, similar to other genres, it is important that there is an authentic compelling narrative that will engage the younger readers. This will also mean that the book has a plot (or storyline) that is intriguing, but also understandable for early readers. Think back to the Zac Power books and how Zac is a 12-year-old spy on all sorts of adventures, or the Dinobot books that bring to life dinosaurs in robot format. Both of these series have engaging plots for younger readers. The books should have characters that are appealing to the readers, so much so, that they want to continue reading about them in other books in the series. Sally Rippin's books mentioned earlier in the chapter have exactly that. Both Billie B. Brown and Jack are characters that children enjoy reading about. These initial ideas match well with what Graves and Liang (2004) found in their study of transitional books: 'In reading the first two pages, we looked for an authentic, compelling narrative voice, an intriguing problem or premise, or an appealing character, preferably all three!' From a text standpoint, the vocabulary needs to be understandable, yet also introduce new words in a manner that newer readers are able to figure out on their own. This can be done in multiple ways. The main way this is done is by putting the new vocabulary in context so that readers are able to use context cues to decode the new word. Sometimes, the illustrations might reinforce the text, thus leading to comprehending the new vocabulary. For example, in the Ivy and Bean series, there are numerous examples of this. In the title *Ivy and Bean Take Care of the Babysitter*, the text describes how Bean moves down the hallway like a spy. Words like 'handrail' and 'pressing' are reinforced by the illustrations, but also the idea of being a spy helps provide the context for how she was moving silently. Finally, with the illustrations, similar to the secret to a good picture book, they must extend and enhance the text. This means that they cannot be the sole form of comprehending the story. While they can reinforce the text, they also need to provide further details that may not be found in the texts. Libby Gleeson's Cleo stories are an excellent example of integrating illustrations beyond a support for what is happening on the page. Instead, they are an integral part of the book themselves. At times, they are a perfect merge between picture books and early novels where some pages contain double-page spreads with illustrations similar to a picture book. While evaluating transitional novels, it is important to recognise that they come in a variety of genres. For example, the titles presented in this chapter alone represent realistic fiction, fantasy and even non-fiction. This means that readers from a wide range of interests can engage with a diverse range of titles to develop their reading skills.

Table 4.1 Evaluation criteria: transitional novels

The book has an authentic compelling narrative.
The book contains an intriguing plot (storyline) that is understandable for early readers.
The book has appealing characters.
The illustrations extend and enhance the text, but do not dominate or simply align with the text.
Rich new vocabulary is introduced in an easily identifiable manner.

CONCLUSION

Transitional novels may not be focused on as much as other genres, but they are still a crucial piece in the process of learning and developing readers. Early readers will find comfort in the early novel structure with the inclusion of chapters, but also the fast-paced action and plot combined with engaging characters and storylines. It is important to remember how these transitional novels are a necessary bridge in early readers' development. By appreciating the essential role these books play in the process of learning to read and motivating young readers, teachers will be able to instil the end goal, which is to create lifelong readers.

ADDITIONAL TITLES

Penny and Her Song, Penny and Her Doll, Penny and Her Sled, Penny and Her Marble – Kevin Henkes

WANT TO KNOW MORE?

Bates, C.C., Klein, A., Schubert, B., McGee, L., Anderson, N., Dorn, L., McClure, E. and Ross, R.H. (2017) 'E-books and E-book apps: considerations for beginning readers'. *The Reading Teacher*, *70*(4): 401–11. Available at: https://doi.org/10.1002/trtr.1543

This article connects early readers and digital books (discussed later in the book). Early reading behaviours and strategies for working with them are discussed, as well as resources for early readers.

Roback, D., Brown, J.M. and Bean, J. (2004) 'In search of new readers'. *Publishers Weekly*, *251*(22): 30–33.

This article presents what different publishers are doing in the field of transitional books for early readers.

Son, E.H. and Chase, M. (2018) 'Books for two voices: fluency practice with beginning readers'. *The Reading Teacher*, *72*(2): 233–40. Available at: https://doi.org/10.1002/trtr.1700

This article provides teaching strategies for working with early readers. There is also an extensive list of books to use with young readers practising using two voices.

REFERENCES

Caravette, L. (2011) 'Portrait of the reader as a young child: assisting the new reader'. *Children & Libraries*, *9*(2): 52–7.

Cianciolo, P.J. (1989) 'No small challenge: literature for the transitional readers'. *Language Arts*, *66*(1): 72–81.

Graves, B. and Liang, L.A. (2004) 'Transitional chapter books'. *Book Links*, *13*(5): 12–16.

Kiefer, B.Z., Hepler, S.I., Hickman, J. and Huck, C.S. (2004) *Charlotte Huck's Children's Literature* (8th edn). New York: McGraw-Hill.

McGill-Franzen, A. and Ward, N. (2015) 'Series books: for seeking reading pleasure and developing reading competence'. In D.A. Wooten and B.E. Cullinan (eds) *Children's Literature in the Reading Program: Engaging Young Readers in the 21st century* (4th edn). Newark, DE: International Literacy Association.

McNair, J.C. and Brooks, W.M. (2012) 'Transitional chapter books: representations of African American girlhood'. *The Reading Teacher*, 65(8): 567–77. Available at: https://doi.org/10.1002/TRTR.01084

Opitz, M., Ford, M. and Zbaracki, M. (2006) *Books and Beyond*. Portsmouth, NH: Heinemann.

Roser, N., Martinez, M., McDonnold, K. and Fuhrken, C. (2004) 'Beginning chapter books: their features and their support of children's reading'. In J. Worthy, B. Maloch, J.V. Hoffman, D.L. Schallert and C.M. Fairbanks (eds), *53rd Yearbook of the National Reading Conference*. Oak Creek, WI. (pp. 308–20).

Szymusiak, K. and Sibberson, F. (2001) *Beyond Leveled Books: Supporting Transitional Readers in Grades K–5*. Portland, ME: Stenhouse.

5

POETRY

WHAT WE WILL LEARN
- What poetry is and the different components of poetry.
- Why it is important to keep an open mind about poetry.
- The different ways to inspire, interest and engage children in poetry.
- The different formats of poetry.

Ah, the poetry chapter! Perhaps you saw the table of contents and groaned a bit when you saw the chapter title, or perhaps you went the opposite way and smiled when you saw that poetry was in this book. These are the two most common responses to poetry in pre-service teachers' heads. 'Why is that?', you may ask. The reason is based on our individual experiences with poetry. Poetry can be powerful, but it can also be quite challenging and at times this causes a resistance to what really is a fun, entertaining and joyful genre. Unfortunately, as Jacobs and Tunnell (2004) note, 'students enter teacher training with an ambivalence toward or a distinct dislike for poetry' (p. 194). This can be quite frustrating because it means that somewhere along the line, the joy of poetry has been lost. The causes for this are hard to determine, but most likely it involved the old school approach of over-analysing a poem. As Janeczko (2003) so perfectly wrote: 'Reading a poem should not be like performing an autopsy, looking at a dead object and figuring out what killed it. Or worse, trying to figure out what it might have been like when it was alive. Good poems *are* alive' (p. 10). Kiefer et al. (2007) continue this sentiment: 'A child responds to the total impact of a poem and should not be required to analyse it' (p. 411). So you, the reader, can relax now, as there will

be no analysis of poems or poetry. The goal of this chapter is to showcase how wonderful children's poetry is and how it can be used to break the cycle of dislike towards poetry or, as Jacobs and Tunnell (2004) write: 'teachers who dislike poetry may have negative effects on children's poetry attitudes' (p. 195). This is a great risk for both pre-service and practising teachers. It is important to be open to poetry and appreciate how it can and should be enjoyed by everyone, especially children. To accomplish this, it is important to define what poetry is.

> ### BUST A MYTH
>
> Every picture book that rhymes is a poetry book.
> It is important to remember that poetry has its own structures and formats; rhyme is just one of those elements. Yes, a rhyming picture book is rhythmic, but making this the sole connection to poetry limits the beauty, complexities and delight that poetry contains.

So what is poetry? This question has been asked many times, and definitions are definitely difficult to establish (Kiefer et al., 2007; Norton, 2003; Temple et al., 2002). In fact, perhaps Temple et al. (2002) stated it best: 'it is impossible to coin a definition of poetry that some poem or other won't slither around' (p. 236). This elusiveness that poetry has confuses many of us as we try to settle upon a common definition. Think about this in relation to picture books that were discussed in the previous chapter. If a picture book rhymes, does that make it poetry? Rhyme is a key component of poetry, but this is also what clouds a definition and why the quote about poems slithering around definitions is true. So what are some key components of poetry? Rhythm, rhyme and imagery are three central elements.

RHYTHM

How a poem flows, or the rhythm of the poem, is an integral part of good poetry for children. This is because children are naturally rhythmical (Kiefer et al., 2007). This is one of the reasons that adults play 'Pat-a-cake' with children or why nursery rhymes are so appealing to them. Think about how often there is rhythm that children move to, sing to or keep time to. Poetry is no different for children.

'Song of the Train' by David McCord is a poem that does an excellent job of capturing rhythm. When this is read out loud, and especially with a choral reading (where multiple people readers read it out loud together), you are able to hear the rhythm that McCord is able to capture through the words and how, when they are read aloud, you hear the sound of a train on the track and the rhythm of this, with the repeated lines of 'clickety clack'. When read aloud, it makes the poem come alive.

'Which Jack?' by New Zealand poet Paula Green is another good example of a poem that captures the idea of rhythm as the poem explores different types of Jacks and plays with the language as well. From a Jack-in-the-box to a Jack-on-the-grass, the creative use of language helps establish a rhythm that flows naturally.

Rhyme patterns are the most common occurrence in poetry and can come in a number of formats. For the sake of simplicity, I will identify two specific patterns: those that follow the ABAB or the AABB format.

A strong Australian example of the ABAB rhyme format is Banjo Patterson's famous poem, 'The Man from Snowy River'. Take a look at the first stanza of the poem:

There was movement at the station, for the word had passed around

That the colt from old Regret had got away

And had joined the wild bush horses – he was worth a thousand pound,

So all the cracks had gathered to the fray.

All the tried and noted riders from the stations near and far

Had mustered at the homestead overnight,

For the bushmen love hard riding where the wild bush horses are,

And the stock-horse snuffs the battle with delight.

Well-known children's poet Shel Silverstein's poem 'Sick' contains the perfect example of the AABB rhyme pattern, with the rhymes of today/McKay and then mumps/bumps. This occurs throughout the poem, but again provides a strong example of a rhyme pattern that children would be able to understand and relate to.

While rhyme is one key aspect of poetry, another connected idea is sound. Two key examples of this would be alliteration and onomatopoeia.

- **Alliteration** is a very common component of poetry and is probably best known with tongue twisters as an example. Repeating the first letter or blend throughout a sentence is the most common form. For example, 'She sells seashells on the seashore.'
- **Onomatopoeia** is more than just a challenging word to say and spell. It represents in word, a specific sound or noise – a cow says 'moo' or when something crashes and we hear the 'bang' when it drops. Those are both examples of onomatopoeia. At times we can see it in different poems, like Susan Green's 'The Greedy Cat'. In the poem, Green describes how the cat eats different foods and the eating noise is represented by the scoff, scoff section in the poem. The *ZzzzZzzz…* section at the end of the poem represents the sound of the cat sleeping. Onomatopoeia within poetry allows the poems and language used to come off the page and assists in visualising.

There is power in the images that poetry evokes as well. While language is the most crucial part of poetry, one must remember that the words in poetry are able to evoke powerful images as well, and this is one of the main mysteries and fascinations about poetry. The poem 'Snowy Benches' by Aileen Fisher evokes images of a park bench in the middle of winter. It encourages the reader to imagine what a park looks like during this time.

When I first read this poem, for whatever reason the image of the snow on the 'laps' of the benches has always stuck with me. This is the beauty of poetry; with limited words, the language must work harder to evoke images in the mind and that is one of the beautiful attributes of poetry. It is one that can be celebrated with children by encouraging them to draw the images they imagine when they read or hear a poem because, as all good teachers know, there is more than one interpretation of a poem. This idea is something that Janeczko (2003) recommends, suggesting that teachers should 'advocate multiple interpretations' and creating these visualisations allows for multiple interpretations. Think about this a bit more. The beautiful thing about poetry, as discussed above, is that everyone can create different images from the same poem. Think about Billie Joe Armstrong from Green Day. When he sat down to write 'Good Riddance (Time of Your Life)', he did not say to himself, 'I think I will write a song that will be played at every graduation, debutante ball and prom.' Instead, when he wrote the song, he had other reasons or ideas in mind. However, people around the globe have all interpreted it differently, which captures the beauty of poetry. We can all have different interpretations of poetry (and even songs) and that is okay. Teachers must remember this as well, as it helps to appreciate poetry.

So let us revisit the main concern addressed at the beginning of the chapter, which is the negative attitude about poetry. One of the key ways to battle the residual negativity towards poetry is to build an appreciation for poetry. This can actually be done quite easily with children, and especially young children. This is because, as mentioned earlier, young children naturally enjoy rhythm, rhyme and sound. This is quite common in young children. Think about the different children's songs and chants they are introduced to at a young age – 'itsy, bitsy, spider' or 'twinkle, twinkle, little star' – and then there are nursery rhymes and Mother Goose. *Over the Hills and Far Away* is collection of all the best-loved nursery rhymes from around the world, compiled by Elizabeth Hammill, and includes illustrations from 77 different artists. This book would be a great way to introduce familiar and new nursery rhymes. These types of literacy experiences are what begin to pave a child's positive path to poetry. It is important to celebrate these encounters early on. It is also imperative to note how these early experiences are all sound related, as young children are introduced to the flow and sound of language. This continues when we explore what it means with poetry. The idea of appreciation is a natural occurrence when we examine, celebrate and enjoy how words flow and sound when they are spoken or read aloud.

However, poetry is not simply limited to rhythm, rhyme and sound; it can be far more sophisticated. Many people may think that just because a picture book rhymes, it is poetry. While there may be elements of poetry within the books, the problem with this idea is that so much is being left out or assumed as well. Rhyming picture books can be used to introduce features of poetry, but this chapter will address more specific forms of poetry. Some books go beyond looking at rhymes, and introduce and celebrate how poetry can be appreciated, and not treated like a dead object, as Janeczko (2003) mentioned earlier.

When teaching poetry to children, it is important to notice and examine rhyme patterns, but it is also necessary to explore other formats of poetry. The following section identifies some key formats of poetry that children should be familiar with. Some of these types are:

- **Humorous verse** is one definite way for teachers and parents to 'hook' children into poetry, and sometimes those reluctant readers. For example, Andy Griffiths's *The Bad Book* and *The Very Bad Book* both contain humorous versions of well-known nursery rhymes, as seen with 'Mary Had a Very Bad Lamb' below. This example has strong connections with the humour chapter, which includes word play as a way to engage young readers.

Image 5.1 Mary Had a Very Bad Lamb by Andy Griffiths (with permission from Pan Macmillan Australia)

- **Ballads** and **narrative** poems are well-known poetry forms. Australia's own Banjo Patterson is very well known for both *Waltzing Matilda* and *Man from Snowy River*, and both of these have new editions, illustrated by Freya Blackwood. *We're All Australians*

Now by Banjo Patterson and illustrated by Mark Wilson introduces readers to a classic poem with very detailed and exquisite illustrations. It celebrates Australia and provides information and detail about the First World War and those who fought in it.

LYRICAL

Lyrical poems can be a tricky format to identify. Most often they contain a rhyme, so it is commonly turned into a broad genre of poetry. However, lyrical poems have a definite flow in their language and a lyrical nature to them. For example, *The Wonderful Things You Will Be* is a lyrical poetry book by Emily Winfield Martin that uses soft rhythms and language flow to create a lullaby-type reading experience for young children to inspire them to be whatever they dream to be. *Where Do They Go?* by Julia Alvarez uses lyrical language to answer the challenging question of what happens when a loved one dies. This format is a good one to use to introduce children to the beautiful nature and language flow of poetry.

Limericks are a well-known and loved format of poetry commonly used for humour, but is not limited simply to humorous verse. They follow the specific rhyme pattern of AABBA. This format may be a little different for children, but it is a very common format and children will see this form quite frequently. *A Natural History of Insects in 100 Limericks* written by Richard Jones contains limericks that are about unusual insects. Combining the humorous poem format with the intriguing idea of unique insects works well.

While a bit older, there is also this humorous title *Loopy Limericks* by John Foster (2012). Although there are few limerick-only poetry books, there are many anthologies that include limericks in them.

Haiku is probably one of the most common forms of poetry that children learn. It has a very structured format of 5 syllables in the first line, 7 syllables in the second line and 5 syllables again in the final line. Traditionally, haikus are around a nature theme. This format has received a lot of attention in recent years, and this is seen in the large number of creatively titled books – for example, *Guyku* by Bob Raczka. The haiku poetry in this title addresses topics such as climbing trees, splashing in puddles and flying kites.

One of this author's favourites is *Wabi Sabi* by Mark Reibstein and illustrated by Ed Young which follows the nature theme by being about a family's cat with the same name as the title of the book. The exquisite illustrations and format of the book (held vertically) provide a captivating reading experience. *Yugen* is another title by Mark Reibstein and Ed Young which tells the story of a mother and son and is another beautiful collaboration.

For those who enjoy this genre, it is worth exploring *H is for Haiku: A Treasury of Haiku from A to Z* by Sydell Rosenberg which contains some good haiku poetry as well truly capturing the inclusion of nature within the poems. The limited text can even capture a squirrel eating acorns on an autumn day.

This collection of haiku poems will have children reflecting on nature and aspects of childhood. *My First Book of Haiku Poems* translated by Esperanza Ramirez-Christensen is yet another title that children could discover with traditional Japanese haikus.

Concrete poems are the most visual of all poems because the words are formed to create the object the poem is all about. There are some amazing concrete poem books for children to discover. *A Poke in the Eye* by Paul Janeczko and illustrated by Chris Raschka is a fun creative title worth knowing. The title poem is structured in the form of an eye test chart. *Wet Cement: A Mix of Concrete Poems* is a 'punny' title full of poems by Bob Raczka. The creative use of words to make the illustrations are fun and hopefully inspiring to children for their own concrete poem creations.

Poems for more than one voice is a type of poetry that was made famous by Paul Fleischman from the United States with his books *Joyful Noise* and *I Am Phoenix*. This creative form of poetry is meant to be read aloud by two voices. Sometimes the voice will have their own line, and at other times they are meant to be read in unison. Challenging himself a bit further, he wrote *Big Talk: Poems for Four Voices*. This is a great way to celebrate poetry and how it sounds when it is read aloud in the classroom while still challenging students.

Boom! Bellow! Bleat! is a book of animal poems for two voices by Georgia Heard that will allow animal lovers to explore this format further. Connecting with the theme of school, *Messing Around on the Monkey Bars* contains poems for two voices all about school by Betsy Franco. An example is found in the poem 'New Kid at School' in which one voice reads the question and another voice reads the answer (in bold). This format for the two voices allows two readers to read the poem together and share the interaction between two students talking about where the new student came from 'Far away' and if they miss their friends, 'every day'.

Finally *Seeds, Bees, Butterflies, and More!* by Carole Gerber is another title with poems for two voices which has a strong nature focus with bees, plants and other insects interacting within some humorous verses meant to be read by more than one voice.

CREATIVE VERSIONS

Mirror Mirror and *Follow Follow* by Marilyn Singer are both examples of poems that are 'mirrored', meaning that you can read them forwards and backwards, and they remain a complete poem. When seen side by side, it is even more amazing. When examining the poems in the book – for example, from *Mirror Mirror* we can see how they are the same poem, but in reverse order. What this does is change the perspective of who is narrating the poem. Using her poem 'In the Hood', for example, on the left side of the page, it could be Little Red Riding Hood's perspective and on the right, it could be the Big Bad Wolf's. That is what makes this clever approach so appealing to teachers and students alike and worth finding and using in your own classroom.

My Bed is an Air Balloon is a lyrical poem by Julia Copus that can be read front to back and back to front. The illustrations are done by well-known illustrator, Alison Jay, and they match the text beautifully.

Dan Brown has 'composed' a number of great lyrical poems in his book *Wild Symphony*. What is impressive about this book is that the reader can scan the QR code in the front of the book or download the app and listen to the music that accompanies each of the poems. This mixed-mode approach is one that will engage readers of all ages and perhaps inspire some budding musicians as well. All these books show the creativity of language and how important it is to celebrate and enjoy poetry with children of all ages.

PICTURE BOOKS OF A POEM

Sometimes picture books are the best format for introducing children to classic poems and poets. For example, we may all know Robert Frost's 'Stopping by Woods on a Snowy Evening'. However, in picture book format with Vivian Mineker's stunning illustrations, it will connect with children on another level. This is also the case with Frost's 'The Road Not Taken', also illustrated by Mineker. Both of these books put a fresh look at well known and loved poems by a highly regarded poet. Chris Raschka has also done this with the book *A Song About Myself* which celebrates the life and work of John Keats in the poet's only work written for children. Raschka's signature style is apparent in the book and again is a way to introduce classic poets to children in a welcoming way.

OTHER POETRY BOOKS TO KNOW

Poetree by Shauna LaVoy Reynolds is a fun idea and play on words in which a young girl writes a poem to a tree and does not expect a response but the tree writes back. The book is a wonderful idea that encourages children to write their own poems and also has a beautiful lesson on friendship. This book could also inspire classroom teachers to grow a 'poetree' in their own classrooms.

Can I Touch Your Hair? by Irene Latham and Charles Waters. This is an absolute amazing book about two children (Irene and Charles) in the same class who end up paired together for a writing project about poetry. Each double-page spread presents the characters' perspectives about similar experiences. The topics deal with such things as shoes, going to the beach, trying to play with others at the playground and getting into trouble at home. Because one child is white and the other is black, through the poems each tells they learn to understand what the other might be experiencing and in the end, become friends. This is a powerful book that captures racial issues in a very positive light.

FREE VERSE

Free verse, or blank verse, is when there is no rhyme pattern whatsoever. This is a poetry format that 'breaks the rules' of poetry and allows for more freedom and poetic licence. Steven Herrick is a well-known and loved Australian poet for young adults and children. His signature style is the free verse form novel where the book is an entire poem without the rhyming format that children may be used to. *Zoe, Max, and the Bicycle Bus* and *How to Repaint a Life* are both examples of this free verse format that are written for older primary school and high school audiences. *Zoe, Max, and the Bicycle Bus* tells the story of a grade five class that starts a 'bicycle bus' to address concerns with the environment, but the book is much more than the unique bus, but a diverse story about friendships within the classroom and so much more. *How to Repaint a Life* shares the story of Isaac who is escaping his old life and an abusive father as he gets off a bus in a small town where he knows no one. When he meets generous individuals and makes new friends, he is able to start life afresh. The free verse format shows readers how poetry does not always have to follow a structure-based format, but still has the ability to tell a powerful story. Australian children's author and poet Sally Murphy's *Roses are Blue* uses the verse novel format to tell the story of Amber Rose and her family as they struggle with tragedy and change. This is another example of the free verse novel that could be connected with Steven Herrick's work to showcase this style of poetry.

Sharon Creech's *Love that Dog (*and its sequel *Hate that Cat*) cannot be recommended enough. In *Love That Dog*, Creech is able to capture Jack's dislike for poetry and sadness with his dog, but also how his teacher Miss Stretchberry is able to turn this all around through poetry and even make him learn that he is a poet himself. Creech uses different poems from Walter Dean Myers and William Carlos Williams to teach and celebrate poetry. In the sequel *Hate That Cat*, Creech again tells the story of Jack, but introduces readers to more formats of poetry as well as poets, as Jack discovers a greater love for poetry. *The One and Only Ivan* (Katherine Applegate) and *Out of the Dust* (Karen Hesse) are both Newbery winning books from the United States that are novels told in free verse. While published some time ago, the books are able to address such controversial issues as animal cruelty and surviving the Great Depression, and are powerfully told stories that show the audience how effective poetry can be in telling stories.

COMPILATIONS

Poetry compilations and anthologies are one of the best ways to introduce children to a wide variety of different formats, poems, poets and topics. Sometimes they can be around a specific theme and other times they are simply a collection of poems. *A Boat of Stars: New Australian Children's Poems* (edited by Margaret Connolly and Natalie Jane Prior) and *The ABC Book of Australian Poetry* (Libby Hathorn) shares poems about the Australian landscape, from towns to country and the bush, as well as the different seasons. Michelle Taylor's *100 Ways to Fly* contains poems that will make readers laugh, challenge them with tongue twisters and explore the way we can play with language, and examine words and sounds all within poetry. All three of these titles are examples of poetry compilations that will introduce children to a variety of wonderful poems, images and ideas that build an appreciation for poetry and its varied features and forms. For example, the poem 'What's in a Few Words?' is full of word play in every line. The poem challenges readers to find words within words. For example, the first line, 'there's an owl in my vowel' allows readers to see how the word owl is within the word vowel. As the poem continues, the lines become more complex and challenging for readers.

Tiger, Tiger, Burning Bright! by Fiona Waters, *Fantastic Football Poems* by John Foster and *I Am the Seed that Grew the Tree* by Fiona Waters and illustrated by Frann Preston-Gannon, are all UK compilations that will interest children with their themes of animals and sport. These are good books to use to showcase a variety of formats and themes for children to learn.

The Proper Way to Meet a Hedgehog selected by Paul B. Janeczko, *Feel the Beat* by Marilyn Singer and *Out of Wonder* created by Kwame Alexander, Chris Colderley and Marjory Wentworth are all compilations from the United States that continue the theme of introducing children to new poets, but are also related to themes and topics that interest them. Again, a compilation of poems is a good way to expand a child's interest in poetry.

In *Wild in the Streets: 20 Poems of City Animals*, poet Marilyn Singer combines both poetry and non-fiction into one book. In this book, readers are introduced to poems about different animals from around the world, such as brushtail possums in Sydney, huntsman spiders in South Africa and pigeons from everywhere. After the poem, there is a paragraph about the animal and where it is found. The poems are in different forms and this is discussed at the end of the book. *In the Past* by David Elliott is another book that combines poetry and non-fiction. Elliott does an amazing job of writing poems about different types of dinosaurs. At the end of the book there is further information about the different dinosaurs as well as the time periods that they come from.

Table 5.1 Evaluation criteria: poetry

Does the rhythm and rhyme of the poetry flow naturally or is it forced? How does the language flow?

Does the poetry include components of poetry such as alliteration, onomatopoeia, repetition?

Does the poetry evoke the senses (touch, smell, taste, and specifically, sight)?

If the poetry contains figurative language, is it appropriate for children (similes and metaphors)?

Does the shape of the poem match the theme and tone in the poem?

Does the poem evoke images?

Is there a clear purpose for the poem?

CONCLUSION

There are a number of great ways that poetry can be celebrated in the classroom.

1. Read a poem a day. Notice how there are compilations that have a nature poem for every day or animal poems for every day. The same can be done in the classroom with students. Read one poem every day. I once suggested this to a children's literature class years ago and heard from a student later who told me she had tried it in her own classroom. She went

on to say that one day she forgot to read a poem. She did not think her students would notice or care, but how wrong she was – they reminded her and made her make up the day as well! Clearly, the class had grown an appreciation for poetry and they let her know.
2. Read a poem during a short break. When students are lining up for playtime or to go home, why not read a poem? They do not need to be long poems, just ones that will engage and interest children. This is a good transition strategy that will also enable students to build their listening skills.
3. Poetry slam: this is one of the easiest ways to celebrate poetry and also encourage children to read aloud in a fun, non-threatening way. Allowing children to read and 'perform' a poem in front of their class will also present them with a number of great new poems and poets. The poetry slam is a positive approach to encourage students to explore and share poems and poets with their classmates and friends.

SO WHAT HAVE WE LEARNED?

Poetry can be a challenging genre, but there are many great poetry books from around the world that can engage, inspire and interest children. It is crucial that teachers are open to poetry and provide positive experiences with the genre. This chapter introduced a number of different formats of poetry and books that highlight those formats. Compilations around different themes and formats assist teachers to introduce and engage readers so that stereotypes about and ambivalence towards poetry can be shattered. By reading and exploring poetry with children in different ways, teachers are able to break down resistance and encourage excitement in an important genre.

ADDITIONAL TITLES

Silly Squid! – Janeen Brian

Did You Hear What I Heard? Poems About School – Kay Winters

The Undefeated – Kwame Alexander and Kadir Nelson

101 Poems for Children: A Laureate's Choice – Carol Ann Duffy

Poetry for Kids – Emily Dickinson

A Little ABC Book – Jenny Palmer

Animal Poems from A to Z – Meish Goldish

This is Just to Say: Poems of Apology and Forgiveness – Joyce Sidman

Thunder Underground – Jane Yolen

Slam Your Poetry: Write a Revolution – Miles Merrill

OLDER READERS

Limelight – Solli Raphael

WANT TO KNOW MORE?

Pullinger, D. (2017) *From Tongue to Text: A New Reading of Children's Poetry*. London: Bloomsbury Academic.

This book delves deeply into poetry for children and how it can be examined and explored even from a theoretical lens.

Sloan, G.D. (2003) *Give Them Poetry!: A Guide for Sharing Poetry with Children K-8*. New York: Teachers College.

This book is a practical guide for teachers of how to connect children and poetry.

Styles, M., Joy, L. and Whitley, D. (2010) *Poetry and Childhood*. Stoke-on-Trent: Trentham Books.

Another book that provides a critical lens for poetry, both examining and celebrating the different formats and themes found in children's poetry.

REFERENCES

Jacobs, J. and Tunnell, M. (2004) *Children's Literature, Briefly* (3rd edn). London: Pearson.

Janeczko, P. (2003) *Opening a Door: Reading Poetry in the Middle School Classroom*. New York: Scholastic.

Kiefer, B.Z., Hepler, S.I., Hickman, J. and Huck, C.S. (2007) *Charlotte Huck's Children's Literature* (9th edn). London: McGraw-Hill.

Norton, D.E. (2003) *Through the Eyes of a Child* (6th edn). London: Pearson.

Temple, C., Martinez, M., Yokota, J. and Naylor, A. (2002) *Children's Books in Children's Hands* (2nd edn). Boston, MA: Allyn & Bacon.

6

NON-FICTION

WHAT WE WILL LEARN

- All about the non-fiction genre.
- The key components found within non-fiction texts.
- The aspects of reading/literacy that are needed in reading non-fiction texts.
- The different forms of non-fiction.
- How the visual is becoming more of a focus in non-fiction.
- What a non-fiction text is.

Throughout the early years of a child's life, they are exposed to a plethora of narratives. Non-fiction, however, is the exact opposite. Instead of focusing on an imagined story, it relies on real life and facts. Early on, scholars in the field of children's literature referred to the genre as 'informational books' (Kiefer et al., 2007), but this has changed to non-fiction. A non-fiction text is one that breaks down factual information for children to easily comprehend. To put this into context, the author of this book had a friend who told him that whenever he needed to learn something new about a topic, he would go to the public library and head straight to the children's section as opposed to the adult non-fiction section. Why, as an adult, did he do this, you might ask? Because he found that children's non-fiction books were able to provide the key information needed and it avoided providing extra information that was not needed. This friend was able to find accurate and authentic information about the topics he was researching, whether it was West Africa, Princeton University or what a buckeye is. What this friend recognised was that in the adult non-fiction section the books were more extensive and sometimes overwhelming with the information. By choosing books about the same topic from the children's section, the friend was able to find the key information that was needed. And that is the beauty of non-fiction texts for children – they provide key information about topics in an easily understandable format.

WHY DO WE HAVE NON-FICTION TEXT?

Children are naturally curious individuals and like to learn as much as they can about whatever topic interests them. Non-fiction allows them an easily accessible format to learn more about a topic that piques their interest. Think about the reading process of children discussed earlier in the book. Children first learn *to* read, and after this is established and they are readers, they read *to learn*. The best genre for learning about new things is non-fiction. As Kiefer et al. (2007) state: 'a non-fiction writer is first a teacher, then an artist, and should be concerned with feeling as well as thinking, passion as well as clarity' (p. 590). It is important to remember, however, that non-fiction texts require different skills for reading.

A key aspect of non-fiction is that it must distinguish between fact and theory. An excellent example of this is Tohby Riddle's *Yahoo Creek: An Australian Mystery*. This book presents information from authentic Australian newspapers about Bigfoot. However, because Bigfoot has never been verified, it presents the fact versus theory argument. Another title that showcases this idea is *Aliens, Ghosts and Vanishings* by Stella Tarakson. Children are introduced to a number of different stories and 'theories', and they must use the facts provided to determine their own beliefs about fact or theory. Regardless of your own beliefs, these titles support the idea of how non-fiction must be clear and not present theories as factual information.

One of the most current elements found in non-fiction is the use of the visual. There was discussion in an earlier chapter about how the visual plays a bigger role in current children's literature, specifically picture books. This is even more apparent in non-fiction. Think about how children are able to see more detailed photographs or even videos of animals in the wild. Technology has allowed this, and non-fiction texts have reaped the benefits. In the past, readers had to make do with limited black-and-white pictures being included to support the text. Now, through the use of technology, the inclusion of colour is much easier. The visuals may have lifelike photos of animals or creative graphs and charts. Regardless of format, it is very clear that non-fiction excels at the inclusion of visuals. *The Illustrated Encyclopaedia of 'Ugly' Animals* is a great example of this idea. *Wild Animals of the North* includes breathtaking illustrations that will not only teach children about animals, but also may inspire them artistically as well.

A creative twist on the visual format is *A Day in the Life of a Poo, a Gnu and You* that uses the comic book format to present a day in the life of various subjects such as plankton, bacteria and the human brain. The engaging visual format will have readers looking for more ways to learn through comics.

Steve Jenkins, an author and illustrator from the United States has a similar style to Jeannie Baker in Australia. He created the illustrations for Mem Fox's *Hello Baby!* He has beautifully illustrated a number of non-fiction books such as *The Shark Book, What Do You Do if You Work at the Zoo?* and *Life on Earth*. Jenkins's creative use of the visual through his use of recycled paper collage is well worth exploring with readers.

Lonely Planet is a well-known publishing company for travel guides. They have a series of books for children as well, and *Airports, Cities* and *Trains* are excellent examples of the strong use of visuals to inform and educate readers. The illustrations have great detail and at times present the inner workings of the topic being addressed.

HOW ARE NON-FICTION TEXTS READ?

Students need to establish their decoding (code-breaking) skills in order to help them decode future texts. 'For all students the most important component of reading development is an understanding of how to apply their knowledge and skills to a new text' (Winch et al., 2008: 120). Educators, parents and children need to be aware of the specific grammar features that are found primarily in non-fiction books. For example, in the non-fiction genre, children are exposed to:

Paragraphs   Information is presented in a structured format using paragraphs with topic sentences.

Subheadings   The information is provided in a structure that requires subheadings to assist in breaking down the text further.

Topic sentences   These first sentences of paragraphs are what provide the key information to be addressed in the paragraph.

Present tense   Because factual information is being presented, readers will be introduced to a lot of present tense verbs.

Technical vocabulary   Factual information will have specific information presented and this will include specific terms or technical vocabulary. In non-fiction books for younger children, these terms may be set in bold or italics, and there may be a glossary at the end of the book.

General nouns   Again, because the information is specific to a topic and only presenting factual information, the reader will see a lot of general nouns. Philip Bunting's *The Wonderful Wisdom of Ants*, which educates readers about the ant world, includes such technical words as drone, queen, pheromones, omnivorous, and much more.

Jeannie Baker's *Playing with Collage* is a perfect example of a book that has many of the grammar features mentioned earlier. Looking at one page from the book, you will see the subheading and paragraph format, as well as the topic sentence and present tense verbs, and even technical vocabulary included in the pages.

Children also need to learn and be exposed to a number of key features found primarily in non-fiction texts:

- Table of contents
- Charts
- Graphs
- Pictures
- Captions
- Index
- Glossary

- Appendix
- Timeline

Daley (2019) writes how 'non-fiction books expose children to a huge variety of text types and visual aids like diagrams, graphs, captions, lists, headings, subheadings and labels' (p. 133). Providing opportunities for children to read and study non-fiction texts allows them to become more familiar with these various features.

Tim Flannery's *Explore Your World: Weird, Wild, Amazing!* is probably one of the best books that showcases so many attributes of a children's non-fiction text. In the Introduction, Flannery presents information about himself which establishes his credibility. Then each section has a table of contents as readers learn about all sorts of amazing aspects from around the world. The multilevels of text, discussed later, will have curious readers poring over the pages to learn more. The personal 'Flannery Files' on some pages will introduce readers to connections the author has personally experienced as well. Another excellent example of a non-fiction text that includes many of these features is *Australia's Wild Weird Wonderful Weather* by Stephanie Owen Reeder and Tania McCartney. The book has a table of contents, many different forms of graphs, glossary, further reading and an index. Yet another title worth picking up is Sandra Morris's *North and South* which explores and compares animals from the northern and southern hemispheres. The entire book exemplifies the characteristics of a high-quality, non-fiction text. The table of contents, glossary, index, and more are featured in this book and the creative approach of presenting information on the top of the page (North) and the bottom of the page (South) highlights how the visual is used effectively to engage readers.

BUST A MYTH

You need to read a non-fiction title cover to cover.

The joy of non-fiction texts, and especially current titles and formats, is that they invite readers to pick and choose the elements they read. By being able to determine what they want to read, children are motivated to read and when rereading the book, will be more encouraged to explore other parts of the book they have not read previously.

Multilevel texts are another key feature found in many non-fiction books. This means that there are multiple forms (or layers) of text that provide separate information. For example, there may be a 'main text' providing the key information, but a page may also include side bars, graphs, 'cool facts', etc. that provide additional information, but this can be read separately from the main text or not at all. Multilevel texts provide readers with the opportunity to read the parts they want to and even skip parts as well. This is vastly different from a narrative in which everything must be read to comprehend the entire story. As Daley (2019) comments about non-fiction texts, 'readers can dip in and out of non-fiction books, making them perfect for reading in small chunks' (p. 132). *The Space Race* by Angelina Yalda is another title that includes almost every key feature found in non-fiction texts: table of contents, glossary, index, graphs, charts and pictures. It is well worth exploring with children to help them understand what these features look like and how they work. *The Bacteria Book*, a DK title by aptly named Steve Mould, will delight readers with all sorts of fascinating and gross facts about bacteria. The format is truly multilevel in how the information is presented, and the reader does not have to read every word on every single page, but can instead pick and choose what they want to read about.

There are some key formats of non-fiction titles and it is important to explore these different forms so that you are able to assist readers with the format, content and non-fiction elements they will encounter. This section presents a number of different titles that address the format.

Non-fiction picture books may sound a confusing idea, but these are quite a common format of informational texts. These books are in picture book format and may even appear to have a story in them. *Kookaburra* by Claire Saxby is one such example. This book presents information about kookaburras, but it appears in almost a story format, and each page has factual information about kookaburras separate from the narrative format. Again addressing the multilevel format, *Searching for Cicadas* by Lesley Gibbes is another title that exemplifies the picture book format. The 'story' is about a boy and his grandfather as they look for cicadas, but each page is full of further facts about cicadas. *Gecko* is a non-fiction picture book that presents the story of a gecko in the wild, as well as providing factual information in another paragraph. The end of the book also has more information about geckos and an index. *Dry to Dry* by Pamela Freeman and Liz Anelli (Eve Pownall Award winner by the CBCA) is another book that exemplifies the picture book format. It tells the 'story' of life in Kakadu, while also including factual information about Australian weather.

Antarctica by Moira Court is a combination non-fiction and counting book about Antarctica. The final four pages provide 'Did you know?' facts about the continent. Sometimes this format can be rather confusing when identifying this type of book. Some may classify this format as 'faction'. However, the main purpose of these books is to inform or present factual information about a topic. *Anemone is not the Enemy* by Anna McGregor and *Argh! There's a Skeleton Inside You!* by Idan Ben-Barak and Julian Frost are both examples of colourfully illustrated non-fiction picture books that will engage young readers as well as provide them with additional factual information at the end of the book. Ben-Barak and Frost have teamed up with *Do Not Lick This Book*, which is created in a similar structure. *Ice Breaker! An Epic Antarctic Adventure* written by Maria Gill is another example of a non-fiction picture book. It tells the story of a New Zealand ship captain and an Arctic explorer who were able to navigate the icy cold waters and icebergs on a challenging adventure. Readers will be intrigued by the true story and enjoy the accompanying illustrations that tell it.

Because young readers (and teachers as well) can be inundated with the huge number of non-fiction picture books, readers must be aware of anthropomorphism. This is when inanimate objects are made to have humanlike characteristics. When this happens, it creates a sense of fiction within non-fiction, thus causing confusion for readers. *Bouncing Back: An Eastern Barred Bandicoot Story* by Rohan Cleaver has the Bandicoot telling the story of how they and their species, on the brink of extinction, were able to find shelter in a rubbish tip. Based on a true story, the book gives the animal the voice of a narrator of the story while presenting factual information, which can lead to misunderstanding. For example, notice what happens in the first few pages: 'We build nests on the ground out of grasses, leaves, and twigs. For you they would be hard to see, but for us, they provide the perfect shelter to protect us during the day.'

While the factual information at the end of the book helps the reader learn more, the narrative-like format, presenting the point of view or perspective of the Bandicoot, can leave readers questioning whether the book is non-fiction or narrative. *Kookaburra* by Claire Saxby provides another example of anthropomorphism. 'In the crinkled shadows night-dwellers yawn, day-creatures stretch and Kookaburra laughs. In a line on a limb with her mate and three young, she leads a sunrise chorus.' Notice how the author subtly uses personification, or human-ike qualities to describe the animal. On the limb with her mate and starting a sunrise chorus are both examples of anthropomorphism. *The Great Lizard Trek* (Felicity Bradshaw) and *Hold On! Saving the Spotted Handfish* (Gina M. Newton) both share information told from the animal's perspective – a lizard and a spotted handfish. The use of first-person narrative in these books can cause confusion for young readers as they must distinguish between narrative and non-fiction. It is important that children are introduced to the concept of anthropomorphism so they are aware of this concept when they are reading.

IDENTIFICATION BOOKS

Sami Bayly's book *The Illustrated Encyclopaedia of Ugly Animals* featured earlier is an example of an identification book in which readers can learn more specific details about a range of ugly-looking animals. Her other titles, *The Illustrated Encylopaedia of Dangerous Animals* and *A Curious Collection of Peculiar Creatures*, will be books that have children reading more about different animals and flipping through the pages to find more and more fun, gross and dangerous animals to learn more about. The illustrations are very inviting as well.

Whose Nose Do You Suppose? by Richard Turner is a great non-fiction book for younger children to identify animals and whose nose belongs to each animal. This would be a good book to introduce the non-fiction genre to younger children.

Well-known non-fiction publisher DK (Dorling Kindersley) has the title *Knowledge Encyclopedia Ocean!* which helps readers identify different creatures in the ocean and more about nearly every aspect of the ocean. The strong use of visuals for every entry will appeal to readers as they pick and choose what they want to learn more about.

First Field Guide to Australian Frogs & Reptiles is a title by Pat Slater that provides a guide for a variety of frogs and reptiles found in Australia. Each entry provides key information about the frog or reptile and a photograph.

As stated earlier, children are very curious, and a country like Australia or New Zealand with a large number of beaches and rockpools will have children exploring all the time. *Rockpools: A Guide for Kiwi Kids* by Ned Barraud is a wonderful title with incredibly detailed illustrations that teaches children more about all the different creatures and items that they will find in a rockpool. The illustrations alone will have a reader looking closely at the book.

New Zealand's Backyard Beasts also written by Ned Barraud is an identification book that will help readers learn more about all sorts of creatures they may encounter in their backyard. There are detailed illustrations for each object and lots of facts about each one that will have readers learning more and more about their surrounds.

Encyclopedia of Animals is a UK title by Jules Howard that goes beyond the backyard and teaches about animals from around the world. The book could be paired with Sami Bayly's books, although the selected species may not be as engaging as the ones Bayly has chosen.

The Big Book of Antarctica by Charles Hope is another example of an identification book that teaches all about Antarctica. The book presents information about the wildlife that lives there, the cold climate and even parts of the history of the continent.

LIFE-CYCLE BOOKS

Life cycles are one of the more common concepts that children are taught in school. *Life Cycles: Everything From Start to Finish* is a truly amazing book published by DK, a well-known publisher of non-fiction books. Readers will explore different life cycles – for example, a butterfly, but also some less common ones too, such as water and volcanoes. *Australian Geographic Discover: Life Cycle* is another title that presents the life cycles of different creatures – for example, butterflies, frogs and wombats. The information is much more basic and able to be presented in a double-page spread. For younger readers, Hachette Australia has titles such as *Tadpole to Frog, Egg to Chicken* and *Acorn to Oak Tree.* Lerner Publishers has a Lifecycle series that will teach readers about such animals as sharks, dogs and bees. The life-cycle concept is one that can be explored in a variety of ways in this format.

EXPERIMENT AND ACTIVITY BOOKS

Peter Macinnis has a number of great non-fiction books, and *Australian Backyard Earth Scientist* and *Australian Backyard Explorer* are terrific titles that will engage readers in a number of ways through activities and experiments that can be conducted, explored, and much more. The 'Did you know?' features showcase how interesting facts can be presented to children and further their learning. This is another example of the multilevel text format discussed earlier. Combined with these titles are George Ivanoff's Survival books, *The Human Body Survival Guide* and *The Australia Survival Guide.* Both of these books share a fun, engaging format that will engross readers to learn more. They also have very interactive pages that are further examples of multilevel text.

Copycat Science by Mark Barfield is a UK title that will be truly fascinating to readers. Connecting with the concept of reliance on the visuals, this book uses a comic book format to teach about a new concept, as well as show the step-by-step process for readers to conduct their own experiments. This is a truly fascinating book that has the potential to inspire future scientists.

SURVEY BOOKS

Many children love the word 'Poo', so with a title like *There's a Zoo in My* Poo, how could a child not love learning about their insides? With an author that is a well-known nutrition professor and interesting content matched with humorous drawings and, of course, poo jokes, children will enjoy reading and learning through this book.

What's Out There? Amazing Plants, Rocks, Creatures, and Cultures that Make Australia Extraordinary written by Nicole Stewart is a very interesting Australian title that will provide an abundance of information about the country. Some will be common knowledge, while others are interesting and fun facts that will have any reader learning more and more about the continent and country.

A Climate in Chaos, written by Neal Layton, is a text that explores the idea of global warming and climate change. It has lots of information about climate change and in the back is a small glossary, as well as three brief biographical information sections on children who have challenged ways to combat climate change.

Well-known non-fiction author Ian Graham, from the UK, has a number of great books. *My Best Book of Spaceships* is a title that will inspire young astronauts to learn more and explore more. *Space on Earth* by Shiela Kalani is a longer non-fiction text that presents information about space and how the science of space ties in with everyday objects such as sunglasses, braces, bike helmets, and more. This book is in chapter format and has interesting side facts about the various topics presented. DK has also published *The Mysteries of the Universe*, a beautifully illustrated and informative book that will have children exploring deeper into space. *The Awesome Book of Space*, written by Adam Frost from the UK, extends the idea of space with intriguing and sometimes unusual facts and information about space. All of these books could be connected to Seymour Simon's books on space from the US.

Back on planet Earth, Lonely Planet Kids has the title *Hidden Wonders*, which explores wondrous places across the globe. Australian children will be interested to see Lake Hellier, Coober Pedy and even the giant pink slugs of Mount Kaputar, and so many more places from around the world. Readers interested in this title can also explore *North and South*, a 2021 book that compares what happens in the world from around the globe between the northern and southern hemispheres. Also branching out beyond space, there is the UK book *The Colours of History: How Colours Shaped the World*, which provides historical references and more to the idea of colours.

CROSSOVER SPECIALISED BOOKS

Everest is a truly interesting book that presents a plethora of information about Mount Everest, while at the same time presenting information about the first two men who climbed to the top. The crossover appeal for this book is between the survey genre and biography. The information and stories are quite intriguing and will have readers on the edge of their seats. This book could easily be paired with *Ice Breaker! An Epic Antarctic Adventure* discussed earlier.

The Happiness Box by Mark Greenwood and Andrew McLean is an example of a crossover specialised book that combines the non-fiction picture book format with biography and a survey book. The book teaches how prisoners of war created gifts for children, and ultimately 'The Happiness Book' which Australian soldier, Sergeant David Griffin, wrote but in the end was never given to the children. It is a remarkable story told well and containing plenty of information about the war and some of the soldiers.

All Aboard! True Train Tales is a crossover book that combines a specialised book about trains and how they work with real-life stories presented by the grandfather in the story. So many facts are presented in the book and they are connected to the real-life stories that grandpa shares. The glossary, further reading and index sections will easily assist readers to learn more about trains and the stories told.

Sometimes there are books that are a little bit about everything, as is the case with *Brain Candy*, presented by National Geographic Kids. The book is full of random facts on a wide range of topics. The colourful photographs throughout the book will have children engaged and sharing many of the random facts they learn. This is similar to a UK title *The Colours of History: How Colours Shaped the World* which explores the impact of colours from around the world.

The Ultimate Animal Counting Book is a combination of counting book and non-fiction book about animals. As children count to one hundred, they are introduced to numerous facts about animals such as Highland cows, zebras, capybaras, penguins, and many more.

Continuing with the beginning book concept crossed with non-fiction is the title *M is for Mutiny* by John Dickson and Bern Emmerichs. This title is an alphabetical history of Australia. Each letter has a paragraph about the topic. Some of the topics addressed are more serious and would be more appropriate for upper primary school. This could be paired with Tania McCartney's *Australia Illustrated*. Both provide information about the country, and the illustrations truly blend well with the text and highlight the qualities of a strong picture book. For older readers who want to learn even more about Australia, they can turn to *The Upside-down History of Down Under* by Alison Lloyd and Terry Denton.

CRAFT AND HOW-TO BOOKS

Lunch at 10 Pomegranate Street is a wonderful picture book that brings an entire apartment building together through the recipes they cook for a common meal. Children will be able to cook and learn new dishes and about different countries through this book. Connecting with the kitchen theme is *The Kitchen Science Cookbook*. This book will have readers trying all sorts of experiments and cooking, such as making a solar cookie oven or microwave cheese, or putting an egg in a bottle, or making it bounce. Food and experiments are a fun way to engage readers in non-fiction.

The Amazing Recycling Project Book written by Sara Stanford is a UK title that will have children begging their parents not to throw anything away. The book shows how to make robots, dragons, cars, elephants, and more from what normally might be tossed into the rubbish bin. *Playing with Collage* by Jeannie Baker, mentioned earlier, is a great title to motivate fans of her work to try their own hand at the collage technique she uses.

Australian weather can be quite unpredictable at times, and it is important to be prepared for whatever happens. *The Bushfire Book* by Polly Marsden is a non-fiction text that teaches readers how to be aware and prepare for bushfires. The book addresses what readers need to know and understand to deal with the ever-changing weather and what it may create.

BIOGRAPHY AND AUTOBIOGRAPHY

The Meet series – *Meet the Flying Doctors, Meet Ned Kelly, Meet Nellie Melba*, etc. – are all part of a series that introduces influential men and women from Australia. The format is one that presents a famous figure from Australian history in a way that will have readers searching for more books and information.

Tania McCartney has a couple of other books that connect with biography, but told with a creative lens. *This is Captain Cook* and *This is Banjo Paterson* are titles that present factual information about influential people in Australia in a fun way. In *This is Captain Cook*, the information is presented in the format of a school play which, as teachers and parents realise, is always a challenge to complete without any disasters. *Amazing Australians in their Flying Machines* by Kerry and Prue Mason introduces readers to specific Australians who have played an integral part in air travel. Continuing with the flying theme is *Born to Fly* by Beverley McWilliams which tells the story of Captain Harry Butler, who was not only a pilot for Australia in the First World War, but he also helped establish Airmail within Australia. The timeline and author's note at the end of the book help readers learn more. *Amazing Australian Women* by Pamela Freeman presents the stories of twelve women from Australian history who have made Australia a wonderful country. From Dame Nellie Melba to Edith Cowan, readers will learn how these twelve women from across the country and through history have influenced different facets of Australian life. Connected with this theme is *High Five to the Boys* providing short one-page summaries about influential males from Australia. Some of the names include AFL star Adam Goodes, very well-known children's author Andy Griffiths, Indigenous singer Archie Roach and celebrated conservationist Steve Irwin. Readers will be introduced to a variety of Australians from all over the country and diverse professions.

Kids Who Did is a non-fiction text by Australian author Kirsty Murray that introduces a number of children who have overcome extreme odds. This can easily be paired with *Rise Up: Ordinary Kids with Extraordinary Stories* by Gareth Moore from the UK so children can see the difference they can make in their world, as well as survive challenges in their lives. To extend this idea further, one can explore the UK title *Survivors* by David Long which tells the stories of young adults and adults who have also survived amazing odds (like a shipwrecked sailor who survived 133 days at sea using shark's blood in place of water).

Stormy Seas: Stories of Young Boat Refugees written by Mary Beth Leatherdale is an excellent title that presents the various stories of refugee children through history from countries such as Cuba, Afghanistan and the Ivory Coast. The book provides the story of the child, what happened to them, as well as information about the different countries they fled.

Little People, Big Dreams is a series of biographies about influential people from around the globe. Some of the titles include David Attenborough, Mother Theresa, Michael Jordan, and many more. The books are written by Maria Isabel Sanchez Vegara and are small and accessible biographies for younger readers.

Will the Wonderkid: Treasure Hunter of the Australian Outback, in the Heritage Heroes Series by Stephanie Owen Reeder is a compelling story about young Will Hutchison who set off with his father and other explorers in search of gold. However, the adventure does not go as planned and the men leave young Will at the campsite as they search for water. In the end, it is Will who finds both water and treasure (opals in Coober Pedy). The tale is an exciting one and each section is full of factual information about Will and his story. The other Heritage Hero titles are also worth exploring (*Lost, Amazing Grace, Lennie the Legend, Marvellous Miss May*).

Matthew Flinders: Adventures on Leaky Ships by Carole Wilkinson tells the story of Matthew Flinders and his adventures as he tried to map the coastline of Australia. This biography includes the trials and tribulations that were faced as he raced the French to accomplish the task. It also includes the courageous cat who sailed with him.

Table 6.1 Evaluation criteria: non-fiction

Is the book factual and up to date?
Does the book provide accurate and authentic information?
Is there an 'About the author' section that shows the author's expertise in the area?
What significant information is included?
Does the book distinguish between fact and theory?
Does the book avoid anthropomorphism?
Content and perspective: is there a clear purpose and identifiable audience? Does the book engage the reader?
Style: what is the clarity and level of difficulty of the text?
Organisation: what is the structure and what reference aid features are there (table of contents, index, etc.)?
What is the impact of the illustrations and do they work with the format of the text?

The evaluation criteria in the table above raise points discussed throughout the chapter. Because non-fiction is based on fact, it is obvious that the titles need to include accurate and authentic information that is also up to date. For example, Harry Houdini is a world-famous magician throughout history, and there are a number of biographies written about him. So, when there is a newer one – for example, by Sid Fleischman in 2008 (*Escape! The Story of the Great Houdini*), the question is, what new material can be provided? In this case, there are unseen photographs and artefacts shared by his widow with Fleischman. Including new material and ideas is critical when the topic has already been well written about.

One key aspect to be aware of with non-fiction text is the author's expertise. While this does not mean that every author needs to be an expert in every field, it is important to be aware of what the author knows about the topic and how they gathered this information. This is commonly found in the 'About the author' section at the end of the book. This section can provide the reader with the author's background – for example, if they are writing about dinosaurs and have a PhD in paleontology – or if the author did extensive research about a specific topic because they wanted to know more about a specific topic – for example, rocket ships and space. Regardless, it is important for readers to be able to identify how authors researched and wrote the book as well, and even providing the reader with resources to learn more.

The criteria of distinguishing between fact and theory as well as anthropomorphism were discussed in depth earlier in the chapter, with specific examples from children's literature titles to connect with the evaluation criteria.

The importance of the visual has also been discussed throughout the chapter, and different examples from titles were included as well. Daley (2019) noted how 'modern non-fiction books rely heavily on good design with eye-catching graphics and varied typography and layout which are intended to make complex concepts more easily accessible and interesting' (p. 132). This idea encapsulates a number of ideas related not only to the visual, but also to the structure and format of the non-fiction text in order to make challenging topics easier to understand. The techniques, formatting and style that are used should also connect with the overall theme of the book. Look at the strong titles that have been shared in this chapter in which the style and format excel at connecting with the book – for example, *North and South* and *Explore Your World: Weird, Wild, Amazing*. Each of these books has incorporated an innovative style and/or format that creates an amazing non-fiction reading experience.

CONCLUSION

Non-fiction is crucial for young children to have experience with so they can both further develop their reading skills and also learn about new topics and ideas. Non-fiction texts require a lot of further skills to navigate successfully and by sharing these texts with children they are able to develop those skills. Many great non-fiction texts are being published for children of all ages. By using the evaluation criteria, you will be able to start to determine what books you would like to include in your own classroom with your own students.

ADDITIONAL TITLES

How Did I Get Here? – Philip Bunting

Australian Birds – Matt Chun

Gold Rush – Jackie French (Fair Dinkum History series, like Horrible Histories)

WANT TO KNOW MORE?

Kurkijan, C., Livingstone, N. and Cobb, V. (2011) 'Inquiring minds want to learn: the info on nonfiction and informational series books'. *The Reading Teacher, 60*(1): 86–96. Available at: https://doi.org/10.1598/RT.60.1.10

Maloch, B. and Horsey, M. (2013) 'Living inquiry: learning from and about informational texts in a second-grade classroom'. *The Reading Teacher, 66*(6): 475–85. Available at: https://doi.org/10.1002/TRTR.1152

Shimek, C. (2018) 'Sites of synergy: strategies for readers navigating nonfiction picture books'. *The Reading Teacher, 72*(4): 519–22. Available at: https://doi.org/10.1002/trtr.1754

Stephens, K. (2011) 'A quick guide to selecting great informational books for young children'. *The Reading Teacher, 61*(6): 488–90. Available at: https://doi.org/10.1598/RT.61.6.6

REFERENCES

Daley, M. (2019) *Raising Readers: How to Nurture a Child's Love of Books*. Brisbane: University of Queensland Press.

Kiefer, B.Z., Hepler, S.I., Hickman, J. and Huck, C.S. (2007) *Charlotte Huck's Children's Literature* (9th edn). London: McGraw-Hill.

Winch, G., Ross Johnston, R., March, P., Ljungdahl, L. and Holliday, M. (2008). *Literacy: Reading, Writing and Children's Literature* (3rd edn). Oxford: Oxford University Press.

FANTASY

WHAT WE WILL LEARN

- Fairy tales and folk tales are early examples of fantasy literature.
- Early traditional literature comes from all around the globe.
- There are two main types of fantasy literature – traditional and modern.
- Believability is a key component of successful fantasy literature.
- There are many themes and components of fantasy.

Children are gifted with strong imaginations. It is this ability to pretend and create imaginary worlds that can make the fantasy genre a natural for children. In picture books especially, children are drawn into new characters and settings that encourage their imagination. Kiefer et al. (2004) support this idea, noting, 'fantasy helps the child develop imagination. To be able to imagine, to conceive of alternative ways of life, to entertain new ideas, to create strange new worlds, to dream dreams—these are all vital to human survival' (p. 308). With these ideas in mind, it is imperative that we as educators encourage the fantasy genre and provide children with the opportunity to engage with fantasy in order to foster their imaginations and open up new possibilities.

The earliest examples of fantasy literature were found in traditional folk tales and fairy tales. And this early folklore has been passed down for generations through the oral storytelling tradition. Temple et al. (2002) acknowledge that those stories were the beginnings of modern fantasy, stating, 'Myths, legends, and folktales are predecessors of the modern genres of fantasy and science fiction. For centuries, the oral tradition of storytelling passed along many tales of magical beings, fantastic occurrences, and imaginative places' (p. 352). Think

back to the fairy tales you remember. What magic elements do you remember? Snow White, for example had witches, magic spells, potions and objects, just as Cinderella had the fairy godmother who transformed her for the ball, and the animals around the house became part of the carriage that took her there. Connecting with this idea of magic found in early fantasy, Kiefer et al. (2007) write: 'folktales, fairy tales, and fables are simple stories about talking beasts, woodcutters, and princesses who reveal human behaviour and beliefs while playing out their roles in a world of wonder and magic' (p. 275). Think about the story of Aladdin and the genie who comes out of the lamp. How many wishes does the genie grant? If you answered three you are correct. Also remember that it is the *Three* Little Pigs, or Goldilocks and the *Three* Bears. This is intentional and a repeated element found in the fantasy literature. All these components are very specific to the genre of fantasy, and will be discussed more in depth later in this chapter. These well-known 'worlds of wonder and magic' have been around for years and years, and many were collected in the Grimm Brothers's first book *Household Stories* from 1812. Galda and Cullinan (2006) acknowledge that 'very few tales were originally intended for children alone' (p. 130). The stories that the Grimm Brothers collected were examples of oral storytelling that connected with so many people, cultures and countries across the globe.

When you study the 'origins' of fairy tales and folk tales, you will find a strong connection with the theory of polygenesis, also known as multiple origins. It is difficult to determine the origin of the stories, and when you explore where these traditional tales come from, you will find their existence in Britain, Germany, Scandinavia, France, Russia, Asia, Africa, South America, the Middle East and India, to name just a few places. It is fascinating to compare different versions of a classic folk tale from multiple countries, such as 'Little Red Riding Hood'. You can see titles such as *Lon Po Po* (Japan), *Pretty Salma* (Africa), *Petite Rouge* (Cajun), *Little Roja Riding Hood* (Mexico). To explore this idea even further, look at Paul Fleischman's titles *Fearsome Giant, Fearless Child* (Jack and the Beanstalk) or *Glass Slipper, Gold Sandal* (Cinderella). These books explore well-known folk tales and present the stories from different countries throughout the book – for example, using Cinderella's name from the different countries (Ashpet, Sootface, Cendrillon, etc.).

Connecting to the idea of innovation in children's literature, the field owes a great deal of thanks to Jon Scieszka and Lane Smith's classics *The Stinky Cheese Man and Other Fairly Stupid Tales* and *The True Story of the Three Little Pigs* which encouraged and celebrated the parody approach to well-known traditional tales. A number of wonderful new twists and variations of traditional folk tales and fairy tales continue to be published each year. For example, well-known Australian children's author Nick Bland has a recent version of *Three Billy Goats Gruff*, which follows the traditional version of the story in which three billy goats try to cross a bridge, but encounter and outsmart the scary troll who lives underneath it. This title could be paired with Richard Jackson's version from the United States, *The Three Billy Goats Gruff: The Full Story*. In Jackson's story, it follows the lead of Scieszka and Smith mentioned earlier, as it provides some innovative ideas in telling the story, with some humorous elements as well. Alice Rex's *Ava's Spectacular*

Spectacles is a clever UK title that teaches a young girl named Ava who does not like to wear her glasses that it is very important to wear them. The story uses well-known folk tale characters as examples of what would happen if they had been wearing theirs. This creative story could easily be connected with a similar story that mixes multiple books and characters, and does not have to be limited to folk tales and fairy tales. *Miss Smith's Incredible Storybook* (and the sequels, *Miss Smith Reads Again!* and *Miss Smith Under the Ocean*) by Michael Garland are all books that bring multiple stories and characters into the book. At first, Zack is unsure of his new teacher, but then Miss Smith turns out to be the best teacher ever, because whenever she opens up her incredible storybook to read to her class, the stories and characters come alive in the classroom. The different books in the series present a number of different stories and have the potential to unlock a number of new stories and authors to children. The fact that Miss Smith wears a Clash badge (button) is an added bonus for music fans. David Ezra Stein's Interrupting Chicken series is a creative way to present and extend nursery rhymes to children. In each of the books in the series, chicken is read folk tales and nursery rhymes, but interrupts the story and adds its own flair to the story. Children will delight in little chicken's antics, while also correcting and pointing out what actually may have happened.

It is important to celebrate all the new variations and twists of these well-known tales. Whether it is exploring culture, gender, setting or even sometimes the morals of the story, it is worth using the schema (prior knowledge) that students must already have with traditional literature in order to introduce the newer versions. It is crucial to pay attention to that last sentence. Children *must* already have the original version of the traditional stories in their schema before introducing them to a new version. For example, before introducing children to the Australian-specific *The Three Little Bush Pigs* by Paul Dallimore, *The True Story of the Three Little Pigs* by Jon Scieszka, mentioned earlier, or even *The Three Pigs* by David Wiesner, children must know the original version in order to understand the humour or the complexities of the different versions. Once the original version of the story is established, only then will children be able to understand and appreciate the creative and innovative takes on the original traditional tale.

Now take a minute to think about the fantasy books or series you remember reading or hearing about when you were growing up. Do you notice how there have always been strong fantasy stories/series through the years? For example, E.B. White's *Charlotte's Web* started this off when we read about how a young girl named Fern could hear a pig talking or a spider that was able to weave words into her web. Madeleine L'Engle's *A Wrinkle in Time* was where readers were introduced to time travelling through 'tesseracts'. Or even the wardrobe that took readers to Narnia in C.S. Lewis's *The Lion, the Witch and the Wardrobe*. J.K. Rowling's Harry Potter series reintroduced the world of magic schools, and wizards and witches, and soon there was another explosion of fantasy novels for children, including Rick Riordan's Percy Jackson series, *Eragon* (The Inheritance Cycle) by Christopher Paolini, John Flanagan's Ranger's Apprentice series, the Rondo series by Emily Rodda and Garth Nix's fantasy book series, to name just a few.

> **BUST A MYTH**
>
> Fantasy and science fiction books are too hard to follow.
>
> Fantasy can be a tricky genre, especially when there are new worlds created and explored. It is crucial that readers give fantasy books at least a few chapters into the fantasy world and be brought into the story, characters and world that is being explored.

When exploring the genre of fantasy, there are a number of traditional elements found within this genre. Table 7.1 showcases this.

Table 7.1 Traditional elements of fantasy

Going on a quest	Finding the Philosopher's Stone
An underdog hero	Harry Potter
The number 3	Dog with three heads (three friends – Harry, Ron and Hermione)
A wise older person (sage)	Dumbledore
Magic	Magic School, magic wands, learning spells and potions (the list could go on and on)
Magic item or power	The wand, cloak of invisibility
Overcoming a fear/obstacle	Being all alone, parents gone
A best friend	Ron Weasley
An enemy	Draco Malfoy
Good versus evil	Harry Potter versus Voldermort

TRADITIONAL FANTASY

You are most likely familiar with J.R.R. Tolkien's *The Lord of the Rings* and *The Hobbit*, and if so, they are prime examples of traditional fantasy, sometimes referred to as 'high fantasy'. These types of fantasy stories include knights, wizards, elves, ogres, dragons, and much more. Think back to your knowledge of King Arthur and the Knights of the Round Table, and you are well into the world of this type of fantasy story. High fantasy will usually have many of the key components from the table above; magic, a quest, wise older sage, and usually a battle between good and evil which takes place in an imaginary world, created by the author. J.R.R. Tolkien's classic work mentioned earlier and Lloyd Alexander's books (*The Chronicles *of Prydain*) were early examples of this format. However, there are other more recent examples that fit this subgenre brilliantly – for example, the Inheritance Cycle series by Christopher Paolini, in which a young boy named Eragon discovers the world of dragon riders; upon this discovery, he joins a long-standing battle between good and evil as he becomes one of the principal fighters against the evil empire.

MODERN FANTASY

Modern fantasy is a story that is grounded in modern times and reality, and then it takes the reader into the fantasy world. Jacobs and Tunnell (2004) believe that 'modern fantasy must have strong, believable characters and should examine issues of the human condition, the universal truths found in well-written books' (p. 88). Think about how this happens with Harry Potter. We meet Harry in a suburb of London, but the main fantasy world comes into play after he boards the train at platform 9 ¾ and is taken to Hogwarts and the magical world that surrounds it. The Rondo series by Emily Rodda is another example of this, in which it is a magic jewellery box that serves as a portal from the modern-day setting into the fantasy world. *Percy Jackson and the Lightning Thief* is yet another example of this. The reader meets Percy in New York City and, similar to Harry Potter, he doesn't know that he has the gift of the power of magic until later in the story. The story is grounded in modern reality and then when Percy enters Camp Half-Blood, the reader enters the fantasy realm. There is, therefore, a big progression from picture books with magical elements to novels.

The 13-Storey Treehouse in the Treehouse series is a good example of modern fantasy with the bonus addition of humour. Andy Griffiths and Terry Denton are at their best with the creation of every child's dream, a treehouse with thirteen levels, and then every sequel adds on another thirteen levels. From an ice-cream parlour, a recording studio, a chocolate waterfall and, in the most recent book, a word-o-matic. The series is fantastical, humorous and overall just a romping good time that children have flocked to around the globe.

The Bad Guys series by Aaron Blabey is another example of a modern fantasy in which traditional folk tale animal villains try to present themselves in a more positive light. The inclusion of police line-ups and police files add to the humour, but the talking animal main characters help showcase the fantasy elements.

FANTASY PICTURE BOOKS

Could almost any picture book be a fantasy? Yes, but in picture books there are a few characteristics that stand out for quality fantasy picture books. One, are strong characterisations. What makes a good book is one in which you believe or relate or accept the character.

For example, Pig the Pug or The Very Cranky Bear, Olivia the Pig, Arnie the Doughnut, or each of the crayons from *The Day the Crayons Quit*, are all examples of strong characters that readers relate to and enjoy going on adventures with. While the list could go on and on, hopefully you understand the idea, that the strong characters found in fantasy stories are ones that are strongly grounded in the fantasy world (for there are no talking dogs, bears, pigs, doughnuts, crayons etc., in case you were wondering), and this is one of the key characteristics that attracts young readers to the genre and, in turn, to the story. Temple et al. (2002) call this 'low fantasy' and write that 'the forms of low fantasy include stories about personified animals, personified toys, outlandish characters and humorous situations, magical powers, extraordinary worlds, supernatural elements, and time slips' (p. 355).

No matter if the characters are relatable, it is important to note that 'low fantasy is actually set in the primary world, but the magical elements of fantasy make the story impossible' (p. 351). This key characteristic is how we are transformed into the fantasy world by a child's imagination. We all remember Maurice Sendak's *Where the Wild Things Are*, and if you don't, you should stop reading this chapter now and find the book. When Max is sent to his room without any supper, the journey to the land of the wild things is found through Max's imagination, although the illustrations make it look as if it is really happening. The Traction Man series by Mini Grey is created through the child's imagination of his action figure Traction Man. The young boy narrates the story and adventures of Traction Man and his sidekick, Scrubbing Brush. Children have vivid imaginations and this series definitely highlights this. Another example is the Australian classic *Animalia* by Graeme Base. As Base's website explains, the book is a 'A fantastical alliterative journey through the animal kingdom with thousands of alphabetically arranged images and ideas to discover along the way' (http://graemebase.com.au). Children will pore over the images and the alliteration alphabet book, but the images have sparked children's imaginations for years.

Curse of the Vampire Robot, a newer title by Graeme Base, is a fantasy-based picture book meant for upper primary students, and explores modern technology, computers, accessories, etc. The story is complex, but includes many elements of fantasy addressed in this chapter with good versus evil, a quest for the protagonist, and a mix of fantasy with technology (modern) and vampires (classic fantasy). Perhaps this newer title best exemplifies what Temple et al. write about how 'fantasy extends reality into the unknown' (p. 350).

The Underhills: A Tooth Fairy Story (Bob Graham) is a wonderful modern Tooth Fairy story in which children are introduced to a family of tooth fairies and how the youngest member learns the trade from his grandparents who watch over him while his parents are 'working' at night. *Trick Number Two* by Nick Bland (illustrated by Stephen Michael King) is a great title with young aspiring wizards who desperately (and impatiently) want to learn magic. The wise wizard agrees to teach them, but only by starting with trick number one. Only one young wizard has the patience to follow through on the trick, and when they do, they learn much more than just one trick.

The Sharey Godmother by Samantha Berger is a fun spoof or parody on fairy godmothers, as readers are introduced to the main character, the Sharey Godmother who is unsure whether she wants to share all the time. While she tries to be different and not share, she learns not only the importance of being who you are, but also the joy that sharing brings.

The Fan Brothers do an excellent job of capturing a more complex fantasy world. Their book *The Barnabus Project* introduces the reader to a fantasy 'world' of inventions. In the laboratory, some feel left out completely or that they are like rejects, but when they all work together and escape, they find they each have their own unique talents, and, by working together, they can survive as a team. Their most recent title, *Lizzy and the Cloud*, tells the story of a girl named Lizzy who goes to the cloud seller at the park and buys her own cloud. She takes care of the cloud until it grows and grows and she needs to let it go. Fantasy is mixed with reality throughout the book that will have readers emphathising with Lizzy throughout.

Kirli Saunders's *The Incredible Freedom Machines* presents the story of the power of books and how they can be someone's incredible freedom machine. The story combines the landscape of Australia with a fantasy machine that can take people anywhere. Matt Ottley's stunning illustrations add to the limited text that is present and combine to make a fantasy world that will have children thinking of their own incredible freedom machine.

Connecting back to what was discussed at the beginning of the chapter about how folk tales were the beginning of fantasy, *The Little Red Fort* by Brenda Maier is a wonderful title that connects easily to the classic tale, *The Little Red Hen*. A young girl named Ruby builds a fort and asks her brothers if they want to help her, and they say no each time. The repetitive text is fun and humorous – for example, her brother José always says 'no way'. In the end, they work together and find a way they can all be part of what Ruby has made.

There are a number of good wordless picture books with strong fantasy elements in them. David Wiesner's *Robobaby* is a comic-book format picture book that blends realistic fiction and fantasy together in the same way that it blends the picture book and comic-book format. The story tells the tale of a robot family which has a new baby on the way, but they need to put the robot together. When they run into technical difficulties, it is the older sister who is able to save the day.

Dan Richards's *Penny and Penelope* is a fun US title about two girls who come together for a playdate. They both have the same doll, but with a stark difference. One calls theirs Princess Penelope and the other Penny, a secret agent. At first their dolls are opposites and do not play well together until they discover that each has their own abilities to help out in a dire situation. This title would connect well with Traction Man mentioned earlier in this chapter.

Journey, *Quest* and *Return* create a wordless picture-book trilogy by Aaron Becker; the wordless format is a great way to introduce the fantasy genre to children in a way that provides them with the opportunity to tell their own fantasy story through the images provided. A young girl who is desperate for an adventure draws a door on her bedroom wall which transports her to an imaginary world where she journeys to find her way home. The following two books continue the story as she rediscovers the magic kingdom she visited in the first book.

One of the greatest challenges to fantasy is being able to s*uspend our disbelief.* As Kiefer et al. (2007) write: 'The literal-minded child finds the suspension of reality a barrier to the enjoyment of fantasy; other children relish the opportunity to enter the world of enchantment' (p. 355). We might need to pause here and break this down a bit more. What does that mean to suspend our disbelief? Well, let's think about that for a moment. One of this author's favourite books is *Arnie the Doughnut.* In this story by Laurie Keller, readers are introduced to a lovely doughnut named Arnie that is made one day at the Downtown Bakery, purchased by a Mr. Bing and taken to his house to be eaten. However, Arnie can speak and talks to Mr. Bing. A talking doughnut, you say? Yes, that is where the reader must suspend their disbelief and say, 'Yes, I believe that doughnuts can talk.' Let us take this one step further. I am also a huge fan of the Star Wars movie series, so in order to suspend my disbelief, I have to say, 'Yes, I believe that there is space travel, and that Yoda exists and provides great wisdom to everyone.' (Think about how Yoda is a perfect example of the wise sage component found in fantasy stories.)

Another challenge for fantasy readers can be getting into the fantasy world created by the author. This is most commonly found in traditional fantasy stories where from the beginning the reader is introduced to a new land which has unfamiliar names and places. Kiefer et al. (2007: 380) describe this: 'many authors of fantasy create believability by setting their stories in an imaginary society where kings and queens rule feudal societies that resemble the middle ages'. While this can be challenging, if a reader is patient and gives the new fantasy world a chance, they are able to enjoy many more adventures. Well-known children's fantasy writer Diana Wynne Jones has written *The Tough Guide to Fantasyland*, and in this book she discusses the very common, and sometimes cliché motifs and elements found in fantasy. Her humorous tone not only points out these very common elements, but also pokes fun at some of these ideas. This is specifically true with the idea of maps of fantasy worlds that are found at the beginning of the books and stories. Most fantasy books with new worlds have a map of the world, as discussed earlier in the paragraph. Some examples of this would be Garth Nix's Old Kingdom series, Christopher Paolini's Inheritance Cycle series, and even Harry Potter has maps to the different parts of the Hogwarts grounds and the neighbouring town of Hogsmeade.

Sometimes there is controversy around fantasy literature – for example, with the Harry Potter series there was discussion about how these books promoted such ideas as magic and witchcraft – but very well-established children's fantasy writer Jane Yolen addresses this best: 'No one reading them—children or adults—is fooled into believing them word for word; that is, the reader does not believe in the actuality of dragons, unicorns, flying horses. But these stories are like points on a map, acting as a guide to life as we actually live it by showing us life as it could be lived' (in Temple et al., 2002: 369). Yolen's words are important to remember. Children appreciate the fantasy worlds, but they do not believe them to actually exist. It is clear that they are imaginary and not real. While they are wonderful worlds to visit, young readers understand that they are a temporary escape from the real world around them.

SCIENCE FICTION

Science fiction is another subgenre of fantasy. It can be science fiction in the truest form with new planets and galaxies. For example, the Hugo-winning *Binti* by Nnedi Okorafor is a good example of this. It can also be found in dystopian stories. Dystopian stories can be defined as those in an imaginary community in futuristic or post-apocalyptic settings that have a totalitarian regime which is governing oppressively. Lois Lowry's *The Giver* is a classic example of this genre in which Jonah becomes the 'Giver' who must hold all the memories of the community, a job he does not wish to keep. This rough 'trilogy' (followed by *Gathering Blue* and *The Messenger*) is a wonderful one to begin with upper primary students as it will have them all guessing what happens to Jonah in the end of the first book. Suzanne Collins's Hunger Games trilogy is a primary example of the dystopian subgenre in which Katniss volunteers to replace her younger sister in the Hunger Games (a dystopian version of the gladiators from the Roman Empire) where children must battle each other in order to survive, all for the 'entertainment' of the upper class in the country's capital. Many readers will find similarities with the dystopian young adult Divergent series in which the main character, Beatrice, must decide her own fate for which of the six factions she will join, something everyone in the world must decide. The choice will determine the rest of her life and may change relationships within her family, as well as with her friends. There are strong comparisons with this title and *The Giver* mentioned above.

The Aurora Cycle series by Australian author Amie Kaufman is a strong example of science fiction in which Tyler Jones, the star student from the Aurora Academy, is able to choose his own squad, but ends up taking the dregs of the academy and even finding himself rescuing a girl that could quite possibly start a war millions of years in the making. All these novels highlight science fiction and will challenge and extend older readers.

THEMES

Many common themes are found in the fantasy genre. Probably the most common one is the battle between good and evil, whether you are a long-time *Star Wars* fan and know the battle between the dark side and the resistance, or just the common battle between those in the empires that keep those under them in the galaxy. The second common theme in fantasy is that the protagonist will undergo a personal transformation that is commonly found on a quest or journey they must take. We could return to the *Star Wars* example and think about how Luke Skywalker underwent his personal transformation to become a Jedi, or we could also look at how Harry Potter or Percy Jackson underwent their own personal transformations in their stories. Finally, a third common theme is that a wise older person (commonly a sage) provides guidance and advice that assists the main character when they are put into a difficult situation on their journey. We could again stay with the *Star Wars* theme and talk about Obi-Wan Kenobi or Yoda who were the wise sages, or we could simply look towards Dumbledore in Harry Potter. Regardless, the idea is the same as these are both wise older people who help the main characters. There are many more common themes that could be explored in fantasy and even more motifs that could be discussed, but for the sake of this book, these three will suffice to get you thinking about the ideas. If you're interested in a humorous take on finding more, look no further than Diana Wynne Jones's book *The Tough Guide to Fantasyland*, which will feature even more examples.

Table 7.2 Evaluation criteria: fantasy

Strong plot that is believable
Convincing characters
Strong and worthy theme
Authentic language matching the fantasy realm
Fantasy elements? Are they convincing? Can readers willingly suspend disbelief?
Believable world? Is the imaginary world logically understandable?

When evaluating the fantasy genre there are several key aspects that need to be addressed. To start with, the plot needs to be strong and believable. Fantasy allows for flexibility within the worlds that are created, but regardless of the story, the plot must still remain strong and believable. This can also connect with the fantasy world that is created by the author. The fantasy world itself must also be believable. This means that the imaginary world is logical and understandable, which means that it makes sense and is not completely mindboggling or beyond comprehension. Connecting further with this idea is an aspect discussed earlier: can the reader willingly suspend their disbelief? Again, for this to happen the fantasy world must have some elements of believability remaining in it. Also discussed earlier is how the characters are convincing and match the style of the fantasy story that is being told. And similarly, is the language authentic to the style of the fantasy? Finally, the overall theme must be strong and worthy as well. Whether that is the strongest theme found in fantasy – good versus evil or another theme – it must be authentic to the plot and the fantasy world that has been created. The diverse titles presented throughout this chapter highlight different aspects of the evaluation criteria.

CONCLUSION

Fantasy is a popular genre with children and one that is changing and developing every year. From the Harry Potter modern-day fantasy to Eragon's more traditional fantasy, to the dystopian Hunger Games and Divergent series, the fantasy genre is constantly appealing to young readers to join new and innovative fantasy worlds. While the stories may be changing, there continue to be strong themes found in fantasy stories. Whether it is magic, good versus evil, personal transformation of the characters, or a wise sage who provides much needed advice in a time of need, they are common themes to emerge. While some readers may struggle to enter into a new world with complicated names or new places, those who persevere will be rewarded with new characters and worlds they will continue to read about. It is important that educators encourage younger readers to enjoy and celebrate new and exciting fantasy books.

ADDITIONAL TITLES

Little Red and the Very Hungry Lion – Alex T. Smith. A parody of the well-known folk tale with a safari twist.

A Damsel not in Distress! – Bethan Stevens

WANT TO KNOW MORE?

Baker, D. (2006) 'What we found on our journey through fantasy land'. *Children's Literature in Education, 37*(3): 237–251.

The article is an exploration into the genre of fantasy, and identifies patterns and themes found within the genre, while also focusing on specific titles and authors.

Levy, M. and Mendlesohn, F. (2016) *Children's Fantasy Literature: An Introduction*. Cambridge: Cambridge University Press.

This book is a further exploration into fantasy literature for children exploring authors and books from the sixteenth century to Harry Potter.

Wynne Jones, D. (2006) *The Tough Guide to Fantasyland.* New York: Firebird.

This fun book by a well-known children's fantasy writer explores key concepts and themes found within fantasy books.

REFERENCES

Galda, L. and Cullinan, B. (2006) *Literature and the Child* (6th edn). New York: Wadsworth.

Kiefer, B.Z., Hepler, S.I., Hickman, J. and Huck, C.S. (2004). *Charlotte Huck's Children's Literature* (8th edn). London: McGraw-Hill.

Jacobs, J. and Tunnell, M. (2004) *Children's Literature, Briefly* (3rd edn). London: Pearson.

Kiefer, B.Z., Hepler, S.I., Hickman, J. and Huck, C.S. (2007) *Charlotte Huck's Children's literature* (9th edn). London: McGraw-Hill.

Temple, C., Martinez, M., Yokota, J. and Naylor, A. (2002) *Children's Books in Children's Hands* (2nd edn). Boston, MA: Allyn & Bacon.

Wynne Jones, D. (2006) *The Tough Guide to Fantasyland*. New York: Firebird.

8

REALISTIC FICTION

WHAT WE WILL LEARN
- The definition of realistic fiction.
- The benefits the genre has for children.
- The techniques that authors/illustrators use to make realistic fiction universal.
- How to evaluate realistic fiction.
- Different themes that are found within the genre.

Kiefer et al. (2007) define realistic fiction as 'imaginative writing that accurately reflects life in the past or as it could be lived today'. This means that it could be connected to historical fiction, as it reflects life in the past. More importantly, it means a realistic story that could happen in the present day and is based on something that could credibly happen. Young children are continually dealing with an ever-changing and challenging world. Realistic fiction is a genre that can help children come to terms with realistic experiences they are encountering and dealing with. For example, starting school can be a new and scary experience for children, and finding books that children can relate to, and see themselves in, assist in working through any challenges that might emerge. Overall, the main goal of realistic fiction is to help children see that they are not alone, that there are other people (children) in the world like them who are experiencing the same things. This is the key aim or point of realistic fiction. This chapter will address a large number of (but by no means all) issues or topics that children from around the world will be able to relate to, including families, school, friendship, emotions, fears, moving away, death/dying, identity and social justice issues. Again, it is critical that children see themselves in the stories they read and are able to think and realise, 'I am not alone, there are other people like me'.

> **BUST A MYTH**
>
> All books must contain a moral or message.
>
> The beauty of children's literature is that many times there is a lesson, message or moral to learn from the story. However, this is not always the case. Similar to the myth in the humour chapter, remember that a book can have an interesting and entertaining story that children can relate to without having a hidden agenda of a message or moral.

There is another key benefit to realistic fiction beyond helping children see that they are not alone, there are other people like them, and that is that realistic fiction can help children learn how to empathise with others. This can happen through stories about feelings, emotions, fears, friendship, and so much more. While the stories help them learn about themselves, they are also able to learn about others around them, in their own families, schools or communities. Australian children's literature illustrator Tania McCartney (cited in Cullen, 2023) warns us:

> I've also noticed an increase in self-help narrative picture books for kinds with 'issues'. Although the concept is important, these books can be saccharin and didactic, and may do more harm than good. Children are so very smart; they recoil from patronisation. Books that empower, comfort and inform children in subtle ways are far more effective---namely books where 'messaging' is built seamlessly and imperceptibly into the narrative. Even well-hidden, kids of all ages get these messages.

While some experts believe that 'there are no animals that talk; no anthropomorphized machines; no ghosts, giants, or supernatural happenings' (Temple et al., 2002), it is important to remember that children's literature, and in particular picture books, use animals as main characters for the key reason that they are universal. Because of this, it is important to include them to assist in telling stories, whether they are realistic fiction or fantasy. As Kasten et al. (2005) note: 'the genre of contemporary realistic fiction includes stories about animals and people that could actually exist along with events that could actually happen in today's world or in the recent past'. As this chapter will highlight, and include, the main characters in realistic fiction can be either human or animal. The main idea is that the story or issue presented could actually happen in today's world.

Evaluating realistic fiction means that the stories being shared in the books must be an honest portrayal of the issues and ideas that children in today's world face in their everyday lives. Making friends, starting school, having fears, worries and anxieties are all examples of this, as are other social justice issues; many of these ideas and more are presented in the sections below. As you read the sections and learn about the books, you will start to see how they are realistic and relatable issues for children across the globe. These issues and more help to expand a child's worldview and allow them to learn and understand more ideas and concepts present in the real world. At times, these may be controversial topics, but that does not mean they should be avoided. Regardless of the topic, it must be addressed appropriately and even invite the opportunity for further discussion and understanding with children. In order for these to happen, however, it means that the stories and books themselves must be realistic and relatable to the child. When the characters in the book are relatable and credible within the story, readers are better able to appreciate and understand the issues or topics being addressed within the pages. For example, characters such as Phoebe's anxiousness to read in front of her peers or William's struggles to make friends, and Cartwheel's difficulty in adjusting to a new country and learning the language, and other features as well. When the reader is able to identify with the character and relate to their struggles, the issues become more real and understandable. It is important to keep in mind the evaluation criteria in the table below as you find realistic fiction titles on your own, so that you will be aware of what will assist children as they read and discover realistic life issues.

Table 8.1 Evaluation criteria: realistic fiction

Honest portrayal of the everyday realities that today's children face.
Today's children relate to the problems addressed in the book.
Has universal associations (children from diverse backgrounds would be able to relate to the issues).
Characters are realistic and credible/relatable.
Stereotypes are avoided.
The book assists in expanding world views and develops an appreciation for a complex and ever-changing society.
Controversial topics are addressed appropriately.

FRIENDS

One of the most common experiences children have is of making friends and the experiences of friendship. *My Real Friend* by David Hunt is a recent title that presents friendship and a lonely young boy who has an imaginary friend (another common occurrence found in childhood) until he makes a real-life friend at school. This title connects very well with Bob Graham's title *Ellie's Dragon*, the story of an imaginary friend that keeps Ellie company as she grows up and makes new friends. She leaves behind her imaginary dragon that has kept her company as she was growing up, and then makes her own real-life friends. She leaves the dragon behind for another child to 'friend' and have on their side as they navigate their own childhood.

How to Make a Friend in 6 Easy Steps by Dhana Fox and *I Just Ate My Friend* by Heidi McKinnon are both humorous stories that address etiquette, as well as making and keeping friends. A shark is the main character in *How to Make a Friend in 6 Easy Steps* and has read a book on friendship and how to make friends. Having double rows of teeth and being told to smile to make a friend is not necessarily a good combination for friendship, but eventually the shark does make a friend. *I Just Ate My Friend* talks about the importance of how we treat our friends (and not eat them). There are strong connections here with Gabriel Evans's *Norton and the Borrowing Bear* where Norton's new neighbour borrows all his prized possessions and does not return them. It is not until Norton has strong words with the bear and tells him this is not how neighbours act, that the bear learns the true value of friendship.

Old Friends, New Friends by Andrew Daddo presents the idea of making friends and the importance of being open to new friendships. A young girl is excited about the new school year to see all her old friends again. But when she walks into the classroom, she sees all new children that she doesn't know. Taking a positive view on this, she decides that she can find all sorts of new types of friends who are important to have in her life. This is a good book to combine the importance of making new friends and starting school.

Frances Watts's *My Friend Fred* is the story of a dog and how he shares the importance of having a good friend, and through the illustrations there are very subtle clues that help the reader learn that the dog has an unexpected friend who is always looking out for him.

Finding François by Gus Gordon takes the importance of having a good friend even further when the reader is introduced to the main character whose mother has passed away and is living with her grandmother. The girl begins a friendship through letter correspondence that helps her deal with the grief she is experiencing, and when François comes to visit, there is hope for the little girl moving forward.

A Perfect Pig is a title that connects with a number of areas – friendship, identity and what we do for our friends. Pig wants to throw the perfect birthday party for his friend, but everything goes wrong and the party is far from perfect. He learns that not everything needs to go smoothly when you have the perfect friend. Similar to *A Perfect Pig* by Katrin Dreiling, there are some titles that cross into multiple themes; *Go Go and the Silver Shoes* by Jane Godwin is one such title. Some of the themes are identity in the family, school and making friends. When Go Go loses one of her brand new sparkly shoes in a stream while her family is exploring the woods, she doesn't know what to do. But a new student at her school might just be able to help when Go Go finds out she found her shoe. Not only has Go Go found her shoe again, she has also found a best friend.

FAMILY

Family is very important to children, and there are many diverse and unique families and family dynamics around the globe, so this is a theme that impacts a large number of children. Whether it is a child's place in the family, or a new sibling, or a new dynamic within the family, children need realistic fiction picture books to help see themselves or their feelings in the books and stories.

New siblings can cause a lot of excitement as well as angst within a family. Many books present the arrival of new siblings, and these books are important for children to read/view because they need to recognise that they are not alone in the feelings of excitement and nervousness they are feeling with a new arrival to the house. *Home in the Rain* by Bob Graham shares the story of Francie and her mother as they drive home from grandma's house. Francie asks her mother what her new baby sister's name will be when she is born. Her mother answers that they do not know yet. Yet during the drive home in a rainstorm, the answer comes to them, and Francie is excited to tell her daddy when they get home. This is a good title that showcases the positive arrival of a new family member. However, sometimes the arrival may not always begin as a positive. Katrina Lehman's book *Wren* tells the story of a young boy named Wren who enjoys peaceful, quiet things. When his new baby sister arrives, who just happens to be the loudest baby in the world, no one in the house is able to quieten her down, so he decides to run away. However, he learns that perhaps the quiet of the country is not exactly what he needs, and soon finds out that he and his sister are a perfect match for each other. This book would pair well with Pat Zietlow Miller's *My Brother the Duck* in which a young girl named Stella conducts a 'scientific experiment' to determine whether her brother is indeed a baby, or perhaps is a duck. This fun and somewhat scientific experiment is an entertaining way to present how children might feel with a new sibling. *A Most Unusual Day* by Sydra Mallery is a story about a child's day at school when she is too excited to focus because today is the day that her newly adopted sibling will be arriving. This story is a nice way to present another way that a new sibling is welcomed into the family. Jane Godwin's book *I'll Always be Older Than You* shares the story of an older sister telling her baby brother how she will take care of him and teach him new things. However, she also reminds him that she will always be older as well.

Sometimes families can present challenges for any child within the family. Where a child's place is in the family can create a number of issues. Anna Walker's book *Tilly* is an example of this. The main character, Tilly, struggles to find a place in her family's new home, as well as her own space. When she finds a secret place to put her special things, she feels at peace, but when the family carpets over her secret hiding spot, she has to adjust and grow with the change. Miranda Paul's book, *Mia Moves Out*, contains a story that connects well with *Wren* discussed earlier. Mia follows Wren's example and tries to run away, as she struggles to adjust to the growing house and the mess that she and her baby brother create. However, similar to Wren, Mia learns that perhaps she and her baby brother are a perfect match and there is a place they can both share together.

Families have many similarities, as well as big differences too. Regardless, the diversity of families should be celebrated, and there are many books that do so in a genuine and authentic way. One of my all-time personal favourites is *Family Forest* by Kim Kane. This book presents the way families are and can be, but does so in a humorous way, presenting big brothers, step-siblings and step-parents, as well as celebrating the diversity within families. Divorce in families can be very challenging, and Anna Walker's book *Hello, Jimmy!* shares this in the story about a young boy named Jack who struggles after a divorce and the challenges of being without his mother when he lives with his dad. When Jack runs away, the boy's father understands the challenges his son is facing, and makes an adjustment in the house. *Family Tree* by Josh Pyke is another strong title that celebrates family and the diversity in families. The book is a good way to present what families are like, and community, and how everyone is a key part of both communities and families.

We are Family by Patricia Hegarty is another title that celebrates families and the diversity within them. The book presents eight different families and showcases the similarities and differences within them. Deborah Kelly's *Me and You* is another great book that presents and celebrates all the people in a child's life, both within the family and within the community. The book helps children appreciate the day-to-day joys that we find within our family and the community around us.

SCHOOL

Many events happen at school that impact the lives of children, and these are universal concepts that children around the world can relate to. Jane Godwin's aptly named *Starting School* would be a perfect fit to present the challenges and worries when starting school, and can be perfectly paired with Kate Berube's title, *Mae's First Day of School*. *Twig* by Aura Parker is a UK title about a young twig (stick) that is a new student at an insect school and is quite nervous. These shared experiences are universal ones that can assist children who are beginning school not to feel alone, and to realise that this is a common occurrence which validates their own feelings.

Some children may worry about what happens at home when they are at school, and the book *Love* by Corrinne Averiss shares this worry. The young girl knows that she is loved, but worries that the love may not extend all the way to school when she is there. Again, this shared feeling of uncertainty while at school is a common one that many children will be able to relate to.

Many children also have the shared experience of a substitute teacher in their classroom. *Dear Substitute* presents letters to the substitute teacher that the students are dealing with. This is a US title illustrated by Chris Raschka, and his illustrations enhance the letters and the events that are occurring in the classroom and the school.

FEELINGS AND EMOTIONS

Children experience a number of feelings and emotions, and picture books that present feelings in an authentic and genuine manner are critical. This means that the feelings and emotions are present, but not the main focus of the book. One 'secret' to be aware of is that when a picture book has a subtitle about a feeling or emotion, most likely the focus of the book is more on the feelings/emotions than on the actual story, plot or character. This didacticism means that the main message in the story is to instruct rather than explore a good story. As Jacobs and Tunnell (2004) write: 'If the lesson becomes more important than the story, the book suffers.' This is important to remember in realistic fiction, but especially in those books presenting feelings that children will all know and experience in the lives. For example, *Mr Huff* by Anna Walker represents the cloud of sadness or depression that might follow us around when we are not feeling 100 per cent. It also presents how we can work through this sadness. Danny Parker's *Sarah and the Steep Slope* continues this theme and presents how we can work through the challenges we face, and how our friends can be there to support us in our time of need. This book would also work well in the friendship section addressed earlier. *Sweep* by Louise Greig presents the story of Ed, who is in a bad mood, a very bad mood that grows and grows. Soon Ed cannot believe how much trouble the bad mood has caused, and the darkness in the illustrations reflect this. Shortly, a new wind/mood blows in and Ed starts to feel better and better, and is rather surprised that he let the bad mood carry him away like it did. This book would be good to show that we are all allowed to be in a bad mood, but it is important to regulate that and then focus on the positive.

Children are facing different experiences for the first time, and this can create a lot of worry – hence, worrying and anxiety are a common feeling/emotion that children have. *Ruby's Worry* by Tom Percival presents this very well as the main character, Ruby, discovers that she has a worry, and that the more she thinks about it, the more it grows, which causes her to worry even more. When she sees a classmate who also has a worry, she (and her classmate) learn that talking about their worries helps to make them smaller and smaller. This book would also connect very well with Kevin Henkes's older title *Wemberly Worried*, as the protagonist, Wemberly, worries about so many different things, especially starting school (an issue also addressed earlier in this book).

FEARS

Fears are another aspect of childhood that we all remember. Whether it is being afraid of the dark, heights, spiders or new situations, most children can relate to being scared of something. Anna Walker's recognisable style is present in *Lottie & Walter* that deals with a child who is afraid to go into the pool. The imaginary whale in the pool is what assists Lottie in overcoming her fear. *Saturday is Swimming Day* is a US title by Hyewon Yum that has the same issue, although how the child overcomes the fear is different. Through her understanding and caring swim teacher, the young girl overcomes her fear of the pool and swimming, and gains confidence as a swimmer as well. Another Australian title directly related to swimming is Andrea Rowe's *Jetty Jumping* in which the main character, Milla, is terrified of what lurks in the water below the jetty while her friends are all carefree about jumping into the water. When Milla accidentally falls into the water, she inadvertently discovers the joys of the water and what is found there, hence overcoming the initial fear of jumping from the jetty.

Boo Loves Books by Kaye Baillie presents the story of Phoebe who is quite anxious and does not like to read to others. When her school class goes to a dog shelter to read to the animals, Phoebe finds the perfect partner in a dog named Boo, whose calming presence helps her overcome the fear of reading to others and she makes a new friend as well.

A very common fear for many children (and even some adults) is the dark. *Light's Out, Leonard* by Josh Pyke is a wonderful title that accurately presents a child's fear of the dark and the problem this presents for parents. Leonard constantly responds 'No!' when told that it is time for the lights to go out. His parents, however, come up with an ingenious plan to convince Leonard that there is no monster lurking anywhere in his room. While the next title is a bit older, *The Dark* by Lemony Snicket is another book about being afraid of the dark. The book presents the challenges that Laszlo faces as he takes on his fear of the dark, even holding a conversation with the dark. In the end Laszlo actually finds that the dark is a friend that in turn helps him to overcome that fear.

Me and My Fear by Francesca Sanna is an excellent title that addresses the common occurrence of children having fears. A young girl conjures up an imaginary friend she calls 'Fear' and that imaginary friend grows bigger and bigger after she moves to a new country to protect the girl and keep her safe, which suggests an immigration/refugee story. However, a new real-life friend helps her deal with some fears, and she learns that she is not alone and everyone has fears. In the end, she discovers how to learn and play at school, even with a fear that may linger from time to time.

DEATH/DYING

Death can be a very challenging issue for children to encounter. Having books that address this issue in different ways can assist with this process. *Olive* by Edwina Wyatt is a perfect title that introduces the concept of death and dying through the story of a young girl grieving the loss of her pet cat. When her family plants an olive tree to remember the former pet, the girl wants nothing to do with it. Through time, however, she learns to accept the loss, and when a young kitten starts to take over the places where Olive used to be, she gradually warms to the new pet.

The Tiny Star by well-known Australian children's author, Mem Fox, presents a title that can really help children understand how death is another part of life through the story of a tiny 'star' (baby) that is welcomed into the world, and grows and becomes a key member of the community. Sadness, but also understanding is reached when the life of the tiny star is celebrated.

Ross Watkins's *One Photo* presents the story of a young family in which the father is facing dementia/Alzheimer's disease and is losing his memory. Using his camera, he takes a plethora of photos as a strategy to help him remember, but also for his family to remember him after he is gone. This book would be a wonderful title to use not only to present death and dying, but also illnesses such as dementia and Alzheimer's.

The Boy and the Gorilla by Jackie Azúa Kramer presents the story of a young boy whose mother has passed away. On the day of her funeral when he is really struggling, he invents an imaginary gorilla that helps him through, as well as cope with the situation. *Henry and Bea* by Jessixa Bagley is another US title that presents a subtle way to address death with children. Henry and Bea are best friends who normally are inseparable. One day, Henry wants to be alone and not be with his best friend. Bea can tell something is wrong, but Henry will not tell her. It is on a class excursion (field trip) that Bea learns that Henry's pet cat had passed away. With this information, Bea is able to assist Henry with his sadness, and help him through the difficult time.

Helen's Birds by Sara Cassidy tells the tale of a young girl named Saanvi who has been good friends with her elderly neighbour, Helen, for years. One day when Helen passes away, movers come and take away her possessions, and soon the house is torn down. All the beautiful birds that Saanvi and Helen enjoyed are gone, which adds to the sadness of losing her friend. Saanvi decides to bring the birds back with her own homemade bird feeders. The format of the book is a wordless graphic novel, and the story unfolds through these illustrations.

Paula Knows What To Do by Sanne Dufft is originally a German title that is a comforting story that presents a young girl grieving the loss of her mother with her very sad father. Understanding that her mother would not want them to be sad forever, she finds a creative and artistic way for both of them to move forward, while still remembering and cherishing the memory of her mother.

REFUGEES (SOCIAL JUSTICE ISSUES)

Realistic fiction also has the ability to address social justice issues, such as refugees. Many of the stories present first-hand narratives of the main character, while others may be reflective pieces of the migration experience. Regardless, they address the social justice issue of refugees. One of the best refugee stories comes from Irena Kobald's *My Two Blankets* in which a young girl named Cartwheel has to move to a new country not knowing the language or anything about the culture. This proves difficult for the young girl as she clings to her old culture (blanket) until she meets a new friend who understands her difficulty and starts to teach her new words, ideas and aspects of the new culture (blanket). The title is a wonderful metaphor for how the blankets are the two cultures that Cartwheel begins to have. *My Beautiful Birds* by Suzanne Del Rizzo is also told from the child's perspective about needing to move to a new country and how the young boy has to leave his precious pet birds behind. As he does this, he finds new birds in a refugee camp that helps calm his anxieties found with the move to a new country. The illustrations are striking and readers can see textures found within them, as Del Rizzo used plasticine and other media to great effect. An excellent title, *The Day War Came* tells the story of a young child whose life is turned upside down when war comes to their country and town, forcing them to flee and become a refugee. When they are finally able to settle into a refugee camp, they learn that war has come everywhere even in the new place they reside. However, the resilience of youth comes through as children come together to ensure everyone is able to attend school.

Watercress by Andrea Wang and *A Different Pond* by Bao Phi both reflect on the migration process and what family life is like after that journey. *Watercress* tells the tale of a refugee family's drive in their new country and when the parents see watercress in the ditch on the side of the road, how they come to a sudden stop and pick all the watercress they can. The young girl is embarrassed by this and does not want to help. During the family dinner in which they eat their new treasure, the girl's mother explains the reasons why watercress is so important to the family and the sacrifices made from leaving their home country. The young girl grows a greater appreciation for her family's history and story. *A Different Pond* has a similar reflective feel as a young boy describes a very early fishing trip with his father. During the fishing trip, he learns of the difficulties the family faced in the migration process and the current challenges of surviving in the new country. *Wishes* by Muon Thi Van has a creative approach to telling the story of the migration journey of a family. The word 'wish' is used throughout every page as it describes the challenging journey the family takes. For example, 'the bag wished it was deeper' or 'the heart wished it was stronger'. Van reflected on their own family's story and the wish aspect captures the challenges that are faced. *Grandma's Treasured Shoes* by Coral Vass is another strong example of a reflective story about how a young girl's grandmother who loves shoes has one specific pair enshrined as a memory of the difficult migration to Australia. The story teaches the young girl about her grandmother's life in Vietnam and the journey to a new country. At the end of the book there is non-fiction information about other stories.

Migrants by Issa Watanbe is a great wordless picture book that focuses on the issue of refugees and migration. The use of animals as main characters highlights the points discussed earlier about universality, and how animal main characters can assist in highlighting realistic issues – in this case, social justice issues.

MOVING

One of the hardest challenges children may face is moving. This could be when they move to a different house, or when a friend moves away, or even when new children move into the neighbourhood. One very specific example of this comes from this author's real life. When my daughter was in grade three, we bought a new house. She was not there when we bought the house and was quite upset because she had no idea we were going to move (although it was only four blocks away and we did not know we would be moving either). Regardless, my daughter was very upset and stressed about the move, and it did take a couple of years before she finally 'settled' into the new house (although we still have to drive by the old house from time to time). This is just an example of how difficult moving can be for children.

Izzy and Frank by Katrina Lehman is a good title to start the topic of moving. Izzy loves living on an island in a lighthouse and has a 'friend' in Frank the seagull. However, when Izzy moves to the city, everything changes for her. She misses the sand, sea and quiet, but most importantly, she misses Frank. How will she cope and adjust? When Frank flies in for a visit, she learns that there are other new friends around her that can help make her new house a home. This book is a good starting point for helping children relate to the challenges of moving. *Florette* by Anna Walker continues this topic and theme. When Mae moves from the country to the city, she has similar experiences to Izzy in *Izzy and Frank*. She misses the country and the wide open spaces. But when she discovers the beautiful garden of green, she learns that she can make a small piece of that into her new home and create her own happiness. *Goodbye House, Hello House* by Margaret Wild is another Australian title that continues the theme of moving from the country into the city. However, this title celebrates both places, while saying goodbye to the country house, the child in the story says hello to the new house and space, and through this the reader is able to see the wonderful side of moving to a new house as well. *My New Home* by Marta Altés is a UK title that also has universal implications as the main character is a raccoon. While the book presents how scary and lonely moving house can be, it also helps readers see that new adventures await in the new house. This is a good title that uses animal characters to present a realistic view of the universal issue/topic of moving.

How I Learned to Fall out of Trees by Vincent X. Kirsch is a US title that helps children learn how to cope with a friend who moves away. Roger and Adelia are best friends who do everything together, but when Adelia has to move away, sadness follows. Before she leaves, Adelia decides to teach Roger one last important lesson – how to climb a tree. The book is a creative approach to moving away, where one character, Roger, is learning one thing, while Adelia is doing another, preparing to move away; they both learn key lessons along the way, and Roger's lesson is how to fall safely.

NATURE

Alison Binks's *Night Walk* is an Australian title that follows a young boy named Caspar as he wakes in the middle of the night during a family camping trip and explores the world around him, observing the animals and terrain. The illustrations and story may remind readers of the now classic American Caldecott-winning title, *Owl Moon* by Jane Yolen (the book could also be paired with *The Night Walk* by Maria Dorléans, a US title that has a similar story about a family going for a nature walk at night). *A Walk in the Bush* by Gwyn Perkins is another Australian title that presents a grandfather taking the family cat for a walk through the bush and exploring the terrain, animals and environment, and enjoying every step of the way, and in particular the birds. These two books do a nice job of celebrating the Australian landscape and environment. *A Walk in the Bush* would be paired well with Tania McCartney's *Ivy Bird* because of the focus on birds. Ivy loves exploring the world, and in particular the birds that she encounters every day. The book follows Ivy along her daily journey; there is information at the end of the book about the different birds that are described.

Rockhopping and *Landing with Wings* both by Trace Balla take the reader on an adventure through Australia and its terrain. The comic-style illustrations make the book a fun read, but also again are strong books that celebrate the diverse landscape that is Australia. *Rockhopping* follows Clancy and Uncle Egg as they explore the Grampians. The comic-book format makes the adventure come alive and explores nature in a creative way. *Landing with Wings* continues the illustrative style as young Mina explores her new community and celebrates all the joys around her.

The Camping Trip by Jennifer K. Mann is a US title that shares the story of a girl's first camping trip with her cousin. She leaves the city and explores the country for the first time, experiencing setting up and sleeping in a tent, as well as sitting around a campfire enjoying the wonderful first taste of a 'smore'. This is a nice way to present the joys of camping for those who have yet to experience it.

Hike by Pete Oswald is a US wordless picture book that shares the story of a father and his child as they leave the city to go for a hike through nature. The illustrations are lovely and present the beautiful adventure and experiences the pair share as they spend time together in nature. The book could be paired with Alison Farrell's *The Hike*, a US title telling the story of three girls who love to go on hikes in the woods. This book takes the reader through that adventure and shows them all the wonderful aspects of nature the girls see along the way. The book does a nice job of linking a fictional hike with the nature they discover along the way.

IDENTITY

Sometimes children struggle with understanding who they are or their place in the world. You may have seen the Olivia series by Ian Falconer. Olivia has no issue knowing her place in the world, and it is her unique personality that entertains readers, both young and old, as she exhausts her parents and sometimes frazzles them with her own unique ways and expectations. *Blue Flower* by Sonya Hartnett is a gorgeous Australian title that tells the story of a young girl who realises that her individual differences are what makes her special. The illustrations are beautifully done and pair with strong text that create a powerful picture book.

Little One by Jane Godwin tells the story of Pippi, who loves her 'little one' (stuffed toy). They go everywhere together and share many adventures, but when 'little one' is lost forever, Pippi must overcome her sadness and loss, and try to discover the world again on her own. While the best friend toy, and even losing that toy, is familiar to many children, the struggle to move on is addressed in Godwin's book and can assist children in understanding that they, too, can move on from the challenge.

Bev and Kev by Katrina Germein tells the story of a giraffe who is always told how tall she is. She becomes self-concious about being reminded of this, in sometimes the most impolite way, so she runs away to be alone. When she thinks she is all alone, she discovers a stowaway on her back, a bird named Kev. Together they form a friendship and Bev learns to appreciate her height and how she can share that with her new friend.

Want to Play Trucks? is a Bob Graham title that captures childhood very well. Two children playing in the sandbox at a playground find their own differences in play, as Alex enjoys playing with dolls and Jack prefers trucks. The disagreement in what to play is a common issue found with children around the world, but so is their ability to compromise and being able to work through it. The illustrations are in Graham's typical style, and an additional story in the background of the pictures adds to the enjoyment of the book.

Jessica Love's *Julian is a Mermaid* and *Julian at the Wedding* (2020) are two books featuring a boy named Julian. In the first book, inspired by the women he sees in his neighbourhood, he wants to be a mermaid and works hard creating his costume. He makes a big mess and is worried what his grandmother will think and say. The wonderful acceptance of Julian in this book is one shining light, while Julian is true to himself and confident in his identity. The sequel *Julian at the Wedding* continues the theme of acceptance as Julian attends a wedding with a new friend, Marisol, and, after the ceremony, they are off on their own shared play adventures. Julian's strong sense of self and acceptance continue to inspire.

Sometimes children can struggle with identity based upon how they look. *Black is a Rainbow Color* is a US title by Angela Joy that celebrates the colour black, but also recognises all the strengths the colour represents, as well as how the young girl narrator is proud to be black. This title would spark a number of good discussion points in a classroom, as well as help children to understand and hopefully empathise with those who may be struggling with identity issues based on similar situations.

COMMUNITY

Sometimes children make connections or have experiences in their local community. You may remember the old song from Sesame Street called 'these are the people in your neighbourhood'. It is important that children are exposed to books like these as well. If you have not seen the Newbery-winning picture book *Last Stop on Market Street* by Matt de la Peña, it is an excellent tale that takes place on a local bus as young CJ and his grandmother travel to the soup kitchen to help as volunteers. During the trip, CJ's grandmother helps him see all the wonderful things around him in his world. It is a very powerful and diverse story that has strong flowing language and imagery. The author and illustrator pair from that book also have *Milo Imagines the World* in which Milo and his sister travel on the train in a similar fashion to CJ on the bus, although Milo draws pictures on the trip. Milo sees everything on the train and the people around him, while his sister's sole focus is her mobile phone. Milo and his sister's destination is the prison where their mother is living. Again, the diversity and celebration of their community and the people around them are what make these two titles so special.

Andrew Daddo's title *Whatcha Building?* tells the story of a young boy who visits a construction site each day and asks for different leftover or discarded materials. The builder gives him something each day and asks 'Whatcha building?' and the boy responds, 'I don't know yet'. In the end, the builder comes to the boy's house to see exactly what the boy is building. The book provides repetitive text that will leave the reader constantly wondering what is being built. *Don't Forget* by well-known and loved Australian author and illustrator pair Jane Godwin and Anna Walker presents advice to children through a book about all the things to remember in life, from making your bed, doing your homework, to lending a hand for a friend. It is a beautifully poetic and illustrated book that reminds children that we all have a place in our community and world, and that we are all happy when we are loved and supported, and provide those same things for others.

CONCLUSION

Realistic fiction is the most common genre for children and the one that is most easily relatable for children. This is because children face many, if not all, of the issues that are found within children's literature. Through reading this genre, children are able to learn, understand, relate and empathise with the issues that are addressed in the books. Realistic fiction is important for children to learn and understand that they are not alone and there are other children like them. There are many common experiences and issues that children face, and this genre is helpful in exposing children to them in a positive manner.

ADDITIONAL TITLES

Poor Louie – Tony Fucile. A new baby comes into the house, told from the perspective of a little chihuahua.

My Papi has a Motorcycle – Isabel Quintero

Jabari Jumps (fear of jumping off the diving board) – Gaia Cornwall

Jabari Tries – Gaia Cornwall

WANT TO KNOW MORE?

O'Connor, B. (2010) 'Profiles and perspectives: keeping it real: how realistic does realistic fiction for children need to be?' *Language Arts*, 87(6): 465–71.

This article, written by a children's author, examines the issue of how real children's literature should be and explores seven different novels in the process.

Tomsic, M. and Zbaracki, M.D. (2022) 'It's all about the story: personal narratives in children's literature about refugees'. *British Educational Research Journal*, *48*(5): 859–77. Available at: https://doi.org/10.1002/berj.3798

This article explores refugee children's literature and the impact it has on refugee students and their own stories.

REFERENCES

Cullen, B. (2023) 'The power of picture books: behind the scenes with ten picture book creators part one'. *Magpies*, *38*(2): 8–12.

Jacobs, J. and Tunnell, M. (2004) *Children's Literature, Briefly* (3rd edn). London: Pearson.

Kasten, W., Kristo, J., McClure, A. and Garthwait, A. (2005) *Living Literature: Using Children's Literature to Support Reading and Language Arts*. London: Pearson.

Kiefer, B.Z., Hepler, S.I., Hickman, J. and Huck, C.S. (2007) *Charlotte Huck's Children's Literature* (9th edn). New York: McGraw-Hill.

Temple, C., Martinez, M., Yokota, J. and Naylor, A. (2002) *Children's Books in Children's Hands* (2nd edn). New York: Allyn & Bacon.

9

HISTORICAL FICTION

> **WHAT WE WILL LEARN**
> - What historical fiction is all about.
> - The role that historical fiction plays in children's literature.
> - How to evaluate historical fiction.
> - The common themes/topics in historical fiction.
> - Discover some of the key authors and illustrators who specialise in historical fiction.

History sometimes has a bad reputation for not being interesting. There are few children who relish the opportunity to open up a history textbook and start reading. However, it is still important that children learn history and about past events. Because children cannot always live or relate to the past, thank goodness that historical fiction exists within children's literature. As Kasten et al. (2005) observe: 'Through historical fiction, students can vicariously live the issues, actions, and emotions of people in previous generations' (p. 178). This is a crucial idea because historical fiction can provide children an opportunity to live indirectly through a character's life or experience. Historical fiction provides children with the opportunity to experience the history and make the events come alive for them. This allows children an opportunity to experience what it was like to protest for equal rights, prospect for gold, be involved in a war, and much more. As Kiefer et al. (2019) note: 'we need to know our history *and* the history of other countries'. This chapter will do just that and encourage teachers to explore historical fiction titles from a number of different countries.

Kiefer et al. (2019) note that 'historical fiction is not as popular with readers as it was a generation or two ago'. However, in Australia and the United States a plethora of great historical

fiction titles is being published, with a significant focus on the two World Wars and ANZACs, as well as many other diverse topics. Even with such a wide variety of books to choose from across Australian and world history, we must be aware of what this genre includes and how we can evaluate historical fiction books.

Historical fiction has the challenging task of being able to blend historical facts and information into an engaging story and format. As Kiefer et al. (2019) write: 'Historical fiction must draw on two sources, fact and imagination – the author's information about the past and her or his power to speculate about how it was to live in that time' (p. 243). While this can be complicated at times, it has been done successfully repeatedly, and Jackie French and Morris Gleitzman are authors who have been very successful writing novels with strong historical connections. This success is exemplified in what Kiefer et al. (2007) note: 'Historical novels for children help a child to experience the past—to enter into the conflicts, the suffering, the joys, and the despair of those who lived before us' (p. 542). While that quote relates to novels, it is important to recognise that there are also a number of great picture books by many different authors and illustrators, and these will be explored throughout this chapter. So, how does one define this genre? Quite simply, 'historical fiction can be used to designate all realistic stories that are set in the past' (Kiefer et al., 2019: 246). Keeping this in mind, we can start to see that the books will be quite realistic, but based on a specific historical time period.

Daley (2019) writes: 'historical fiction personalises accounts of past atrocities, which helps us to develop greater empathy than if we were to read a strictly factual account of the same historical context' (p. 117). For example, in Australia the story of the Stolen Generation has led to a number of good books that include the topic and provide an opportunity for children to learn more about the experiences through the stories being told (this is one place where avoiding stereotypes is important; children must be able to recognise the facts and details of the situation while avoiding stereotypes that may be included).

What constitutes a quality historical fiction picture book title? McDonald (2018) describes the genre as historical realism and writes that the 'texts describe events from a specific time and place as experienced by characters who hold values, attitudes and beliefs from the historical period' (p.14). There are several elements to keep in mind when exploring titles from this genre and the table below addresses several of the criteria to look for in a historical fiction title. A quick summary of these highlights is that, first and foremost, a historical fiction title must accurately blend fact and fiction together while also telling an engaging story. Galda and Cullinan (2006) describe this as, 'good historical fiction is grounded in facts but not restricted by them' (p. 213). The content of the historical elements must also be accurate and authentic, including the language and, in the case of picture books, the illustrations as well. Also, a quality historical fiction title will have notes and/or background information from the author to provide the reader with the opportunity to learn even more or to discover what inspired the story, as well as the resources the author used to find information.

Table 9.1 Evaluation criteria: historical fiction

Does the author blend historical fact and fiction together accurately?

Is there a solid balance between providing historical information and a fictional narrative?

Is the language authentic for the time period?

Do the illustrations accurately reflect the time period and the content of the story?

Is there an author's note? Background information?

Are stereotypes avoided?

Does it tell a good story?

EQUAL RIGHTS

Across the world there have been issues with equality and civil rights. This was found in Australia with the Stolen Generation. While some of these books are found in the next chapter (Indigenous literature), it is important to highlight them here as well.

Stories for Simon by Lisa Sarzin introduces the reader to Simon who unwraps a beautiful boomerang, and from this learns about the Stolen Generation and National Apology Day. The book would be a good way to introduce children to these topics and help them understand the impact these issues had on different members of Australian society. *Sorry Day* by Coral Vass tells the story of a young girl who goes to the Sorry Day ceremony with her family. During the ceremony she sees (imagines) different Indigenous people from the past and their experiences while the apology is being read. This is a powerful book that highlights a big issue that has impacted and continues to impact Australia. *Say Yes, A Story of Friendship, Fairness and a Vote for Hope* by Jennifer Castles shares how two girls who are best friends and do everything together soon learn that they are not allowed to be friends, simply because one is Aboriginal. The book includes details of the vote on the referendum in 1967 that changed this rule, and also includes further information at the back of the book about the Constitution and what changes were made.

The push for equal rights is not limited to Australia, as there are many examples of it from the United States as well. Opposition to the injustice of slavery was a very early example of this in US history and James E. Ransome's *The Bell Rang* is a solid example of this. Each day starts with the plantation manager ringing the bell and the slave family's daily routine begins. Each day it is the same, except one day when the girl's brother Ben is not there when the bell rings because he has tried to escape. While the family is sad that he has run away, they are also hopeful that he has been successful and reached the north, so that he will finally be free.

While there is a plethora of books about slavery that deal with the issues around that topic in the South, *New Shoes* by Susan Lynn Meyer (2016) describes unfair treatment due to segregation and the search for justice. A girl goes shoe shopping with her family, but because she is the youngest in the family, it usually means that she gets the hand-me-downs. But when her older sister's shoes do not fit her, she acquires her own new pair of shoes. The experience at the shoe store highlights inequality at its worst, when the girl and her mother must wait for a white mother and daughter first before they can be served. This historical example of equal rights is a powerful lesson for children. *Let the Children March* by Monica Clark-Robinson is based on a real historical event when thousands of children marched for equal rights in Birmingham, Alabama, after hearing Martin Luther King Jr speak. The book provides an excellent example of how the fight for equal rights was not limited to adults, but that children took a stand as well.

Continuing this theme of equal rights, *Overground Railroad* by Lesa Cline-Ransome is about the journey, or migration, north into states where segregation did not exist in the US. In the book, young Ruth Ellen describes each leg of her family's journey from the deep South to Penn Station in New York City. Cline-Ransome also weaves in elements of the book *Narrative of the Life of Frederick Douglass*. The book does a good job of providing information about African Americans migrating north to a different life.

IMMIGRATION STORIES

There are a number of good immigration stories that introduce specific historical aspects of Australian history. *Beth: The Story of a Child Convict* by Mark Wilson, and the two other books in the trilogy – *Never Lose Hope* and *The Little Wooden Horse* – all tell stories about child convicts who were transported to Australia, and the challenges and experiences they faced. The trilogy will challenge older primary school readers as they are introduced to the hardships, trials and tribulations these children faced. From a more recent time, *Ten Pound Pom* by Niall Griffiths informs the reader about the Assisted Passage Migration Scheme from the 1950s and 1960s, and relates the story of the author's migration to Australia.

A Cat Called Trim tells the story of Trim, a cat that Matthew Flinders found on the ship the *Reliance*. The story presents 'Trim's story' and the adventures that he and Flinders faced as they sailed to different parts of the world.

Immigration stories are not limited to Australia, and there are many stories from America as well. For example, *Gittel's Journey* written by Lesléa Newman is an immigration story in which a young girl named Gittel must immigrate by herself to America. She has her cousin's address on a piece of paper, but when she arrives at Ellis Island, the ink has run and it is now illegible. Gittel must now try to find her family in a new world. Although the publication date is a bit older, *The Matchbook Diary* by Paul Fleischman is an interesting twist on an immigration story. A young girl asks her great grandfather about the different matchbooks he has and the objects they hold. As he goes through each one, it tells a different part of his immigration from Italy. A more recent immigration story comes from Doyin Richards with *Watch Me.*

The book tells the story of the author's father's immigration story to America. The more modern experience in the book presents the realistic fiction-type experiences that match Kiefer et al.'s quote earlier about how historical fiction is about 'realistic stories set in the past'.

HISTORY IN GENERAL

Farmhouse by Sophie Blackall (who has also written and illustrated *Hello Lighthouse*) tells the story of a farmhouse in the country (based on the author's own experience of buying an old farmhouse). Through the illustrations the reader/viewer is able to see what life looked like and how the farmhouse (and world) changed through the years. One example of this are the modes of transportation, with the horse-drawn plough early in the book and then a car at the end taking one of the original children away from the farmhouse to visit her sister. *The Hundred-Year Barn* by Patricia MacLachlan is another good title that would match with *Farmhouse* as it shows the life of the barn and the changes it witnesses when a young boy sees it being built, and then after he grows up into a young man and takes over the family farm. This theme of someone or something witnessing history through the years continues with *What Did the Tree See?* by Charlotte Guillain which tells the story of an oak tree and what it witnesses through the years as life changes and passes by them. From being a part of the woodlands, to witnessing the Industrial Revolution, this tree has seen a lot. The book has a timeline at the back which also helps the reader identify the different events it has observed through history. *Oscar's American Dream* by Barry Wittenstein tells a story from the unique perspective of a corner shop in New York City and the different shops it becomes through the twentieth century. What begins as the barbershop of newly immigrated Oscar changes hands through the years and shows what happens through history in New York City. The book is a good cross between an immigration story and the perspective of an inanimate object – in this case, the corner shop that was originally a barbershop.

Sometimes history in general can be aligned with a specific person that has an influence on people's lives and for the purposes of this book, most likely children. *Miss Franklin: How Miles Franklin's Brilliant Career Began* by Libby Hathorn tells the story of Stella Miles Franklin and her job as a governess in the country. She does not take well to the position and longs to be a writer. When she decides to write a book, it becomes a success and thus begins her journey as an author, leading to both the Miles Franklin Award and the Stella Award in Australia. You could pair this one with the US title *That Book Woman* by Heather Henson (2008), which shows how certain people in history can have such a powerful impact on us.

AUSTRALIAN HISTORY

Australia has a number of historical landmarks, and the Sydney Harbour Bridge is one of the most famous. *To the Bridge* and *The Day We Built the Bridge* are two stories that present this significant landmark in different ways. *To the Bridge* presents the story of Lennie and his horse Ginger Mick and their journey in 1932 to see the new bridge. *The Day We Built the Bridge* shares the building of the bridge through the eyes of a boy as he grows into a young man, and through his life sees the vision of the bridge become a reality and the process it took. The stunning illustrations are a strong aspect of the storytelling in this book.

The Gold Rush was a significant event in Australian history. Both *Eureka! A Story of the Goldfields* and *Gold!* present this story and these events. *Eureka! A Story of the Goldfields* shares the story of Molly and her father as they become gold prospectors during the great gold rush. Also illustrated by Mark Wilson (presented earlier), the illustrations are outstanding and readers will learn much about the difficult times the gold miners experienced. *Gold!* by Jackie Kerin is about four friends who become prospectors dreaming of finding gold. They, too, experience the challenges of prospecting, but have a positive outcome as well.

The Shop Train written by Josie Wowolla Boyle shares the story of a young girl and her mother and the trips they took to meet the Tea and Sugar train that ran between South Australia and Western Australia. The train provided supplies, stories and excitement for residents in remote areas between the states. The book would pair very well with Jane Jolly's book *Tea and Sugar Christmas*, in which within the story of a young girl waiting for the Christmas train, which only came once a year, there is also non-fiction information about the trains and what they looked like and included. Jolly has also written *Radio Rescue*! telling the tale of a remote family living on a farm in the outback. When they get a new radio with pedals and everything, they are finally able to communicate easier with their neighbours. However, when an emergency happens, the young son must use the new radio to try to save his father. The book is another example of living in remote areas of Australia, as well as the Royal Flying Doctors.

Wild Bush Days by Penny Harrison shares the story of two young girls exploring the Australian bushland and remembering the famous lady bushranger, Jessie Hickman. As the girls go through different areas of the bush, the story and illustrations match up with different aspects of Jessie Hickman's life as well. This book would pair well with *King of the Outback* by Kristin Weidenbach, which also deals with a historical figure from the outback. Sidney Kidman left home at thirteen and dreams of becoming one of the greatest cattlemen in Australia. Sidney's story is a great rags-to-riches one that provides another strong outback experience.

The Friendly Games by Kaye Baillie tells the story of the Melbourne Olympics and the impact of the racial tensions from around the world. Schoolboy John Wing has an idea to challenge this and writes to the Olympic Committee for a suggestion for the closing ceremonies. This book tells more about the Melbourne Olympics and can provide guidance for current racial issues as well.

Where's Jessie? by Janneen Brian tells the story of Bertie the bear, a young child's (Jessie) teddy that is lost as they travelled across Australia to Alice Springs. The cameleers who travelled across the Australian outback are the ones who take Bertie around Australia, as the common refrain through the book is 'Where's Jessie?'. Poor Bertie endures a flash flood, an eagle, getting left behind, until finally a good Samaritan Indigenous boy reunites Bertie with Jessie.

Flood, Fire, Cyclone and *Drought* tell the different stories of how these natural phenomena have influenced Australia. The latest book *Pandemic* is timely, as it tells the story of the Spanish flu and how it impacted the entire world. This is a good book to include when talking about pandemics and Covid-19, and how the world responds to such experiences. This matches well with what Kiefer et al. (2019) wrote: 'stories of the past help children see that times change, nations rise and fall, but universal human needs have remained relatively unchanged'. This series by Jackie French helps show children that there are shared experiences and there are similar as well as new ones to respond to them.

WAR

FIRST WORLD WAR

There are numerous books that can be used to introduce the two World Wars, and with the centenary of the battle of Gallipoli, there are many excellent books to explore. *The Good Son: A Story From the First World War* tells the difficult story of a young man who temporarily deserts the army to visit his mother and ends up paying the ultimate price. The illustrations are photographs of painted lead figurines. The exquisite detail in the illustrations are amazing in themselves, but, coupled with the storyline, the book is well worth reading. *Alfred's War* recognises the part that Indigenous Australians played in the First World War, sharing the story of Alfred who returns home after being injured in battle and how he adjusted to life after the war. This title provides long overdue recognition of the Indigenous Australians and their contribution in the war.

When the War is Over (Jackie French) presents the impact of war from the First World War to present-day conflicts in Afghanistan and beyond. The illustrations are powerful and the connections to wars through the years provides younger readers with the opportunity to explore and learn more about the history of different wars. *The Anzac Tree* is the perfect companion to French's book, as it presents a number of short stories about children who have loved-ones fighting in wars from the First World War up to the conflict in Afghanistan. The end of the book has brief information about each war.

I Was Only Nineteen is a picture book combining the well-known song that is sung at almost every ANZAC day vigil with the Vietnam War. This title from 2019 provides an opportunity to expand the discussion of war and introduce another significant war in world history.

Never Forget by Clare Hallifax has outstanding artwork actually painted by those observing the First World War around them. It details what the men and women experienced during the war. The artwork adds to the power of the book.

This is Where I Stand (Philippa Werry, 2021). This New Zealand title presents the story of a young man as a statue as he reflects on what he saw in war. This book presents a different perspective on who is telling the story, and still includes information and history about the war.

The ANZAC Billy tells how 'billys' (which were metal bucket 'care packages' for the ANZACs) were filled and sent to the soldiers in the war. This title would work well with younger readers who are learning about the war and how Australia cared for soldiers in war.

The Anzac Violin is another New Zealand title to include, telling the story of Alexander Aitken, a solider who plays the violin everywhere he goes. One day he sets off to the battle at Somme and is seriously wounded. Based on a true story, children will be able to learn more about the war and how soldiers kept their spirits up and supported one another.

Message in a Sock is another strong story from the First World War, based on a real-life experience between a soldier and a young girl. The young girl's mother knits socks for the soldiers and the girl writes a message in each one. The gorgeous collage illustrations connect well with the story. *My Name is Henry Fanshaw* is another New Zealand title that is told from the perspective of Henry, the teddy bear from the No. 75 Squadron of the Royal New Zealand Air Force, as he tells stories about members of the squadron. Intrigued and interested readers can find Henry in the Air Force Museum of New Zealand. This book could connect well with *Anzac Ted* listed at the end of this chapter.

A Soldier, a Dog and a Boy is a beautifully written story about a soldier who meets a stray dog and brings him along as a mascot. It is a very powerful story based on a photograph from the First World War of a young French orphan being smuggled out of France. *Stubby: A True Story of Friendship* (2018) is a wonderful story about a stray dog joining an army training session. It is a rather light-hearted story that will have children strongly connecting to Stubby, while also learning about the challenges that soldiers faced during the war. *Bunny the Brave War Horse* (2015) is based on a true story about a former police horse and the two brothers who rode him during the First World War. The book presents the realities of war, but Bunny's presence helps subdue some of the issues presented. There is information at the end of the book from the author that includes dates and details about the First World War, as well as maps of the areas from the book.

Well-known historical fiction children's author Mireille Messier (*Finding Winnie*) wrote the book *Sergeant Billy: The True Story of the Goat Who Went to War*, based on a true story about a goat that was adopted by a platoon of soldiers. The goat had a number of experiences such as headbutting soldiers, eating secret documents and even becoming a decorated war soldier. The book is a fun way to share unique aspects of what happened during the First World War.

Shooting at the Stars by John Hendrix shares the experience a young soldier has on Christmas Eve during the First World War when German and Allied soldiers had a Christmas truce, not only ceasing fire, but also celebrating Christmas, singing carols together and even exchanging gifts before returning to their own trenches and going back to the realities of war. At the back of the book the author provides more information about the war, the truce and even a photograph taken at the time.

Poppy Field (Michael Morpurgo, 2018) is a UK title, longer than a normal 32-page picture book, which delves deeper into the history of the poppy and its symbolism. This is a good book to use to extend the learning of war and memorials. It also has nice background information at the end. *Christmas Truce* and *Where the Poppies Now Grow* are all part of a series of books presenting different aspects of the First World War, written by Hilary Robinson. Also written by Hilary Robinson, *Peace Lily* recognises the nurses who served during the war. *Where the Poppies Now Grow* celebrates all the soldiers who served, *Flo of the Somme* acknowledges the animals that risked their lives, and *Christmas Truce* tells the story of the truce during the war. All the books present different aspects of the First World War.

SECOND WORLD WAR

Charlie's Swim by Edith Wright is based on the fascinating true story of an Indigenous man named Charles D'Antoine who jumped into the water to save a woman and her child when the Japanese bombed Broome during the Second World War. This captivating story is one that shows the impact and different roles that many Australians had in the war.

Flapper, VC is a fascinating story about how carrier pigeons helped carry messages during the Second World War. Mark Wilson's illustrations are on display again, and he has found another interesting historical story to tell as well.

Tucky Jo and Little Heart by Patricia Polacco tells the tale of Tucky Jo who was only 15 years old when he enlisted in the army. When he is sent to the Pacific, he befriends a young girl and her family who help him with such things as insect bites, and they share a mutual kindness as he shares his rations with the family. When war hits home, Tucky Jo is able to help even more. The book is based on a true story and helps children learn that there can be kindness in many forms, even during war. Both the characters meet each other again, much later in life, and the kindness continues again. *Nicky & Vera* by Peter Sis tells the story of Nicholas Winton and how he saved hundreds of children from the Nazis during the Holocaust. This book tells the story of one of the children he saved, Vera Gissing. This title can teach children more about the Holocaust. *The Whispering Town* is a book about a Danish fishing village that shelters and assists a Jewish family during the Holocaust. It is a powerful story during a very difficult time in history. In a short graphic novel entitled *Hidden: A Child's Story of the Holocaust*, a grandmother tells her granddaughter a story that no one else in the family knows: how neighbours and friends hid her from the Nazis and saved her from the concentration camp. This would be a good title to use with upper primary school students. The book would connect well with *They Called Us Enemy* by George Takei, a graphic memoir telling the story of George's family experience as Asian Americans in internment camps in the United States during the Second World War. This graphic memoir would pair well with *Write To Me: Letters from Japanese American Children to the Librarian They Left Behind* by Cynthia Grady. It tells the story of a librarian in San Diego, California, who realises that many of her young patrons will be sent to internment camps. Before many of them leave, she gives them postcards and books and tells them to write to her. The powerful story presents many issues of war and human rights during wartime.

The Cat Man of Aleppo by Karim Shamsi-Basha and Irene Latham is based on a true story that happened during the Syrian civil war. When war struck Aleppo, many of the residents fled for their safety. However, one resident stayed behind to help those who remained and keep them safe. One day, he heard the cries of cats and brought them to safety. Soon, he had rescued more and more cats. News of his good deeds spread and donations poured in. He now has an animal sanctuary.

CONCLUSION

Historical fiction is an excellent way to engage children in history while engrossing readers in the story. By ensuring that the stories are historically accurate and authentic, teachers can encourage children to return to this genre. It is important for teachers to understand how to evaluate and select titles that are quality examples of the genre. Whether the history is specific to Australia or other parts of the world, historical fiction has the potential to educate children about the past, while also preparing them for the future. No matter where a child is in the world, or what they are interested in through history, there will most likely be a book for them to learn more. This is a genre that deserves exploration and, with all the amazing titles from Australia, it is well worth more recognition and attention.

ADDITIONAL TITLES

Digger: The Dog Who Went to War (2015) – Mark Wilson

One Minute's Silence – David Metzenthen

The Soldier's Gift – Jane Tanner

Anzac Ted – Belinda Landsberry

The Afghanistan Pup – Mark Wilson

An Anzac Tale – Ruth Stark

Lest We Forget – Kerry Brown

Roly the Anzac Donkey – Glynn Harper

The Last Anzac – Gordon Winch

WANT TO KNOW MORE?

McTigue, E., Thornton, E. and Wiese, P. (2013) 'Authentication projects for historical fiction: do you believe it?' *The Reading Teacher*, *66*(6): 495–505. Available at: https://doi.org/10.1002/TRTR.1132

This article presents teachers with an opportunity to critically examine historical fiction and reflect on its believability and influence for learning about history.

Wilson, K. (2008) 'The past re-imagined: memory and representations of power in historical fiction for children'. *International Research in Children's Literature*, *1*(2): 111–24. Available at: https://doi.org/10.3366/E1755619808000264

This article presents a critical analysis of historical fiction and points out the influence the genre can have on learning about historical events, and even 're-imagining' what happened in the past.

Wilson, K. (2011) *Re-visioning Historical Fiction for Younger Readers: The Past through Modern Eyes*. London: Routledge.

For those interested in the article above, the author has written a book delving into historical fiction further, and exploring the influence and impact it can have on children when they read historical fiction.

REFERENCES

Daley, M. (2019). *Raising Readers: How to Nurture a Child's Love of Books*. Brisbane: University of Queensland Press.

Galda, L. and Cullinan, B. (2006) *Literature and the Child* (6th edn). Belmont, CA: Wadsworth.

Kasten, W., Kristo, J., McClure, A. and Garthwait, A. (2005) *Living Literature: Using Children's Literature to Support Reading and Language Arts*. London: Pearson.

Kiefer, B.Z., Hepler, S.I., Hickman, J. and Huck, C.S. (2007) *Charlotte Huck's Children's Literature* (9th edn). McGraw-Hill.

Kiefer, B.Z., Tyson, C.A., Barger, B.P., Patrick, L. and Reilly-Sanders, E. (2019) *Charlotte Huck's Children's Literature: A Brief Guide* (3rd edn). New York: McGraw Hill Education.

McDonald, L. (2018) *A Literature Companion for Teachers* (2nd edn). Newtown, NSW: Primary English Teaching Association Australia.

10

INDIGENOUS LITERATURE

> **WHAT WE WILL LEARN**
> - All about Australian-specific children's literature.
> - The key features of Indigenous literature.
> - How country, community, culture, people and language connect with Indigenous literature.
> - How to evaluate quality Indigenous literature.

There are many identifiable characteristics to Australian children's literature. These could include specific vocabulary, landmarks, cities and locations, or even specific 'Aussie' traditions. Throughout the chapters in this book, there have been some Australia-specific titles – for example, *Three Little Bush Pigs, Big Bad Bushranger, Goldilocks and the Three Koalas* – as well as those that feature Australia specifically – for example, Leigh Hobbs's *Mr Chicken Goes to Australia*. This celebration of Australia as a country and its people is important for children for a multitude of reasons. One is that they are able to recognise key features of their home country. Two, they are able to learn more about their own country. Third, and perhaps most important, children are able to celebrate the unique and wonderful features that are found in Australia.

Mem Fox started this celebration of Australian culture years ago with *Possum Magic*, when Poss and her grandmother set off on a journey across Australia, and specific Australian food is centre to the story and its resolution. Mem Fox was then at it again with *Koala Lou* featuring Australia-specific wildlife (koalas) as a main character. It is important to note that this was not the first time this happened. However, it led to international recognition as *Koala Lou* is a prime example of a well-loved and celebrated universal story about the love a parent has for their child.

Dirt by Sea by Michael Wagner is a fun comic-book formatted title that takes the reader along on a father and daughter road trip to explore all states in Australia. The young daughter misheard the national anthem and thought the line was 'our home is dirt by sea'. The father decides to help his daughter see the entire island of Australia and the book does exactly that. The adventures they experience are a wonderful way to show young readers highlights of every state across Australia. *Our Country: Ancient Wonders* by Mark Greenwood is a title that explores fourteen different wonders across Australia. Each state and territory is included in the wonders and will have readers learning more about Australia. A fascinating example is Lake Mungo in New South Wales and the fossilised footprints and remains of people dating back 42,000 years. The end of the book includes further information about the wonders and Australia. This book would pair very well with Roland Harvey's books about Australia.

Roland Harvey is well known for his books that include geographic landmarks in Australia, ranging from *To the Top End, In Our Bush* and, a more recent title, *Off We Go Around Australia.* What these books provide are opportunities for children to see Australia beyond their window, town or even state. Readers can also explore books such as Tania McCartney's *The Gum Family Finds Home* which invites the reader to join a family of koalas on a cross-country road trip, as both the Gum family and the reader learn more about Australia.

It is crucial to also celebrate and explore Indigenous literature as well, as they are the first peoples of Australia. Recently, there has been a wonderful explosion of quality Indigenous children's literature, both written by and featuring Indigenous people.

Early on, Indigenous children's literature had a more Dreaming (Dreamtime) story focus. There was also a large amount of partnerships between well-known children's authors and illustrators with schools in Indigenous communities, and this provided some much-needed attention. Now, however, there is an exciting growth within this genre. With more authors and illustrators being published and even an Indigenous-specific publisher (Magabala Books), there are many more high-quality books that are worth exploring. As Ross Johnston 2017) notes: 'The growth of Indigenous publishing houses has made it possible for many more books by Indigenous writers to be produced' (p. 172). This is a delightful development and is a huge benefit for all readers within Australia and across the globe.

BUST A MYTH

All Indigenous books are related/connected to Dreaming (Dreamtime).

One of the best developments in the field of children's literature is a focus on Indigenous Australian children's literature. In the past decade alone, there has been a stronger focus on publishing Indigenous Australian authors, illustrators and stories. This means that a plethora of quality books is being published that go well beyond the traditional Dreaming stories.

This section will have a strong focus on picture books because this is a genre that provides creators with many different opportunities to experiment with different approaches. As Ross Johnston (2017) writes: 'Picturebooks, with their visual and verbal freedoms, are well suited to stories that juggle and jumble pasts, presents and futures, and differing ideas of time and place' (p. 172). One key feature to explore in Indigenous titles is the use of the bird's-eye view. As Ross Johnston identifies:

> In Aboriginal art, the perspective is aerial—looking down on the picture from above. Thus some of the circular patterns and animal tracks that seem to go off the top of a page, for example, suddenly make sense to the Western-trained eye. This overhead perspective conceives of land as unchangeable and of the individual as part of it, as intimately related to it. Perhaps it also implies that land and country are not just to be viewed, but to be known beyond the viewing. (p. 163)

This can be seen in several pages of Bruce Pascoe's book *Found*, which describe a young calf that has lost its family and is surrounded by horses. One specific image from this book is found in a double page spread which highlights the power of the bird's eye view by showing a scared young calf being circled by a number of horses.

Table 10.1 Evaluation criteria: Indigenous literature

Promotes positive cultural discussion
Avoids stereotypes
Tells a good story
Appropriate and authentic language
Illustrations are authentic and accurately reflect the culture.
What about author's note? Or something about the author? To show where they are from? But is this needed for authenticity?

There are a number of different features to consider when evaluating Indigenous literature, as shown in Table 10.1. One of the key aspects is how/if the book promotes positive cultural discussions. The many different titles shared throughout this chapter are key examples of how this can be done. (*Welcome to Country* by Aunty Joy Murphy and *Hello and Welcome* by Gregg Dreise are two examples that showcase the positive cultural discussion.) While the text is one key feature of the book, it is important to evaluate the illustrations as well, and with these they need to be authentic and accurate. Of course, one of the main criteria would be the most simplistic – does it tell a good story? Finally, one last point to consider would be information about the author. While this can provide authenticity about the author or illustrator, it also can provide context for the story or artwork.

Indigenous cultures have a very strong connection to country. The Australian curriculum recognises how Indigenous peoples 'celebrate the unique belief systems that connect people physically and spiritually to Country/Place' (www.australiancurriculum.edu.au/f-10-curriculum/cross-curriculum-priorities/aboriginal-and-torres-strait-islander-histories-and-cultures/). This and the importance of language within the Indigenous communities is why in this chapter, where possible, each author and/or illustrator also recognises where they are from within the vast Indigenous communities and Australia.

BOOKS FOR YOUNGER READERS

While there are a number of titles in this chapter that could fit perfectly into other genres, the aim of including them here is because they deserve to be recognised and celebrated, and deserve more attention. *An A to Z Story of Australian Animals* (2020) by Sally Morgan (Palyku people of the eastern Pilbara region of Western Australia) is an excellent alphabet book featuring different Australia animals. *Joey Counts to Ten*, also by Sally Morgan and illustrated by Ambelin Kwaymullina (Palyku people of the eastern Pilbara region of Western Australia), is an outstanding counting book. Kwaymullina highlights each animal being counted so young readers can easily identify and count the correct number. *Can You See Me?* by Sue Briggs and Bev Harvey and illustrated by Bronwyn Houston (Wunna Nyiyaparli people of the Pilbara) uses specific prepositions (over, under, above, etc.) to assist young readers in expanding their vocabulary. Venetia Tyson's *My Lost Mob* (Quandamooka woman from North Stradbroke Island area of Queensland) is a wonderful story about a young emu as they search for their family, asking different animals along the way for assistance. Some readers may make connections between this book and the classic children's picture book *Are You My Mother?* by P.D. Eastman. This Indigenous title expands on that idea and presents an Australian perspective on that story. *Colours of Australia* by Bronwyn Bancroft (a proud Bundjalung woman) introduces young readers to different colours with a descriptive verse connected to each colour. All these books are strong examples of beginning books (see Chapter 2) with Indigenous perspectives and illustrations. As discussed in Chapter 2, beginning books assist young readers in learning new concepts. The books listed above introduce concepts such as the alphabet, counting, vocabulary, animals and colours, while including Indigenous culture and language.

REALISTIC THEMES

As mentioned earlier about books in this chapter, the following books could fit in the realistic fiction chapter as they are all realistic narratives that introduce relatable real-life events, feelings, situations and dreams. This also connects well with what Neale and Kelly (2020) write: 'story carries more weight in the Aboriginal world, as history does in the Western world' (p. 39). This importance of story is quite apparent when one looks at the stories told in the following titles. This also highlights the idea that Freeman and Lehman (2001) wrote about how multicultural literature 'is a way to learn about other cultures, to bring people together, to travel the globe, to bridge our differences, and to rejoice in our common joys and triumphs'. The following titles connect well with those ideas and present not only common joys and triumphs, but differences as well.

Australian Rules Football (AFL) is quite popular around Australia and *Going to the Footy* by Debbie Coombes celebrates how people go to football all across Australia. Whether it is by foot, car, bus, aeroplane or other ways, the simplistic text in the book celebrates the common tradition of travelling to football games. Children of all ages will relate to dreaming of owning a special item, whether it is a toy, a pair of shoes or a bicycle. *Billie and the Blue Bike* by Ambelin Kwaymullina (Palyku people of the eastern Pilbara region of Western Australia) tells the story of how Billie works and saves her money in order to buy the blue bike of her dreams. The book provides a wonderful universal lesson about the importance of working and saving your money in order to achieve a goal.

Every child has a playful side and imagination is one of the true joys of childhood. *Molly the Pirate* by Lorraine Teece (Elder of the Alayawarra people from Central Australia) and illustrated by Paul Seden (descended from the Wuthagi and Muralag people of North Queensland), tells the swashbuckling pirate adventure of Molly who has always dreamed of being a pirate. The story is based upon what she imagines and plays one morning while her mother works around the house. Children will be able to relate to and appreciate the imaginative pirate adventures that Molly shares with the reader. Another book that fits well for its imagination and playfulness is *Steve Goes to Carnival* by Joshua Button (Walmajarri people of the Kimberly Region in Western Australia). This is a clever story about a gorilla in Rio that escapes from the zoo in order to find jazz music. As he wanders through the town in search of his favourite zookeeper, he discovers different places as well as the music he craves. The book is a fun story that showcases an Indigenous author and his creativity.

We all have dreams and children are no exception, especially when it comes to characters such as Batman, Spiderman or Ironman. *I Want to be a Superhero* by Ambelin Kwaymullina (Palyku people of the eastern Pilbara region of Western Australia) and Breanna Humes (Noongar, Gunditjmara, Wiraderjiri, Jawoyn) shares the dream of one child who has always wanted to be a superhero. Through minimal text and unique illustrations, children will relate to the dream of having superpowers and what it would be like to be a superhero.

Continuing with the football theme discussed earlier, there is Paul Seden's (Wuthathi and Muralag people) and Karen Briggs's (a descendant of the Yorta Yorta people from the junction of the Goulburn and Murray rivers in Northeast Victoria), *Kick With My Left Foot*. Young children learning to read will appreciate the simple, repetitive text in the story of a young boy learning to play Aussie Rules Footy. While the character struggles to kick with his right foot, he overcomes this when he learns he has even better skills with his left foot. This book will help children learn to read, as well as learn resilience in overcoming challenges.

My Deadly Boots by Carl Merrison (a respected Jaru/Kija man) is another title that incorporates footy into the story. A young boy saves up his money to buy a brand new pair of colourful footy boots, which he calls his deadly boots. When they arrive, he wears them everywhere. As he does this, he discovers the challenges he faces, from jealousy among friends, to police not believing that they are his own. In the end, he learns that boots or not, he himself is deadly, in a good way. Continuing the connection with the football theme, *Rocky and Louie*, written by Phily Walleystack and Raewyn Caisley, and illustrated by Dub Leffler (descended from the Bigambul people of South-West Queensland), is a story about two brothers, Rocky and Louie. Rocky is the older brother who teaches Louie all about country and different cultural traditions. When Rocky announces that he is going to chase his dreams of playing professional footy, Louie is devastated. However, Louie gives him a parting gift that reminds Rocky of how to return home. This is a special story of the bond between brothers, as well as the importance of following your dreams.

Crabbing With Dad, another title by Paul Seden and most likely autobiographical, is a story about a day spent fishing and crabbing. The simple text shares the adventures of a day on the water with dad as they catch mud crabs for dinner. Children will enjoy the adventure as well as learn a bit about the crabbing process along the way.

Many children will remember the fear of being lost from their parents or family. *The Lost Girl* (2017) by Ambelin Kwaymullina tells that exact story about a girl who loses her way in the country. However, she utilises what she has learned from her family about the country and survival, and is able to find her way home again. This story is one that will help children see the connection between the country and the importance of learning about it in order to take care of oneself.

FAMILY

Main Abija My Grandad is by Karen Rogers from the Ngukurr community in Southeast Arnhem Land in the Northern Territory. The book shares the author's memories of growing up and how her grandad taught her many things, and how she remembers those things and has even taught them to her own children and grandchildren. It is another strong example of the importance of family and country. The book is written in both English and Kriol. It would also pair well with *Shirley Purdie* written by Shirley Purdie, a prominent leader in Warmun community. The book tells about Shirley's life and the strong influence her family had on her childhood, and how she became a famous painter. The book would pair well with *Main Abija My Grandad*, as it connects strongly with family and is bilingual – in this case, English and Gija.

I Remember, by Joanne Crawford (descended from the Nhunda people of the Geraldton area of Western Australia), is a memory story about how her family used to go camping in the same spot each year. The book shares the memories of the journey to the spot where they camped and all the different things they did while they were camping. It is a strong example of the importance of family and country together.

Mum's Elephant is by Maureen Jipiyiliya Nampijinpa O'Keefe (a Kaytetye-Warlpiri woman). In this book the author revisits one of her mother's prized possessions, an old teapot that she called her elephant. The story shares how important the teapot was to her mother and how she treasured it.

Found by Bruce Pascoe (Yuin, Bunurong and Tasmanian Aboriginal heritage), illustrated by Charmaine Ledden-Lewis (Bundjalung people) mentioned earlier in this chapter, tells the story of a young calf that loses its family and 'mob'. The young animal tries to find its family and the metaphors throughout the book could lead to many excellent discussions about such topics as family, community and even the Stolen Generations.

MORALITY AND VALUES

As discussed earlier in the book, some children's literature has a strong moral or message that can be taught through the book. There are some Indigenous titles that do exactly this in a way that maintains a strong connection to culture. Gregg Dreise (Kamilaroi and Euahlayi heritage, southwest Queensland and northwest New South Wales) is one such example, having five books in a series that are described as morality tales based on dreaming stories. *Mad Magpie, Cunning Crow, Kookoo Kookaburra, Silly Birds* and *Awesome Emu* are all different books that contain a specific moral. *Mad Magpie* addresses the issue of bullying as well as remaining calm during challenging times, and the importance of music. *Kookoo Kookaburra* is the second book in the series and tells the story of a kookaburra that delights all the other animals with funny stories. When he runs out of stories, he resorts to making fun of his friends and learns the importance of kindness, especially with one's friends. *Cunning Crow* teaches the idea that beauty is found within. The book tells the story of how birds found their colour, but when a crow was jealous of the colours of the other birds, his plan to change his colour did not turn out as he had planned. *Silly Birds* is the first book in the series and teaches the lesson of listening and being a good leader by doing the right thing. When an eagle and a turkey team up and start to do silly things, it takes some time before the eagle realises the error of their ways, learns the important life lesson that 'you cannot fly like an eagle when you hang out with turkeys', and begins to listen and lead. *Awesome Emu* is the final book in the series that teaches about confidence and even overconfidence. When a young emu believes that it is able to run and fly the fastest and furthest, it learns a very hard lesson. This series connects well with what Ross Johnston (2017) writes: 'Aboriginal narratives of the Dreaming connect animals and landscape to personal, familial, regional and spiritual community' (p. 163).

Aunty Fay Muir (Boonwurrung Elder) and Sue Lawson have written a series called Our Place, illustrated by Lisa Kennedy (coastal clan, the Trawlwoolway people of North East

Tasmania), including the titles *Family* and *Respect*. *Family* connects back to what was discussed earlier in this chapter about the importance of country, place, community and people, as it shares different ways that family connects with country and other people in their own place, which creates a true sense of community. The text is brief yet powerful – for example, 'Family. Stories and songs' and 'Family. Kinship that bind. Showing the way'. *Respect* continues this idea as it represents the Indigenous culture within the country and how respect is needed throughout every aspect of our lives. The text is similar to that found in *Family* in that it is brief but poweful – 'Our way is respect. Respect for stories that shimmer through tall grass' and 'Respect for Elders gathered beside dancing fire, for Ancestors always with us'.

Grandfather Emu and *Bobtail's Friend* are part of a Dreaming series of books written by Rhonda Collard-Spratt (a strong Yamatji-Noongar woman) and Jacki Ferro. The first title is the dreaming story of how Mother Yonga Kangaroo got her pouch, as well as the importance of helping people. The story is about how grandfather emu is hungry and thirsty, but other animals in the bush are not willing to help him, but mother kangaroo does. In *Bobtail's Friend*, Balharda the bobtail is excited to wear her new necklace of wildflowers, but a group of Bidi-Bidi butterflies change that when they make fun of her. Balharda is sad and follows the river, meeting others and learning the value of friendship along the way.

STRONG CONNECTION TO COUNTRY

A strong connection to country is a key component of Indigenous culture and a number of titles are able to do this and represent different parts of Australia. *Wilam*, written by Aunty Joy Murphy (Senior Aboriginal Elder of the Wurundjeri people), is an absolutely gorgeous book. The illustrations are simply amazing and the inclusion of the Woiwurrung language makes the book stronger. The glossary at the end of the book helps make the book even more powerful and meaningful. *Welcome to Country* (2016), also written by Aunty Joy Murphy and illustrated by Lisa Kennedy, provides the Wurundjeri insights into the traditional Welcome to Country. The illustrations are intricate, the details similar to those in *Wilam*, and are representative of what would be found in Wurundjeri country. This book would pair perfectly with *Hello and Welcome* by Gregg Dreise, which presents/teaches/celebrates the acknowledgement and welcome to country. Because Dreise's book and illustrations present a Queensland focus, both of these books would provide insightful perspectives of the Welcome to Country tradition.

Bronwyn Bancroft, well-known author and illustrator, shows a wonderful appreciation to country in her book, *Coming Home to Country*. Bancroft's distinctive illustration style is apparent throughout the book as the text reflects her deep appreciation for culture and country. The text matches well with the strong illustrations – for example, 'I ease into a palette of leaf green, red rust, yellow ochre, deep blue and crimson and walk with our people'. This title would connect very well to *My Culture and Me* by Gregg Dreise. The style and content are similar to Bancroft's work, but the book also highlights and recognises the importance of culture, country, people and community.

Baby Business by Jasmine Seymour (a Dharug woman belonging to the Burubiranggal people) is a beautiful picture book that shares the Indigenous smoking ceremony tradition of welcoming a baby into the world and country. The book weaves Dharug words into the story and shows the different ways that the smoking ceremony teaches the baby about its place in the community and country.

Open Your Heart to Country, also by Jasmine Seymour, is a powerful book about celebrating country and being open to celebrating it. The book is written in both English and Dharug, and while the text is brief, it is quite powerful and inspirational. 'Open your heart to Country. Let place soothe your lonely feet' and also, 'Your skin might have many names. You might be far from home'. The book is a celebration of both culture and country. This is a wonderful title to incorporate with children to help them learn the importance of country and Indigenous culture.

Somebody's Land (Adam Goodes, Adnyamathanha and Narungga man and community leader) shares a strong connection to country and who the country belongs to. The book looks at the history of Australia before and after the English came to the country. The repeated lines: 'When the white people came, they called the land Terra Nullius. They said it was nobody's land. But it was somebody's land' establishes the history of the land and how the Indigenous people were on the land long before the white people came. The book is part of a series that also includes *Ceremony* and *Back on Country*, both of which integrate Adnyamathanha words into them. *Ceremony* shows readers the process of getting ready for a celebration and invites them to see and enjoy what happens during the celebration. *Back on Country* shares the story of two young children who are on a road trip with their mother to visit their Nana back on country. The children meet family members, learn new native vocabulary as well as traditions. The three books capture the importance of country, culture and family.

Looking After Country with Fire: Aboriginal Burning Knowledge with Uncle Kuu was written by Victor Steffensen (descendant of the Tagalaka people). This title provides information about how Aboriginal people have used fire for centuries for such things as telling time, identifying places and even to help the environment. The book does an outstanding job of sharing the importance of country and how to take care of it.

Story Doctors, written by Boori Monty Pryor (Father, originating from the Juru people from the Bowen Region; his mother is from the Gurubana Moiety group from the Kunggandji Nation) and illustrated by Rita Sinclair, from Marreba North Queensland, is a powerful acknowledgement and recognition of country and culture, and of the importance of respect for both. The main message of the book is that we must all listen and respect the land and country of Australia in order for people to sustain its beautiful elements. This book is an excellent connection with Ross Johnston's idea that 'traditional Indigenous Australians have a profound sense of before-ness that is at once past, present and future' (p. 162).

NATURE-RELATED

Brother Moon by Maree McCarthy Yoelu, a Wadjigany woman from the western Wagait region in the Northern Territory, and illustrated by Samantha Fry, descended from the Dagiman people from Katherine, is a beautifully illustrated story about the moon told by the grandfather to his grandson. The rhythmic text throughout adds a special layer to the story as the grandfather tells all the ways that the moon assists him in his life. This is a wonderful book in the way it connects with nature.

Little Bird's Day by Sally Morgan and illustrated by Johnny Warrkatja Malibirr, a Yolnju man from Ganalbingu, is a day in the life of a bird and the adventures it faces throughout the day. Dealing with the weather and other animals, the bird flies through the day until it is reunited with its family and has a comfortable place to rest for the night. *The River* by Sally Morgan is a celebration of country and nature. The narrator introduces the reader and tells all the things they can see and hear both in and around the river. This is a wonderful title for younger readers to introduce different sights along the river. Following along with Morgan and Warrkatja Malibirr's theme and format is *Thank You Rain!*, again a celebration of nature and what is seen during a rainstorm. The book is intended for younger audiences to share what is found during the rain.

Ninni Yabini by Cheryl Kickett-Tucker (highly respected Wadjuk Noongar Traditional Owner) is a story of a young egret (baby swan) named Yabini. After the family nest was swept away in a storm, the parents had to build a new one. Yabini sees a willy-wagtail and follows it and soon becomes lost. Scared and alone in the dark, Yabini follows a little star in the sky and is happily reunited with her parents. Yabini learned a very important lesson: 'You must never follow a willy-wagtail. He will get you lost and then you will be all alone'.

ABC Dreaming by Warren Brim, descended from the Djabugah people of far north Queensland, is a strong example of a good alphabet book. It presents different items present in the author's rainforest in Queensland. The book has one-to-one correspondence with the object and word on each page, and introduces common and new objects as well – for example, ant, kookaburra, quandong fruit and zamia palm, so the book definitely passes the Zbaracki test for alphabet books.

Backyard Bugs by Helen Milroy, descendant of the Palyku people of the Pilbara region of Western Australia, is a book for very young readers that presents bugs that children would find in their own backyard, such as earthworms, crickets, caterpillars, butterflies, and much more. *Backyard Bugs* is a concept book that teaches about bugs that children might encounter. Milroy has also written *Backyard Birds*, which is the same idea but with birds that children can find in their backyard.

HISTORICAL FICTION

Alfred's War is by Rachel Bin Salleh who is descended from the Nimunburr and Yawuru peoples of the Kimberly region of Western Australia and illustrated by Samantha Fry who is descended from the Dagiman people from Katherine. This book recognises the sacrifice that Indigenous soldiers made during the First World War. It is a story about Alfred who was injured in battle and sent home. He was not honoured like other soldiers or provided with government support and instead wanders the country. This book is a good way to begin the discussion about how there were many soldiers who sacrificed so much and represented Australia during a difficult time.

Strangers on Country, illustrated by Dub Leffler, descendant of the Bigambul people of Southwest Queensland, is a mix between fiction and non-fiction. The book is broken into chapters and tells stories about three shipwreck survivors and escaped convicts who are taken in and cared for by different Indigenous peoples. Another unique feature of this book is that each story is broken into two perspectives, one from the Indigenous people and one from the stranger to the land. At the end of each chapter is factual information that connects with the story.

Free Diving by Lorrae Coffin (Nyiyaparli and Yindijibarnadi people of the Pilbara region in Western Australia), and illustrated by Bronwyn Houston (Wunna Nyiyaparli people of the Pilbara) is another historical fiction picture book. It tells the story of those who used to free dive (deep diving without scuba-diving equipment) for pearls and acknowledges the dangers of this occupation. There is a song at the end of the book that connects directly with the story.

Boomerang and Bat by Mark Greenwood tells the story of the first eleven, a group of Indigenous men who learned the sport of cricket, and then were taught even more by a coach from England who took them to England. While in England, they dazzled the spectators and opponents with their fine cricket skills. The book is a solid example of historical fiction based on a real-life experience.

POLITICS/SORRY RELATED

Well-known Indigenous singer/songwriter Archie Roach, along with his wife, Ruby Hunter, (Ngarrindjeri woman), created an engaging and powerful picture book version of his song, 'Took the children away'. The illustrations in the book are done by Ruby, and there are real-life photographs of both the author, illustrator and their family throughout. The book would be a strong introduction to the Stolen Generations, as well as to the music of Archie Roach.

Day Break by Amy McQuire (Darumbal and South Sea Islander woman from Rockhampton, Central Queensland) connects Australia Day with the Indigenous perspective. The book is able to provide different perspectives while continuing to highlight the importance of country. The book would assist in introducing Indigenous culture as well as political discussion about Australia Day and how it may have different meanings to different people in Australia.

Sorry Day by Coral Vass and illustrated by Dub Leffler shares the story of Maggie and her mother as they go to hear Prime Minister Kevin Rudd issue an apology about the Stolen Generations. When Maggie loses her mother in the large crowd, there are echoes of children being taken from their families, but the memories of those around her help with the reunion. This title would be a good way to introduce a number of topics and themes to primary school children.

BOOKS FOR OLDER READERS

Ubby's Underdogs by Brenton E. McKenna (Yawuru people of the Kimberley Region of Western Australia) is a graphic novel series that tells the story of Ubby and her mates. The series takes place in Broome in the 1940s, and Ubby and her underdogs experience a number of adventures. The books weave in myths and legends as well as Australian history from the 1940s in Western Australia.

Azaria is a picture book for older readers that presents the story of the disappearance of Azaria Chamberlain and the national media attention, trial and conviction of her mother. It is a powerful book highlighting the perspective of Azaria's mother. Given the serious topic and a major injustice, it would be better used with upper primary and lower secondary pupils.

The First Scientists by Correy Tutt (a proud Kamilaroi man) is an outstanding non-fiction book all about the cool inventions and innovations from Australia's First Peoples. The book is divided into sections sharing how the Indigenous people understood astronomy, engineering, chemistry, tracking, and much more. The book is a wonderful way to celebrate the inventions and innovations that have been around for centuries.

Bindi (2020) is a free verse novel by Kirli Saunders, a proud Gunai Woman. The book tells the story of 11-year-old Bindi from Gundungurra Country, and the adventures she and her friends face with school, assignments, a drought and a bushfire. Readers will be drawn into the free verse format, as well as connect with the main character and the challenges she faces.

Black Cockatoo by Carl Merrison and Hakea Hustler is a short novel for independent readers. The book tells the story of a girl named Mia who rescues a Black Cockatoo from her brother who has injured it. As she tries to nurse the bird back to health, she learns more about her family and in turn herself. Through the process, she discovers her own inner strength to deal with the challenges and world around her.

CONCLUSION

Australian children's literature presents exciting stories across many genres that is specific to Australia with its content, language, food, geography and cultures. There are many wonderful and exciting titles to explore, and in recent years there has been a strong increase in the publication of books written and illustrated by Indigenous peoples. These books can be used with students from across many ages and across a number of genres as well. Incorporating these titles, authors and illustrators into classrooms is an excellent way to introduce children into country, places, communities, peoples and languages across the great country of Australia.

ADDITIONAL TITLES

The Great Lizard Trek – Felicity Bradshaw

Nintirringanyi Ngurra Ku – Annette Robinson Roxanne Sharpe

We all Sleep – Ezekiel Kwaymullina (Sally Morgan)

Tom Tom – Rosemary Sullivan

Shake a Leg – Boori Monty Pryor and Jan Ormerod

WANT TO KNOW MORE?

Bradford, C. (2007) *Unsettling Narratives: Postcolonial Readings of Children's Literature*. Waterloo, Canada: Wilfrid Laurier University Press.

O'Neill, A. (2011) 'Aboriginal Australian and Canadian First Nations Children's Literature'. *CLC Web: Comparative Literature and Culture*, *13*(2). Available at: https://doi.org/10.7771/1481-4374.1742

Sheahan-Bright, R. (2011) 'Red, yellow, and black: Australian Indigenous publishing for young people'. *Bookbird*, *49*(3): 1–17. Available at: https://doi.org/10.1353/bkb.2011.0045

Xu, D. (2016) 'The gift and the ethics of representing Aboriginality in Australian children's literature'. *Australian Aboriginal Studies*, 2: 33–45. Available at: https://doi.org/10.3316/ielapa.520678193064738

REFERENCES

Freeman, E.B. and Lehman, B.A. (2001) *Global Perspectives in Children's Literature*. New York: Allyn & Bacon.

Johnston, R. (2017) *Australian Literature for Young People*. Oxford: Oxford University Press.

Neale, M. and Kelly, L. (2020) *Songlines*. Melbourne: Thames & Hudson Australia.

DIGITAL TEXTS

> **WHAT WE WILL LEARN**
> - What a digital text is.
> - All about ebooks.
> - The characteristics of good ebooks/digital texts.

There has been a lot of development in the field of digital texts, especially in the past ten years. These developments can be seen beyond the past decade, but it is in this time that there has been a major shift or focus in the use of digital texts. Courage (2019) supports this: 'it is important to note that ebook technology has evolved dramatically over the past decade'. This has been especially true in libraries around the world, and even more so since the global pandemic influenced remote learning and access to literature. Some may argue that there is a battle between the two formats of traditional print-based books and the newer digital texts and that eventually digital texts will replace the traditional print-based original. It is important to be aware that it may be best to forget this unneeded divide. Courage (2019) contends

> that print-based resources and e-books are not mutually exclusive, nor is technology a substitute for print. Rather, traditional print books and e-books seem to play different roles in the literacy process, and eliminating this false dichotomy offers children more opportunity for diverse types of literacy experiences.

Even with all these changes, it is important to explore and understand what digital texts are and how they can be used, interpreted and understood. It is important to begin with the definition of what digital texts are.

EBOOKS

First, when one looks at the definition of books, it is important to acknowledge how the definition of books, and text in general, has been changing rapidly for years, and there are many who suggest that the definition of a book or even text, should be expanded (Cope, 2001; Opitz et al., 2006). Diving deeper into this idea is when one introduces digital texts into the discussion. When this happens, the definition gets even more murky. As Sargeant (2015) notes: 'the lack of clarity surrounding the term ebook has not assisted in establishing a comprehensive understanding of the ways that digitisation has altered the picture book' (p. 461). Courage (2019) supports how difficult the definition can be, writing, 'although these formats may have some differences, the research literature has investigated all of these formats under the broad umbrella of "e-books" as technology has developed over the years'. With this in mind, it is important to try to define what a digital text is and break down the different components. For example, one of the most classic terms for an ebook is the contraction of the phrase 'electronic book', which is exactly what an ebook is – 'an electronic representation of a book' (Garrish, 2011). ebooks therefore can simply be a digital replica of a printed book, but they can also include imagery, low levels of interactivity or more complex hypermedia links as well. Another type of digital text is a 'book app', which, according to Sargeant (2015), is more of a 'sales category and is used to describe a type of digital book'. Book apps, however, are more of 'a fusion of written text, visuals, audio and interaction design' (Sargeant, 2015: 461). This fusion leads to a plethora of formats that can include a number of interactive features presented later in this chapter. Courage (2019) agrees that there can be confusion between the definitions, writing, 'the distinction between "e-books" and "apps" is not always obvious and likely rests more on the intended outcome or goal that on any difference in format or structure'. Courage also reminds us 'that not all e-books have multimedia features, such as animation, narration, or interactive, touch-screen components'.

So, with some basic definitions in place, one can start to look more closely at what this all means, and more specifically what digital texts look like. Currently, ebooks, as found in most libraries, are the basic digital replica of a printed book, but may also have an option of having the book read to the reader. One of the main benefits of this format is ease in access. One is no longer limited to owning a Kindle or eReader in order to access and read these books. Most libraries use a different platform that allows easier access to the book – for example, Libby and Borrowbox. These can be accessed via a tablet, phone or eReader, but regardless, public libraries are striving to make access simpler. Overall, Sargeant (2015) writes that enhancement can be a good word to describe digital books, noting, 'the term now appears to characterise a broad variety of detail relating to the digital book' (p. 461). Whatever format these digital texts come in, it is important to explore them in more detail, with specific titles as examples.

BOOK APPS

As one delves deeper into digital texts, the 'book app' is the next major category that will engage readers, especially older ones in upper primary school and above. One of the major issues to be aware of with book apps is that their longevity can be limited. For example, when one looks at an article found in *The Guardian* from 2015 exploring the top ten book apps, half of them no longer exist. However, exploring some of these is definitely worth the investment in both time and even money. *Device 6* is an interactive story that blurs the lines of genre, text and format. The story is about a girl named Anna who wakes up in a castle on a distant island and has no idea where she is or how she got there. The book is told through the story, puzzles and images. The blend of format will engage readers/viewers as they work to help Anna and solve the mystery. *Blackbar* is also an interactive ebook that includes puzzles and allows readers to capitalise on the use of censorship to tell the story and engages the reader/viewer into solving the mystery. There are some similarities between this title and *Device 6* in the concept of the story and interaction of the reader. An interactive ebook/game is *80 Days*, which puts a new spin on the classic book *Around the World in 80 Days*. In this 'book', readers race around the world using whatever mode of transport they can. Readers will need to be aware of health, finances and, most importantly, time, as they work their way around the globe. This adventure story would be a good one to use to introduce readers to the classic novel it is based upon as well. *A Wise Use of Time* is a 260,000-word interactive science fiction novel. The story allows readers to freeze time in order to do things such as ransack casinos, rescue celebrities or even escape death. However, every moment of time that readers freeze causes more stress to their bodies. Readers are able to actively engage in the adventure and get to decide if they help the city or join the mobsters and become even more corrupt. Moving-tales.com are ebooks that will engage readers in the various traditional stories. For example, *The Pedlar Lady of Gushing Cross* is available for $3.99 (AUD) which is based on a a thirteenth- century Persian poem. The book features music, read-aloud options and a built-in dictionary support. Moving Tales also has an ebook trilogy for $7.99 (AUD) which includes *The Pedlar Lady of Gushing Cross, The Unwanted Guest* and *This Too Shall Pass*. The same features found in the stand-alone book are also available in the trilogy.

Meet Millie is an interactive picture book for younger readers. The story is read to the reader and the text is highlighted as it is read. Young readers will enjoy the use of an actual dog within the 'illustrations', and there are interactive electronic lift the flaps or pull tabs. The story of the author's dog will have readers of all ages enjoying the hijinks of Millie and what she is up to.

Weirdwood Manor is a series of six books that tell the story of three young children with special abilities that they are learning to harness and develop. Oliver, Celia and Eugene all come together to Weirdwood Manor to meet their hero, eccentric writer and inventor Arthur Weirdwood. Adventure and mystery abounds throughout the books as the main characters are thrown into different worlds and the books are reminiscent of Harry Potter and the Golden

Compass. The books have interactive features that provide readers with the opportunity to engage with the story through solving puzzles, as well as the mystery.

A less intense book app than discussed earlier would be Rockford's Rock Opera. For those who are fans of music, this story is one that integrates music (in a musical-type format) as it tells the story of Moog, a boy from London, and his dog Rockford as they go on a fantasy-based adventure to share the secrets from the Island of Infinity. The stories are available with a read-along which allows younger readers to follow the text that is highlighted as it is read.

The Fantastic Flying Books of Mr. Morris Lessmore was the book that started it all for interactive books, and especially with augmented reality in children's books. The app for this book by William Joyce used augmented reality and a phone's camera to make the pages of the actual physical book come off the page. While the app is no longer available, the concept started a tidal wave of creativity within the ebook format. Another title by Joyce was *The Numberlys*. Again, the app for the book is no longer available; however, it is important to note that these books were the hallmark for the use of augmented reality in children's picture books.

Wild Symphony, a picture book by well-known author Dan Brown (*The Da Vinci Code*), is a musical interaction where readers download an app that uses augmented reality to hear the actual symphonic music that accompanies each page, as well as animals, in the book. For example, the page with kangaroos includes bouncing music and there is music for the cats on their page, all composed by the author.

AUGMENTED REALITY (AR) BOOKS/FEATURES

The Ghostkeeper's Journal and Field Guide is a novel that has an app called Ghost-o-Matic that makes the book come alive. The Society for the Pursuit of the Reputedly Undead, Namely Ghosts! is an organisation that captures ghosts, but its key new ghost catcher, Ag, is missing, and all that remains is his field guide (the book itself). The book and the app work together to bring the ghosts to life, and readers will use the field guide and app to help solve the mystery and find Ag.

Wonderscope is another augmented reality app that makes stories come alive. For example, the story *Little Red: The Inventor* will have children interacting with the characters within the stories and working with them as part of the story. The only issue is that the reader/viewer has to read words out loud, so children will need to know the words and the vocabulary in order to engage with the app.

INTERNET TEXTS

Inanimate Alice (www.inanimatealice.com) is a well-established book which is available on the internet. This is a story about a young girl who travels around the world with her family, but her father has gone missing. The text uses a variety of formats with story, text, music and images all playing an active role in the storytelling. While in the past access to the story was free, there is now a $10.00 fee for access. Dust Echoes (www.abc.net.au/education/collections/dust-echoes/) consists of twelve chapters or stories and is presented by the ABC (Australian Broadcasting Company). The stories contain Dreaming stories from Central Arnhem Land. They are animated stories that combine moving images and music in order to tell the tales. There are guiding questions and teacher guides connected to each one. Flightpaths.net is another internet text in a similar format to inanimatealice that tells the story of Yacub who is on his way to Dubai to find a job and earn more money. Yacub's story collides (literally) with a mother in England who is on her way to get groceries. Their meeting combines the characters and the stories and will leave readers/viewers with more questions than answers, but is also a very intriguing plot and ending to engage readers to create the future chapters on their own.

Storybox is one more collection of books that is well worth knowing and subscribing to. The individual fee is $5.99 (AUD) a month. The subscription price varies accordingly with schools, libraries, universities, families, and more. The books are animated in places, yet also provide actual pages from the books themselves. The books are read by well-known Australian celebrities, and some titles are even read by the authors themselves.

There are a number of great 'free' book apps – for example, 'Skybrary', 'Epic!' and 'Vooks', to name just a few. The use of quotations is intentional, as some of these apps do have a cost associated with them. There are many great good points to this type of book app. For example, Matteson (2016) presents teachers with a number of benefits for using ebooks – specifically, their interactive read-aloud features, the enhancement of non-fiction texts, ease when everyone needs a copy of a book, and the ability to engage reluctant readers. The resources listed here will provide you with good options that meet many of these benefits. Skybrary is a BookApp connected with RIF (Reading is Fundamental), an organisation in the United States that promotes reading. The app provides children with a curated library containing hundreds of stories to interest, engage and connect with children. There is a free trial period and then there is a $4.99 (USD) monthly fee. 'Epic!' is another free book app that has over 40,000 books to read. There are many well-known titles for children to read (*Where the Wild Things Are, Goodnight Moon, The Invention of Hugo Cabret, Watercress*, to name a few). There is a free membership which allows access to one book a day. Educators can get a free subscription and parents can pay for access to more daily titles by paying $6.67 (USD) a month. 'Vooks' is another book app that helps children connect with a variety of different books (some titles include *I am (Not) Scared!, Curious George*). The books are animated and read aloud, with the text being highlighted as the word is read. For families, there is a seven-day free trial, then it is either $4.99 a month or $49.99 for the year. The best news, though, is that for teachers, it is *free*! This allows teachers to access the large electronic library for free on one device.

Table 11.1 Evaluation criteria: digital texts

Features

Do the special features help the reader/viewer engage with the characters better?

Do the visual/audio elements add/enhance the text?

Do the effects add to the features of the story?

Do the functions enhance the experience?

Is there an easy set up/navigation of the 'tools'?

Audio effects

Is the speed of the read-aloud appropriate for the age level?

Is the expression used appropriate?

Are the sounds clear and distinct?

If there is 'tracking' of the words, does it follow easily?

Visual effects

Do the images match the theme of the text?

Are the images overwhelming to the reader/viewer?

Overall

Is the text enjoyable to 'read'?

Do children enjoy it?

BUST A MYTH

Digital texts can do a lot of things that hardcopy books cannot, so they are better.

Digital texts do offer a number of features that traditional books do not. However, reader beware! Bells and whistles are not the only feature that make a quality book. While they can engage readers in multiple ways, they can also distract. It is critical that we remember that the purpose of a book is to tell a good story. A strong balance is important when exploring the format of books.

Walsh (2013) asks: 'Do we need new ways of evaluating these texts?' Because there are so many complexities found within the texts, the answer is a resounding 'yes'! The evaluation of digital texts can be divided into different sections. The first is related to the special features (multimedia, audio/animation/touch screen elements) in the digital text. The key evaluation here is whether or not the special features enhance the text as well as the reading experience. This concept can be addressed further with the idea of whether the features help readers connect with the characters as well.

Addressing the enhancement features more specifically, one can start to examine if the audio features are effective and beneficial to the reader/viewer/listener. For example, many digital texts have a 'read to me' feature. With this feature, it is important that the read-aloud uses appropriate expression and a speed that is appropriate to the age level of the text. Some digital texts will highlight the text as it is being read aloud (similar to what you might see in a karaoke experience). If this is the case, then it is important that the highlighting of the text follows the speed of the voice reading the story aloud. At times, the highlighting can be done either too quickly, leaving the reader/listener lagging behind, or too slowly, leaving the listener waiting for the narration. Another aspect of the audio is how the sounds are heard. The sounds (sound effects) should be clear and distinct and not confusing or distract from the story itself. A key category for a digital text is also one that is important in picture books as well, and that is the use of images. The visuals in digital texts should match the theme of the text, but not be overwhelming to the viewer/reader. The images should also avoid being drab or uninspiring to the reader/viewer.

Finally, from an overall perspective, the digital text should be enjoyable and engaging to read, but not distracting or dull. This idea of avoiding distraction from the features is one that Hirsh-Pasek et al. (2015) recommended when stating how digital texts 'must be engaging and this is accomplished through keeping children's minds "on task" and not distracted'. Sargeant (2015) also warns that designers of digital texts 'can also distract users by including inter textuality and animation that is tangential to the narrative or central theme' (p. 464). Perhaps Courage (2019) sums it up best, stating, 'well designed digital picture storybooks integrate illustration and narration so that each complements the other and, together, they provide an enhanced multimedia text experience that may help story comprehension'. So, while it is crucial to ensure that the digital texts are engaging and beyond a simple 'enhancement' of the print-based format, ultimately, like any text, the digital text should provide enjoyment to the children reading them.

CONCLUSION

It is important to be open to new forms of text and the definition of text, and even books in general. One of the key benefits of digital texts is the ease of access, also the ways in which they encourage interaction with the reader. While this chapter presented a number of benefits that these types of books present, it is also important that teachers are aware of how the interactive/enhancement features found in these types of literature may distract readers, their engagement and the comprehension of books. Courage (2019) notes: 'it is clear that good, well designed content presented on interactive digital media devices can enhance reading, language, science and social skills, and teach factual information about the world for all school aged children'. Through this chapter, we learned how to evaluate these types of books and some quality titles, websites and book apps to explore. Finally, it is important to remember, that there is not a competition between digital and traditional print-based text. Each has their strengths, and children of all ages need positive experiences with both types of texts to grow and develop as readers.

WANT TO KNOW MORE?

Green, M. (2019) 'An investigation of augmented reality picture books: meaningful experiences or missed opportunities?' *Journal of Educational Multimedia and Hypermedia, 28*(4), October.

Augmented reality in picture books was a big area a few years ago. This article explores the experiences provided and what works and what might be missing.

Kim, J.E. and Hassinger-Das, B. (eds) (2019) *Reading in the Digital Age: Young Children's Experiences with E-books: International Studies with E-books in Diverse Contexts*. Literacy Studies (LITS, 18). New York: Springer.

This book is an edited volume addressing many issues associated with digital texts. There are many practical suggestions in different chapters.

Mygind, S. (2022) *AR Books for Children*. Available at: https://thewritingplatform.com/2022/05/ar-books-for-children/

This is an online article that includes features of AR books, as well as a number of different AR books that were created a few years ago.

REFERENCES

Blumberg, F.C. and Brooks, P.J. (eds) (2017) *Cognitive Development in Digital Contexts*. New York, London: Academic Press.

Cope, B. (2001) 'New ways with words: print and etext convergence'. In B. Cope and D. Kalantzis (eds) *Print and Electronic Text Convergence* (pp. 1–15). C–2–C Series. Altona: Common Ground Publishing.

Courage, M. (2019) 'From print to digital: the medium is only part of the message'. In J.E. Kim and B. Hassinger-Das (eds) *Reading in the Digital Age: Young Children's Experiences with E-books*. New York: Springer.

Garrish, M. (2011) *What is EPUB3?* Sebastopol, CA: O'Reilly Media.

Guardian, The (2015) 'Interactive book apps – ten of the best'. Available at: www.theguardian.com/technology/2015/sep/14/ten-best-interactive-book-apps-ios-android

Hasinger-Das, B., Dore, R. and Zosh, J. (2019) 'The four pillars of learning: e-books past, present, and future'. In J.E. Kim and B. Hassinger-Das (eds) *Reading in the Digital Age: Young Children's Experiences with E-books*. New York: Springer.

Hirsh-Pasek, K., Zosh, J.M., Golinkoff, R.M., Gray, J.H., Robb, M.B. and Kaufman, J. (2015) 'Putting education in educational apps: lessons from the science of learning'. *Psychological Science, 16*: 3–34.

Matteson, A. (2016) 'When an ebook is the best book'. *School Library Journal*. Available at: www.slj.com/story/when-an-ebook-is-the-best-book

Opitz, M., Ford, M. and Zbaracki, M. (2006) *Books and Beyond*. London: Heinemann.

Sargeant, B. (2015) 'What is an ebook? What is a book app? And why should we care? An analysis of contemporary digital picture books'. *Children's Literature in Education, 46*(4): 454–66. Available at: https://doi.org/10.1007/s10583-015-9243-5

Walsh, M. (2013) 'Literature in a digital environment'. In L. McDonald, *A Literature Companion for Teachers*. Newtown, NSW: Primary English Teaching Association Australia (PETAA).

12

HUMOUR

> **WHAT WE WILL LEARN**
> - How humour engages readers.
> - Different elements of humour found in children's books.
> - Elements of humorous books that not every reader may see.
> - The benefits of humorous literature and its inclusion in the classroom.

What is the number one motivator for engaging young readers? Humour! 'Humour is probably one of the most popular genres among children who are learning to read' (Zbaracki, 2015). This chapter is designed to educate teachers and future teachers about why humorous literature is so important to include in the classroom, and how it can impact and engage children to become readers (and hopefully life-long readers). Daley (2019) writes: 'Humour engages children (particularly reluctant readers) as they are naturally playful and generally laugh far more than adults. Humorous literature harnesses the exuberance and wonder of young with words and ideas' (p. 113). Landsberg (1992) continues this idea: 'Laughter is the reward that lures the most reluctant reader.' Take a moment to think about this idea of how laughter can lure readers. Have you ever noticed a small group of students gathered in the back of the classroom that are all gathered around a book and laughing? What was your first response? 'Hey, what are you doing?' Perhaps you then thought to yourself, 'I wonder what's so funny?' If you have answered 'yes' to those questions, then you are seeing the importance of including and celebrating humorous literature. In fact, 'Encouraging this genre of reading and allowing these shared moments help spread the intrinsic motivation to read' (Opitz et al., 2006: 97). However, intrinsic motivation is just one benefit of humorous literature. There is also a very strong social factor to humour, which is found with the desire to share the humorous

books with peers. The well-loved and popular Australian children's author Andy Griffiths (2014) noted: 'Young people interact with their peers and foster friendships through humorous literature as they enjoy sharing the laughs with their peers.' Because there is both personal and social implications for humour, it is critical that humour is given the respect it deserves and engages as many readers as possible. Griffiths continues this discussion and notes how he began writing and sharing his own stories with his students. 'I started writing down silly little stories, provocative stories, about bums growing arms and legs and running away. And they laughed . . . "This is cool, sir! Can I write a story like that?" I said, Yeah! And I'll photocopy them and we'll put them in a book in the library and look, you've just become authors' (www.abc.net.au).

There is much that can be gained from the use of humorous children's literature in the classroom. Authors have long recognised that humour has great power to hook their young readers. Many children's literature authors from around the world have acknowledged this. Former Children's Literature Laureate Jon Scieszka from the United States acknowledges, 'The main role of humor in my stories is to motivate readers (who might not otherwise be too keen on reading) to want to read' (Zbaracki, 2003). Reflecting on his own writing and the impact for the readers, children's author Gordon Korman stated: 'What's in it for the reader? And my answer is always that the payoff is the next laugh' (Zbaracki, 2003). Andy Griffiths discussed this and pointed out how this works in his own writing: 'I've always loved making people laugh, particularly children. I love telling them something that's completely preposterous as if it actually happened to me. You're playing a game of make believe . . . If it has also the effect of turning them on to books and improving their literacy, these are wonderful, almost secondary benefits of that activity' (ABC News, 2019).

It is clear that authors understand the importance and benefit of humour and have specific reasons and motivations for writing within this genre. With so many benefits to using humorous literature, it is possible to reverse Michael Cart's (1995) belief that 'Humor is the Rodney Dangerfield of literary forms: It gets no respect!'. It is time to celebrate and share the laughter of children and also show them that laughing is just another aspect that makes reading enjoyable and could even be (gasp!) easier than they thought.

There are many benefits to using humorous texts in the classroom. Probably the number one factor, as mentioned earlier in this chapter, is motivation, both intrinsic and social (Zbaracki, 2003). One of the best places to find humour is in picture books, which have been the main focus throughout this book. What makes them such a wonderful resource is the interplay between text and illustrations. Most times, the reader is able to be in on the joke that the main character does not 'see'. A wonderful example of this is in *Duck and Penguin Are NOT Friends* by Julia Woolf.

Throughout the story, Betty and Maud are presented as best friends with their own stuffed toy (Duck and Penguin). The girls think their toys will be best friends as well, but the illustrations show a different perspective. Again, the reader is in on this information while the main characters, Betty and Maud, are not. Another title that showcases this idea is *Nine Lives Newton* by Alice McKinley. This UK title will have readers laughing, as a dog named Newton thinks he has nine lives because of a sign he read. Unfortunately, he did not see the whole sign, so he is constantly being saved by his feline friend. Readers are in on the joke as they see what each sign actually says and Newton continuously puts himself into danger.

Another example of this is in Chris Haughton's book *Maybe*. In this story, three monkeys are told explicitly by their mother not to go to the mangoes because the tigers are near. Of course, the monkeys are cheeky and curious, so they go explore where the mangoes are. While they do not see the tigers hidden in the bushes, the reader does. Again, this shows the interplay between text, images and the humour that the reader understands, but the main character does not. Another of Haughton's books is *Shhh! We Have a Plan* could also be paired with this title as the illustrations again allow the reader to see what the main characters do not.

Figure 12.1 Forms of humour in humorous literature

Through much research and reading of children's literature, the author of this textbook was able to create five categories of humour that greatly appeal to young readers (and in reality readers of all ages). The categories are: 1. Humorous characters. 2. Poking fun at authority. 3. Physical humour. 4. Incongruity. 5. Humorous discourse or language play. Each of these five will be discussed in more depth, with specific connections to children's literature.

HUMOROUS CHARACTERS

In her book *Laugh Lines: Exploring Humour in Children's Literature*, Mallan (1993) notes the humorous character as a key aspect of humorous children's literature. Many characters from literature fit this category well. Memorable characters include Pig the Pug, the cranky bear, Amelia Bedelia, Pippi Longstocking, Lilly, Tacky, Billie B. Brown, and many more. These characters are memorable because of the many different situations they experience. For example, Pig is a pug (dog) that is greedy and selfish, learning the hard way that sharing might be a safer option than living his self-centred lifestyle. Tacky the penguin tricks penguin hunters and saves his fellow penguins through humorous incidents. Amelia Bedelia takes everything literally, and Billie B. Brown learns to grow up by making a few mistakes here and there, reminding us all of how challenging and funny growing up can be. There are many different reasons that children are able to relate well to humorous characters such as these. One reason is that, as Monson (1978) notes, 'It concerns the laughter that comes from a "sudden glory" at discovering we are better or smarter than others . . . character humor is often directed toward a comic character who is so stupid or absent-minded as to be ludicrous' (p. 5).

Mr Chicken All Over Australia is the latest in the series of Mr Chicken books and exemplifies Monson's point about the ludicrous. While Mr Chicken has travelled the world (Rome, London and Paris) and destroyed many famous cities and landmarks, he is very much loved and welcomed in Australia. His adventures take him all over the country, with so many children pleading with him to visit them. True to form, Mr Chicken makes every visit memorable and children will get excited to try to find themselves close to wherever Mr Chicken visits, no matter where they live.

Pig the Pug by Aaron Blabey is a well-known humorous character in Australian children's literature. Pig is able to break the social norms in a funny way that appeals to young children. Both the storyline and the big bright pictures will lure readers in and make them fans of Pig, the cute, but selfish and poorly behaved Pug. *Rodney Loses It!*, an energetic title from Michael Gerard Bauer, introduces a humorous character, as well as a clever play on words in the title. Rodney is a rabbit that loves to draw, but when he loses his special pen, 'Penny', it causes him a lot of angst and stress as he tries to find it. That is where the play on words in the title comes into play. Readers will love closely inspecting the illustrations to find where the pen may be.

Bad Crab by Amelia McInerney is a great example of a humorous character. Crab is very ill tempered and is snapping at everyone with his claws in this wordless picture book. This means that the illustrations alone must 'bear the burden of narration' to revisit what Huck wrote years ago. The illustrations depicting Crab are what hold the humour, as he is not aware of what the other sea creatures are planning, and this is mainly focused on his eyes. This is a wonderful example of what is identified in the evaluation criteria with regard to features of humorous text, and the importance of how the illustrations provide a lot of the humour. This is a fun book that could be paired well with Jon Klassen's trilogy of hat books for a hat trick– *This is Not My Hat*, *I Want My Hat Back* and *We Found a Hat*.

Scott Tulloch's *Keep an Eye on this Kiwi* is another fun title in which the reader knows what is going to happen to the main character, without the kiwi knowing. The build-up is fun and the gross (fart humour) will have readers laughing and wanting to reread the book.

Goodnight Already! by Jory John shares the story of a bear trying to go to sleep who is always interrupted by his neighbour, the duck. Readers will enjoy the interplay between the two main characters and how their personalities come out in the illustrations. Children will relate to the excuse of not being tired, while adults will relate to bear just trying to sleep.

POKING FUN AT AUTHORITY

Numerous researchers have found how authority figures lay victim to humour in children's books (Mallan, 1993; Landsberg, 1992; Nilsen and Nilsen, 1982; Monson, 1978; Bateman, 1967; Wolfenstein, 1954). This attack upon authority can be directed at teachers, parents, even children's peers. Mallan (1993) contends: 'Teachers are the obvious choice for exaggerated portraiture in children's books, for children are experts when it comes to telling tales about this group' (p. 9). Many books have the teacher bearing the brunt of the humour, yet they are simply one of many adults that hold this burden. Nilsen and Nilsen (1982) describe this idea with adolescents: 'The teenager's need to achieve independence tempts writers to portray adults as coming out on the short end of their dealings with teenagers' (p. 62). In much humorous literature, many adults are never able to match wits with a child. Children love the idea of overcoming the authority that holds them in check, similar to the characters they meet through literature. Think how Roald Dahl did this repeatedly in *Matilda* in which Miss Trunchbull and even her parents are poked fun of or overcome in different situations. Pippi Longstocking is another classic example of a character who challenged authority. The power struggle that occurs within these battles is described by Gail Munde (1997): 'Many of the humorous fiction choices by children involved stories that either placed the main character in a position of power or allowed the main character to vent frustration at being powerless' (p. 222).

Mum for Sale by Zanni Louise is a fun book that pokes fun at parents who spend too much time on the phone and do not notice their children. This book brings back the adorable penguin Errol. He continues to ask his mum for something, but she is too busy on the phone to assist. He then decides to try to sell her, and she remains oblivious to this. In the end, he discovers that he needs his mother to open the jar of jelly beans he just traded her for. The humour in this book is found in Errol's idea of selling his mum, the illustrations and the limited text. Many children (and parents) will delight in the process of trying to get an adult's attention when they are on the phone.

Another way that authors poke fun at authority is when the fourth wall is broken down and there is more of an interaction between reader and text. By engaging with the reader, and at times the narrator, the main character in the book is actually poking fun at the 'authority', the reader or narrator who is telling the story. Laura and Philip Bunting's title, *Another Book about Bears*, breaks down the stereotype of bears in books, and within this story the narrator and bear engage with one another. This fun and entertaining title will have children enjoying how bear changes the rules and creates a whole new story. Children will be laughing about yet another book about bears, although this one contains a whole new twist. Deborah Underwood's *The Panda Problem* is another fun and creative book that breaks down the fourth wall and has the reader directly interacting with the text and the author. Panda does not do everything the 'reader' says, and this creates a very entertaining interaction and story that will have readers laughing and enjoying the exploits and ideas from Panda.

PHYSICAL HUMOUR

Physical humour is a category that is found quite frequently in children's literature. Smith (1967) made this point years ago: 'Probably the most common of all sources of children's humor is the physical situation with its obvious elements of contrast and surprise' (p. 207). Bateman (1967) speculates that this idea of physical humour is one that appeals to children because it is easy for them to visualise what is happening in the story (discussed further in Chapter 2). By creating a visual picture of the character or situation, the children can better see the humour and, in turn, better understand the story. Physical humour also includes the visual appearance of a character, and extreme exaggeration is a writing strategy in describing characters.

Everyone surely remembers the childhood game of Duck, duck, goose. There has now been a (word) play on that game in picture books, most recently with the Australian title, *Duck, Duck, Moose* by Lucinda Gifford. With very limited text, children will enjoy watching what happens with Moose in each picture and try to determine the twist at the end. This could be paired with a book with the same title *Duck, Duck, Moose* published in the United States in 2014 written by Sudipta Bardhan-Quallen. In this title, the ducks and Moose are friends, but Moose has a tendency to accidentally ruin all the wonderful ideas that the ducks have.

What about a new and different idea – zombie rabbits in a children's picture book, for example? Impossible, you say! Well, *My Dead Bunny* is able to do exactly that. When a young boy tells about his late bunny, readers learn all about Brad:

My dead bunny's name is Brad,

his odour is extremely bad.

He visits me when I'm in bed,

but Bradley wasn't always dead.

Children will enjoy the rhyming text and silly idea of a zombie bunny, but the illustrations will complement the concept and have children not scared or worried, but enjoying the fun illustrations.

Another fun but rather disgusting idea that children will be laughing and squirming about is when they meet the cockroach that joins a young girl's birthday party in *Your Birthday was the Best!* by Maggie Hutchings. Readers will delight in the adventures and how oblivious the cockroach is to what is actually happening in the illustrations. Children will be hoping to be invited to next year's birthday party to see what the cockroach does next. Readers will enjoy the sequel as well, *Your School is the Best*, which has the cockroach hitching a ride to the child's school, leading to similar results found in the first book.

We have all had neighbours who may have rubbed us the wrong way at times. *Goodnight Already!*, mentioned earlier, introduces readers to two neighbours, Bear and Goose. Bear is trying to sleep yet Goose is constantly trying to come over and keep him company because he himself cannot sleep. What ensues is a funny and enjoyable interaction between neighbours in which Bear finally ends up losing his cool. There is a lot of physical humour throughout the book in the exchanges between the characters.

Let's face it, drawing can be tricky. *I Can Only Draw Worms* by Will Mabbitt helps release that stress and introduces a number of different worms that can all be identified, and if we do not have enough, we can cut one in half! Readers will enjoy the interaction between text and illustration, as well as what the illustrator does to only draw worms. This book could be paired with *I am Not a Worm* by Scott Tulloch. A caterpillar has a debate with a hungry lizard about if he is a worm or not. The back-and-forth discussion will have children laughing, but the ending will surprise them as well.

INCONGRUITY

What do you *not* expect to see in life? This is what incongruity is, and one of the best examples in children's literature is a penguin wearing a Hawaiian shirt. The Tacky the Penguin series by Helen Lester states that 'Tacky is an odd bird, but a nice bird to have around'. This final sentence is so true when describing Tacky, a Hawaiian shirt-wearing penguin that breaks the norms of not just penguins, but of almost any creature. This series has Tacky and his icemates on many adventures that will have readers laughing and wanting to read more about him and his friends. The incongruity of what we expect penguins to be and act like as well as Tacky's zany antics are what make the character, stories and series so enjoyable for readers. Continuing this idea of penguins and incongruity is Sean Avery's *Frank's Red Hat*. Frank is a creative penguin who makes a red hat. His fellow penguins are not as fond of the hat as he is, especially when something surprising happens. However, the seals all love Frank's creation and it leads to Frank creating another clothing item. The fun incongruity of what happens in the icy land will again have children chuckling. Ideas like these are what incongruity is all about, and it is rife in children's literature. American children's literature author (and former vaudeville magician) Sid Fleischman discovered this many years ago and reflected on this: 'I depend a great deal on surprise for my humor. The unexpected can make us laugh' (Zbaracki, 2003).

A recent title that accomplishes this to great effect is Philip Bunting's *Not Cute*. Not only would we not expect a quokka to dress up as a different animal so he does not look 'cute', we would not expect him to take on a crocodile and survive! The ending of the book and quokka's interaction with a snake will leave the reader completely surprised.

A chicken who likes to travel the world, but looks like an uncooked roast chicken? Leigh Hobbs's Mr Chicken series, discussed earlier, also highlights the idea of incongruity as the chicken visits different places around the world in the books and never knows the mayhem and confusion he causes wherever he goes.

Laurie Keller is known for her humorous books that combine text and illustrations in a very funny manner. Her creative character, Arnie the Doughnut, is just one of the fun books that entertains younger readers, and her newer title, *Potato Pants*, continues that pattern. A potato's journey to find a new pair of pants presents many humorous twists and turns, and will have readers laughing with the story, word play and the illustrations.

HUMOROUS DISCOURSE/LANGUAGE

Language play is a category of humour that has been identified by both researchers and critics (Mallan, 1993; Landsberg, 1992; Shaeffer and Hopkins, 1988; Whitmer, 1986; Nilsen and Nilsen, 1982; Smith, 1967). Whether it is young children just learning the language or a child in the adolescent years, word play appeals to them all. McGhee (1979) found this in young children as they began to learn new words and master language. Landsberg (1992) describes how this fits with children's literature and the young child: 'Linguistic invention is another form of humor that wears equally well. Indeed, the earliest forms of humor in children's literature are nursery rhymes, with their absurd juxtapositions and delight in patterns of rhythm, sound, and rhyme' (p. 37). Early on in their development, children are drawn to the words. Children listen to words until they become cognitively ready to play with them. One aspect of children's early play with words is to create nonsense words that rhyme with known words (McGhee, 1979). One of the most common ways that humour and language are combined in picture books is through puns, or language play. For example, *7 Ate 9* by Tara Lazar, mentioned below, is chock full of puns and word play throughout the book. The title alone highlights the word play. However, the opening pages of the text showcase this as well:

As a Private I, I'm used to his type—numbers.

They're always stuck in a problem.

But I knew about this 7 fella. He was odd.

Told through the voice of a Private I (pun intended), the detective must solve a mystery involving a number of different numerals (pun intended again). Children will enjoy the play on words, as well as how the detective solves the mystery. The word play here with numbers and language is quite funny and will engage readers. The sequel to this book, *The Upper Case: Trouble in Capital City* continues the fun with word play but changes from numbers to letters. *Bad Apple* by Huw Lewis and Ben Sanders is a fun rhyming text about a bad apple. The text goes through a number of different fruits and objects that Bad Apple meets and the not so pleasant outcomes of the meetings. The language play is fun, especially when he meets orange, that was never going to work out, since there are no words that rhyme with orange.

Heath McKenzie, has a fun way of playing with language and baboons with the title *Butt Out!* There are numerous examples of word play; the personal favourite of this author is, 'sun's out, bums out!'. Children will giggle at the constant reference to bottoms, but may also be interested to know that baboons really do have bare bottoms.

Humorous language is not limited to puns and word play. Readers can also learn from fun and silly language or words. For example, *You're Called What?*, a title by Kes Gray, is a fun way to see a humorous book provide a plethora of facts as well. A number of real-life animals with crazy names request their names be changed at the Minister of Silly Animal Names, and who could blame them? With names such as Pink Fairy Armadillo, Shovelnose Guitarfish and even Bone Eating Snot Flower Worm, wouldn't you want your name changed as well? Children will delight in the silly names and the fun illustrations, but will also be amazed to learn actual facts about these real-life animals.

Some humorous titles have direct interaction between text and reader that do not necessarily fit the five categories discussed earlier. In these titles, the book directly asks the reader to do something. For example, in Hervé Tullet's *Press Here*, the text directs young readers to press the coloured dots on the page to create the change in the book. It also has the reader shake and tilt the book and the pages respond accordingly. This direct interaction is unique and creates a fun experience for the reader. B.J. Novak's *The Book with No Pictures* has the direct interaction between the reader and the audience. In a read-aloud experience, the book would be making the reader say embarrassing things to the listener ('I am a robot monkey' or 'my only friend in the whole wide world is a hippo named Boo Boo Butt'). The book will have children who are listening to the book read aloud howling with laughter at what has to be read. The title is accurate – there are no illustrations in the book. John Kane's book *I Say Boo, You Say Hoo* carries this idea further in which the text and the reader have a call and response that includes fun word play as well. For example, the text tells the listener (reader) that when they say 'boo', you say 'hoo'. The interactions with what is being said in response to what the listener hears or sees creates hilarious experiences that will have young children actively engaged and laughing at what happens.

EVALUATION CRITERIA

Table 12.1 Evaluation criteria: humorous books

The text and illustrations work together to create the humour.

The illustrations present humour addressed at the reader to be 'in on the joke'.

The main character is a key element of the humour.

Language play (puns, tongue twisters, etc.) helps make the book funny.

There are elements of gross humour, but it is not over the top (farts, underwear, bottoms, etc.).

The humour builds with each page culminating in a hysterical conclusion.

The illustration provides humour that is not obvious or addressed in the text.

Physical humour is addressed through the illustrations

The book makes you laugh *a lot*!

When evaluating humorous books, it is important to address a number of different criteria. As found in all picture books, and discussed in the picture book chapter, it is crucial that the text and illustrations work together to tell the story, and, in the case of this genre, the humour is generated through both medium (text and visual). This was discussed earlier in the chapter with the focus of how the illustrations help the reader see aspects that the main character may not see or understand. Sometimes, though, the illustrations are the exact opposite of what the text states. For example, in Jon Klassen's first book in the hat series, *This is Not My Hat*, a little fish is narrating the story and saying what is happening and about how the big fish will be feeling, but the illustrations show the exact opposite of that. This adds to the humour found in the story and illustrations. Another aspect also addressed earlier is that the main character is a focus of the humour. This does not mean that they need to be the only focus, but the main character would enhance the humour. This can be found in a number of ways, as shown through this chapter, and most likely will lead to being a memorable character such as the very cranky bear, or Pig the pug, or even Tacky the penguin.

Language is another key element found in good humorous titles. For example, one of the titles mentioned earlier, *7 Ate 9*, presented in the word play/language play section earlier, is a perfect example of this. The pun and language play is apparent in the title alone. Sometimes gross humour plays a role in good humorous books as well. For example, *Butt Out!*, shared earlier has 'bum humour' in it, but it is not over the top. Sometimes the inclusion of words such as bum, fart, underwear and poo are solely used to try to interest young readers because it includes taboo words or ideas and draws readers in, not because the story is good, but because the taboo idea will appeal to young readers. It is important to pay close attention to these books and identify what their purpose is. For example, Dav Pilkey's classic book *Dog Breath* shares the story of a dog with horrendous breath. Clever word play is included throughout the book, creating a humorous idea and outcome as well. The book could be compared with *Walter the Farting Dog* by William Kotzwinkle and Glenn Murray. The idea is the same about a dog, but in this case Walter's farting is what causes the issues, and there is no word play throughout the story. Understanding the gross humour as well as how and why it is included is important for humorous literature.

However, probably the most important criteria for a humorous book is that it makes the reader laugh a lot. As has been discussed and presented throughout this chapter, when a book is funny, it makes us want to share it with others, and read it again and again. That is one of the key benefits of humorous books. We enjoy it and are motivated to read. Whether it is the illustrations, language play or the characters in a book, all of these have the power not to only make us laugh, but to read and reread books as well as share them with our students, friends and colleagues, and that is what reading is all about.

CONCLUSION

Humorous children's literature has a lot of power to engage and motivate readers. The key elements of physical humour, poking fun of authority, humorous characters, incongruity and word play are all key elements of humour found in books across the globe. Using humorous books in the classroom is a way to motivate the most reluctant readers to read. Children are not the only ones who enjoy humour and laughing as they read. Humorous literature also encourages social interaction when children are wanting to share what they find funny. It is important to embrace the humour and perhaps in the end, you yourself will be laughing with your students. Perhaps a grade four student in my research study about humorous children's literature summed it up best, 'Funniness runs in the human race. I mean books are written to make people laugh or for people to understand history and if half of the books written are to make people laugh, we don't live forever so we can't read all the books so we just want to read the ones that are really funny' (Zbaracki, 2003).

FOR OLDER READERS

Laugh Your Head Off 4 Ever (and the first book is called *Laugh Your Head Off*) – various authors

The Treehouse Books – Andy Griffiths and Terry Denton

OTHER TITLES TO KNOW

The Runaway Pea – Kjartan Poskitt

The Bad Bunnies' Magic Show – Mini Grey

The Lost Dad's Home – Eric Veille *Encyclopedia of Grannies* – Eric Veille

Mr Bunny's Chocolate Factory – Elys Dolan

Eat Your People – Kes Gray

The Couch Potato – Jory John (other books in the series *The Bad Seed, The Good Egg, The Cool Bean*)

Pea + Nut! – Matt Stanton

Errol! – Zanni Louise

Read the Book, Lemmings! – Ame Dyckman

Thank You, Mr. Panda – Steve Antony

Beast Feast – Emma Yarlett

WANT TO KNOW MORE?

Cross, J. (2011) *Humor in Contemporary Junior Literature*. London: Routledge. Available at: https://doi.org/10.4324/9780203832943

This book examines humour in children's literature more closely using humour theories and literary criticism to analyse patterns in literature.

Loizou, E. and Recchia, S.L. (eds) (2019) *Research on Young Children's Humor: Theoretical and Practical Implications for Early Childhood Education* (1st edn). New York: Springer International Publishing. Available at: https://doi.org/10.1007/978-3-030-15202-4

This book explores humour in children and different formats for this humour, with one chapter focused specifically on children's literature.

Nwokah, E.E., Hernandez, V., Miller, E. and Garza, A. (2019) 'Playing with words: Dav Pilkey's literary success in humorous language'. *American Journal of Play*, *11*(2): 222–46.

This article focuses on language in humorous books, specifically examining Dav Pilkey's work and how his use of humorous language influences the books he writes.

REFERENCES

ABC News (2019) 'It takes two: Andy Griffiths and Terry Denton', 25 July. Available at: https://www.facebook.com/watch/?v=211771579758787

Bateman, R. (1967) 'Children and humorous literature'. *School Librarian and School Library Review*, *15*: 153–6.

Cart, M. (1995) *What's So Funny? Wit and Humor in American Children's Literature*. London: HarperCollins.

Daley, M. (2019) *Raising Readers: How to Nurture a Child's Love of Books*. Brisbane: University of Queensland Press.

Griffiths, A. (2014) www.abc.net.au/radionational/programs/sundayextra/andy-griffiths-on-writing-outlandish-lyrics-funny-stuff-for-kids/6865800

Landsberg, M. (1992) 'Liberating Laughter'. *American Education*, *16*(3): 34–48.

Mallan, K. (1993) *Laugh Lines*. Dunstable: Ambassador Press.

McGhee, P. (1979) *Humor: Its Origin and Development*. New York: Freeman.

Monson, D. (1978) 'A look at humor in literature and children's responses to humor'. Paper presented at the annual meeting of the International Reading Association, Hamburg, Germany.

Munde, G. (1997) 'What are you laughing at? Differences in children's and adult's humorous books selections for children'. *Children's Literature in Education*, *28*(4): 219–33.

Nilsen, D. and Nilsen, A. (1982) 'Exploration and defense of humor in young adult literature'. *Journal of Reading*, *26*(1): 58–65.

Opitz, M., Ford, M. and Zbaracki, M. (2006) *Books and Beyond*. London: Heinemann.

Shaeffer, M. and Hopkins, D. (1988) 'Miss Nelson, knock-knocks & nonsense: connecting through humor'. *Childhood Education*, Winter: 88–93.

Smith, J. (1967) *A Critical Approach to Children's Literature*. New York: McGraw Hill.

Whitmer, J. (1986) 'Pickles will kill you: use humorous literature to teach critical reading'. *The Reading Teacher*, February: 530–4.

Wolfenstein, M. (1954) *Children's Humor: A Psychological Analysis*. Bloomington, IN: Indiana University Press.

Zbaracki, M. (2003) 'A descriptive study of how humorous children's literature serves to engage children in reading'. PhD. thesis, The Ohio State University, Columbus.

Zbaracki, M. (2015) *Writing Right for Text Types*. Oxford: Oxford University Press.

13

FUTURE LEANINGS

> **WHAT WE WILL LEARN**
> - Where the field of children's literature is headed.
> - How the visual is becoming more of a focus in children's literature.
> - What innovative approaches are being seen in children's literature.

By now you have read and learned about a plethora of children's books, authors, illustrators and genres. You have learned the different features that each genre includes, as well as key evaluation criteria that can be used within these genres. So what more can you learn? In this case, it is about where things are headed and where should they be headed in children's literature. If you think back to the first chapter, you read about visual literacy and how that is a newer component found within the area of literacy. With that in mind, a focus on the visual will continue to be an emphasis for the future. But there is more than that as well. You have also seen a number of great titles and authors and illustrators from different cultures, and that will continue to be an emphasis in the field of children's literature.

FOCUS ON THE VISUAL

Let us start with the focus on the visual. With that start we can go back a few years to an undergraduate children's literature class I was teaching, when a student answered a discussion question of 'children's books are or should be . . .' by responding, 'groundbreaking'.

This answer has stuck with me for years and the discussion from the class after the answer was equally as influential. Regarding where children's literature is headed, the answer continues to be relevant. Groundbreaking is an accurate way of discussing where things should go, in a number of ways. In Chapter 1 there was great discussion about visual literacy and its importance in classrooms and reading around the globe. Walsh (2013) addresses this as well, stating: 'Readers are engaged in reading in a different way. Not only are they processing multimodal elements but they are also being active in their participation.' Walsh is not alone in this belief about the changes to reading. Sipe (2011) also posits: 'postmodern picturebooks afford readers the possibility of being co-authors; they seem to invite an even higher level of intellectual engagement from reader than traditional picturebooks' (Sipe, 2011: 247). The changes to reading, comprehending and engaging with books is crucial to explore and build an awareness, because it is being found in more and more books and genres throughout children's literature. The multimodal elements of literature and picture books in particular are aspects that have been discussed and seen in various titles throughout this book. We have focused primarily on picture books because 'while they may appear to be simplistic in format, picture books provide a plethora of complex structures and strategies for reading, viewing and comprehension' (Zbaracki and Geringer, 2014). For decades, picture books have developed and changed, and have at times increased in complexity, and this will continue to be the case. Sipe (2011: 239) supports this notion:

> Picturebooks, along with these other invitations to 'new literacies' are both re-inventing themselves and transforming the way we view the processes of reading and seeing, inviting us to think of ourselves – especially our identities as readers/viewers – in new ways. All art both informs us and has the potential to transform us.

As you have explored the different titles throughout this book, hopefully you have seen exactly what Sipe is saying, and you were transformed in different ways through the written and visual techniques you have encountered. This focus on the visual and the multimodal features found in not only picture books, but throughout all children's literature deserves further attention, but first it would be better to be open to expanding our definition of literature.

Reviewing Eliza Dresang's definition may be the best place to start as she created the concept of 'radical change', writing extensively about where literature was headed twenty-five years ago. Some of Dresang's ideas have flourished while others have faded to the background. However, her definition of literature is paramount. 'Literature is writing, illustration, or other graphic representation demonstrating excellence of form or style and expressing ideas of widespread or long-term interest' (Dresang, 1999: 5). Think about this for a minute and reflect on those key ideas of writing, illustration, and, specifically, graphic representation. Notice how those three elements are ideas that have been presented throughout the book in various forms and formats. We have seen a wide range of examples that incorporated the text and visual in different ways. The term 'graphic representation' is key here, because it emphasises how the visual can be incorporated, however that exploration was done within the confines of a genre. As discussed earlier, and will continue to be examined below, it is critical we are aware that sometimes these categories may need to be blurred as well.

There has been, and will be, lots of discussion about the defining or creating of formats and the blurring of these lines. However, the one constant that remains is the focus on the visual. It is beyond simply saying that a book has sequential art and is a graphic novel or a comic book, and this is where the innovative style is found. Sipe (2011: 249) recognises this, noting:

> The distinctions among comics, graphic novels, and picturebooks are blurring. I predict that this trend will continue, until the distinctions become less and less useful, and we begin to think of picturebooks, comics, and graphic novels as forms of 'sequential art'.

In fact, with these new innovative approaches, lines and distinctions are not the only things being blurred, but categories and genres are blurring as well. Zbaracki and Geringer (2014) recognised this after reading Kate diCamillo's Newbery Medal winning *Flora & Ulysses: The Illuminated Adventures* and from examination of that title and looking back at Brian Selznick's Caldecott Award winning *The Invention of Hugo Cabret* and they started to explore how the use of the visual was being used beyond simply for illustration of the written text. Examining more and more titles, they created the term 'blended narratives'. Blended narratives are texts that combine the features found in picture books, comics and graphic novels, along with the traditional novels that readers know. 'A key component of blended narratives is that they contain narratives that are told through two aspects on equal footing: the text and the visuals (illustrations)' (Zbaracki and Geringer, 2014, p.289). When one opens the covers of *Flora and Ulysses: The Illuminated Adventures* and starts reading, you are met with a comic that introduces part of the story and then moves the story forward before Chapter 1 even begins. This blurring of categories, and in essence creation of a new genre, is found in many other titles since – notably, Andy Griffiths and Terry Denton's Treehouse book series in which the images and text work together telling the story, but then also standing alone to advance the story. This is also present in Aaron Blabey's Bad Guy series, in which there are traditional chapters, as one would expect to find in a novel, but then the illustrations are present to advance the plot. Both of the elements work independently to move the story forward. It is important to note how the use of visuals continues to create a more complex and engaging reading experience.

As mentioned above, the term 'blended narratives' was conceived after reading two award-winning books. This begins to establish that children's literature committees are giving more recognition to genres bending formatting as well, and in some cases truly encouraging and supporting blurring the lines of genres. For example, notice how in 2008 the Caldecott Award was given to Brian Selznick's *The Invention of Hugo Cabret*. The book was over 500 pages long and does not have the traditional look of a picture book. The title has traditional chapters of text, but within the chapters there are multiple pages of illustrations that must be viewed before the text picks up exactly after the last illustration and continuing the narrative from that point. What this means is that all pages must be read in order to comprehend the story and how it is being told. Selznick has used this technique in other titles as well, *Wonderstruck, The Marvels*, and his most recent title, *Big Tree*. Talking about *The Invention of Hugo Cabret*, Sipe writes: 'we can see in the choice of this innovative book a sterling example of the blurring of genres and formats that I have described' (2011: 250). It is important to remember that the Caldecott Award is given to the most outstanding picture book. Continuing this idea of blurring genres is Matt de La Peña's *Last Stop on Market Street*, which was awarded the Newbery Award in 2016 and is a traditional picture book. Readers are reminded that the Newbery Award is given to the most outstanding writing, which is normally found in a novel, but in the case of the 2016 winner, the committee believed that a picture book was the most outstanding writing. More recently, *New Kid* by Jerry Craft was awarded the Newbery Medal in 2020 and is a graphic novel. What starts to show here is that award committees are now recognising the need to blur or even expand the definition of genre and format of books. Sipe (2011) connects with this idea of genre blurring when he writes and questions, 'Another example of the blurring of the formats is the Australian author/illustrator Shaun Tan's (2007) *The Arrival* . . . Is this book a very long wordless picturebook? A wordless graphic novel? An imitation of a film? A wordless, cell-less comic book? Again, the categories we have constructed do not do justice to this book' (p. 250). Sipe's words are spot on in this discussion. As literature continues to blur the lines of format and genre, as found in Tan's, Selznick's and diCamillo's work, it is important to acknowledge and respect that these new formats are not simply sequential art-related. Instead, it is examining and exploring the innovative approaches and appreciating the way they expand the intended audience, as well as our own personal understanding of reading and viewing.

The focus on the visual is not limited to narratives. One can look at *Older Than Dirt* by Don Brown and Michael R. Perfit. In this book, readers are introduced to information about Earth, geology and non-fiction, but in the format of a graphic novel. The use of sequential art is a unique approach to teach a content specific topic. This innovative approach for presenting non-fiction information connects to the groundbreaking idea, and highlights how authors and illustrators are continuing to explore visual formats and techniques to bend genres.

OTHER INNOVATIVE TITLES TO EXPLORE

Another creative and innovative title is Jon Sceiszka and Mac Barnett's *Battle Bunny*. This title is what can be termed an innovation on text. The book is in the size, shape and format of a traditional Little Golden Book. However, the original story is one that the authors created together, called 'Birthday Bunny'. The innovation on text was done by an imaginary child named Alex, who decided that 'Battle Bunny' would be a better version of the bland and trite 'original' story, so readers will see Alex's changes to both text and illustrations done with black ink throughout the book. The creative idea is one that could inspire children of all ages to create their own stories based on existing titles.

Again, continuing the concept of the creative use of the visual, one can look at Australian children's author and illustrator Philip Bunting's work, many of which have been seen throughout this book – for example, *Mum for Sale* and *Bad Crab*. In his work, his focus on the visual includes wordless 'flow-chart'-type illustrations as seen in *Mum for Sale*. There are also wordless frames throughout *Bad Crab* that contain subtle changes that readers/viewers must focus on to see what has changed or the focus is. In the non-fiction title *The Wonderful World of Ants*, Bunting uses a number of different visual literacy techniques to present and teach interesting facts about ants. The use of a flowchart again is present, as is a back-and-forth diagram that uses the visual quite creatively. The inclusion of humour assists in engaging readers as well.

Another innovative title and approach, or format, is *Space Band* by Tom Fletcher. What appears to be the standard novel, or even blended narrative, is much more than that. The book is about three children who have their own rock band and are competing in a battle of the bands. The only problem is, they are not the best musicians, and a second problem emerges as when they start to play, they are beamed to outer space. The band must work hard to win the battle of the bands in outer space in order to return home. What makes this book unique, beyond the illustrations that work like a blended narrative, is that Fletcher has also written the songs found in the book and his band McFly recorded them so children can listen to 'Space Band' as well.

Sipe's idea that categories do not do justice to some books is quite true and matches well with the titles shared in this section and even how the multimodal features being found in children's literature sometimes goes beyond the visual.

MULTICULTURAL LITERATURE

Another future leaning that deserves attention is a focus on multicultural literature. You will notice in this book that there is no multicultural chapter. That is because throughout all the chapters and genres there are multicultural titles, authors and illustrators included. The focus for the book is to be inclusive within and across all genres. Yes, there is a chapter focusing on Indigenous titles, as well as authors and illustrators, and the reason is that in the present it is important to celebrate so many quality titles that are published, as well as share the outstanding creators of these titles. Because this chapter is titled Future Leanings, the hope is that in the future these books can be incorporated into each chapter and that the field of children's literature continues to grow and respect all the quality books that are being created.

In discussing multicultural literature and its importance, Winch et al. (2010) introduce its best writing: 'story is a connector, and all cultures have stories that can fill schools and lives richness and diversity' (p. 638). Story is indeed important and children deserve to see themselves in a story so they are able to relate to what they are reading. Tomsic and Zbaracki (2022) note this in discussing what children's author Jacqueline Woodson wrote on this: 'I realized that no one but me *can* tell my story' (Woodson, 2003: 43) and when this is facilitated through a published book, significant possibilities emerge. All children deserve to see themselves in the books they read and this must be recognised throughout the field of children's literature. Fortunately, Kiefer et al. acknowledge how there has been an increase in titles, noting: 'In recent years, we have seen an increase in the number of books for children that highlight or include diverse material' (2019: 13).

While her focus is on African American literature, renowned children's literature, academic Rudine Sims Bishop (2012) puts forth her thoughts on the future of that area and also shows the direct connection with teaching: 'Assuredly, African American children's literature will continue to evolve and change as American society changes. But to this point, it appears to have been created to tell stories that have not been told before, stories that need to be told. Stories are a way of knowing as well as a way of teaching' (Bishop, 2012). Again, the theme comes back to stories and providing children the opportunities to read a wide and diverse range of books. These main ideas shared capture exactly what multicultural literature is all about, and whether it is sharing the lives and perspectives of diverse characters, or even sharing events and ideas from history, it allows the reader the opportunity to see and understand more about the world around them. Freeman and Lehman (2001) sum these ideas up best, stating how multicultural literature 'is a way to learn about other cultures, to bring people together, to travel the globe, to bridge our differences, and to rejoice in our common joys and triumphs' (p. 428).

At the present time, the recognition for diversity is being seen more especially with award winners. For example, *We Are Water Protectors* won the Caldecott Award in 2021 and the illustrator Michaela Goade became the first non-white woman to win the Caldecott Award. *Watercress* by Andrea Wang won the Caldecott Award in 2022. These two examples help show the increase in diverse titles being published, as well as greater recognition for these titles and their creators. This is not limited to the United States, though. *Young Dark Emu: A Truer History* won the CBCA Eve Pownall Award in 2020, and Jasmine Seymour won the award for best new illustrator in the same year for her title *Baby Business. Sorry Day* by Coral Vass won the Children's Book Council Award and Eve Pownall Book of the Year in 2019 as well. When one explores novels as well and the Newbery Award winners, there is an even greater appreciation when one explores titles such as *Freewater* by Amina Luqman-Dawson (Newbery Award winner in 2023), *The Last Cuentista* by Donan Barba Higuera (Newbery Award winner in 2022), *Merci Suárez Changes Gears* by Meg Medina (Newbery Award winner in 2019), and *The Crossover* by Kwame Alexander (Newbery Award winner in 2015). All these winners highlight how a much needed change and recognition of multicultural literature is happening, and the hope is that this continues on into the future. Zbaracki and Geringer (2014) note that 'children's literature is ever evolving, reflecting the values of the culture in which it is embedded'. The hope is that with multicultural literature the evolution and reflection of the cultural values continues to progress.

FUTURE LEANINGS

> ## BUST A MYTH
>
> ebooks are going to take over hardcover books, so why keep reading them?
>
> This is a myth that has been circulating for well over a decade that ebooks will take over reading. While there are many great features and some innovative ideas in ebooks, traditional hardcover books are still being published and the industry is adjusting well. Similar to the digital texts chapter, it is important to celebrate the innovations that not only work well in digital texts, but also recognising the many qualities and innovative features the traditional book has to offer as well.

CONCLUSION

So there you have it! With knowledge about the different genres of children's literature and exposure to a wide range of authors and illustrators, you will be able to build a classroom library and add to your teaching toolbox so that you can be ready to share new and exciting, and, dare I say, ground-breaking books with your students. The hope is that you have built a solid base of understanding of children's literature, and through time you will continue to build your knowledge and explore more books, authors and illustrators. As Goldstone (2001) wrote: 'why should children's books remain static in form and design? Individuals who work with children and books need to be cognisant of the changes and rejoice their vibrancy and creativity'. Enjoy the journey of finding new titles to read to your students and exploring the creative ideas and approaches not only to storytelling, but also information learning. Hopefully, all this new knowledge will inspire your students in their reading (and literacy) journey, and perhaps even inspire the author within them who might one day become authors of their own books in the future.

ADDITIONAL TITLES

Iguana Boy (series) – James Bishop

Ratbags (series) – Tim Harris

WANT TO KNOW MORE?

Nel, P. (2017) *Was the Cat in the Hat Black? The Hidden Racism of Children's Literature, and the Need for Diverse Books*. Oxford: Oxford University Press.

This book challenges different aspects of children's literature, specifically racism within the field. It is a great book to explore if you are interested in delving deeper into the field.

Wolf, S.A., Coats, K., Enciso, P. and Jenkins, C.A. (2011) *Handbook of Research on Children's and Young Adult Literature*. London: Routledge.

This book presents research in the field of children's literature from around the world. It is a good resource to learn more about the field, as well as hear from authors and illustrators themselves.

REFERENCES

Bishop, R. S. (2012) 'Reflections on the development of African American children's literature'. *Journal of Children's Literature*, *38*(2): 5–13.

Dresang, E. (1999) *Radical Change: Books for Youth in a Digital Age*. New York: H.W. Wilson Company.

Freeman, E.B. and Lehman, B.A. (2001) *Global Perspectives in Children's Literature*. New York: Allyn & Bacon.

Goldstone, B.P. (2001) 'Whaz up with our books? Changing picture book codes and teaching implications'. *The Reading Teacher*, *55*(4): 362–70.

Kiefer, B.Z., Tyson, C.A., Barger, B.P., Patrick, L. and Reilly-Sanders, E. (2019) *Charlotte Huck's Children's Literature: A Brief Guide* (3rd edn). London: McGraw Hill Education.

Sipe, L.R. (2011) 'The art of the picture book'. In S.A. Wolf, K. Coats, P. Enciso and C.A. Jenkins (eds) *Handbook of Research on Children's and Young Adult Literature*. London: Routledge.

Tomsic, M. and Zbaracki, M.D. (2022) 'It's all about the story: personal narratives in children's literature about refugees'. *British Educational Research Journal*, *48*(5): 859–77. Available at: https://doi.org/10.1002/berj.3798

Walsh, M. (2013) 'Literature in a digital environment'. In L. McDonald, *A Literature Companion for Teachers*. Newtown, NSW: Primary English Teaching Association Australia, PETAA.

Winch, G., Ross Johnston, R., March, P., Ljungdahl, L. and Holliday, M. (2010) *Literacy: Reading, Writing and Children's Literature* (4th edn). Oxford: Oxford University Press.

Woodson, J. (2003) 'Who can tell my story?' In D.L. Fox and K.G. Short (eds) *Stories Matter, the Complexity of Cultural Authenticity in Children's Literature* (pp. 41–5). Champaign, IL: National Council of English Teachers.

Zbaracki, M.D. and Geringer, J. (2014) 'Blurred vision: the divergence and intersection of illustrations in children's books'. *Journal of Graphic Novels and Comics*, 5(3): 284–96. Available at: https://doi.org/10.1080/21504857.2014.916225

INDEX

Page numbers in *italics* refer to figures; page numbers in **bold** refer to tables.

7 Ate 9 (Lazar), 160–161, 163
10 Clumsy Emus (Allen), 29
The 13-Storey Treehouse (Griffiths), 93
80 Days (book app), 145
100 Ways to Fly (Taylor), 71

An A to Z Story of Australian Animals (Morgan), 24–25, 132
The ABC Book of Australian Poetry (Hathorn), 71
ABC Dreaming (Brim), 138
Abela, D.
  Wolfie: An Unlikely Hero, 42
Abey, K.
  The Alphabet of Peculiar Creatures, 25
  Jurassic Pug Knows Shapes, 30
Adventures of Cow (Korchek), 48
Ahlberg, A.
  The Gaskitts series, 57
A is for Australia (Lessac), 26–27
Alexander, K.
  The Crossover, 172
  Out of Wonder, 72
Alexander, L.
  The Chronicles of Prydain, 92–93
Alfred's War (Bin Salleh), 123, 139
Aliens, Ghosts and Vanishings (Tarakson), 76
All Aboard! True Train Tales (Deeves), 83
The All New Must Have Orange 430 (Speechley), 45
Allen, E.
  10 Clumsy Emus, 29
Allen, P.
  Who Sank the Boat? 38
Allergic Alpaca (Thomas), 27
alliteration, 65
Alpha Pups! (Beer), 23
alphabet books, 23–29, **26**, 132, 138
The Alphabet of Peculiar Creatures (Abey), 25
Alphabetical Tashi: A Story Told in ABC (Fienberg and Fienberg), 23
Alphablock (Franceschelli), 26
Altés, M.
  My New Home, 111

Alvarez, J.
  Where Do They Go? 68
Amazing Australian Women (Freeman), 84
Amazing Australians in their Flying Machines (Mason and Mason), 84
The Amazing Recycling Project Book (Stanford), 83–84
American Library Association (ALA), 59
Anderson, D.
  Little Quack, 28
Andreae, G.
  Be Brave, Little Penguin, 40
Anelli, L., 79
Anemone is not the Enemy (McGregor), 79
Animalia (Base), 23, 94
Anisa's Alphabet (Dumbleton), 26, *27*, 41, 45
Another Book about Bears (Bunting and Bunting), 158
Antarctica (Court), 79
anthropomorphism, 79–80
The ANZAC Billy (Saxby), 124
Anzac Ted (Landsberry), 124
The Anzac Tree (Booth), 123
The Anzac Violin (Beck), 124
Applegate, K.
  The One and Only Ivan, 71
Archer, P.
  A Hippy-Hoppy Toad, 11
Are You My Mother? (Eastman), 132
Argh! There's a Skeleton Inside You! (Ben-Barak), 79
Arnie the Doughnut (Keller), 96
The Arrival (Tan), 43, 44, 45, 170
Asher, J.
  The Ghostkeeper's Journal and Field Guide, 146
augmented reality (AR), 146
Aurora Cycle series (Kaufman), 97
Aussie Animal Opposites (Lea), 30
Aussie Bites series, 56
Aussie Nibbles series, 56
Australia Illustrated (McCartney), 83
The Australia Survival Guide (Ivanoff), 81–82
Australian Backyard Earth Scientist (Macinnis), 81
Australian Backyard Explorer (Macinnis), 81

Australian children's literature, 129–130, 140–141.
    See also Indigenous literature
Australian Geographic Discover: Life Cycle (AG), 81
Australian history, landscape, and environment
    beginning books and, 24–27, 28–29, 30
    folk and fairy tales and, 42
    historical fiction and, 120, 121–123
    illustrations and, 48
    non-fiction texts and, 80–82, 83, 84–85
    poetry and, 67, 71
    realistic fiction and, 111–112
    transitional novels and, 56
Australian Rules Football (AFL), 133
Australia's Wild Weird Wonderful Weather (Reeder), 78
authority figures, 155, 157–158
autobiography, 84–85
Ava's Spectacular Spectacles (Rex), 90–91
Averiss, C.
    Love, 106
Avery, S.
    Frank's Red Hat, 159–160
The Awesome Book of Space (Frost), 82
Awesome Emu (Dreise), 135
Azaria (Coote), 140
Azúa Kramer, J.
    The Boy and the Gorilla, 109

Baby Business (Seymour), 137, 172
Back on Country (Goodes), 137
Backyard Birds (Milroy), 138
Backyard Bugs (Milroy), 138
The Bacteria Book (Mould), 79
Bad Apple (Lewis and Sanders), 161
The Bad Book (Griffiths), 67
Bad Crab (McInerney), 156, 171
Bad Guys series (Blabey), 93
Bad Guys series (Blabey), 169
Bagley, J.
    Henry and Bea, 109
Baillie, K.
    Boo Loves Books, 108
    The Friendly Games, 122
    Message in a Sock, 124
Baker, J.
    Belonging, 43
    Circle, 43
    Mirror, 42–43
    Playing with Collage, 77, 83–84
    Window, 43
A Ball for Daisy (Raschka), 43

Balla, T.
    Rockhopping and Landing with Wings, 112
ballads, 67
Bancroft, B.
    Colours of Australia, 132
    Coming Home to Country, 136–137
Bardhan-Quallen, S.
    Duck, Duck, Moose, 158
Barfield, M.
    Copycat Science, 82
    A Day in the Life of a Poo, a Gnu and You, 76
The Barnabus Project (Fan Brothers), 95
Barnett, M.
    Battle Bunny (with Scieszka), 170–171
Barr, L.
    When Numbers Met Letters, 29
Barraud, N.
    New Zealand's Backyard Beasts, 81
    Rockpools: A Guide for Kiwi Kids, 81
Barrows, A.
    Ivy and Bean series, 60
Base, G.
    Animalia, 23, 94
    Curse of the Vampire Robot, 94
Bat vs Poss (Moses), 38, 47
Bateman, R., 158
Battle Bunny (Scieszka and Barnett), 170–171
Bauer, M. G.
    Rodney Loses It! 13, 156
Bayly, S.
    A Curious Collection of Peculiar Creatures, 80
    The Illustrated Encyclopaedia Ugly Animals, 76, 80
    The Illustrated Encyclopaedia of Dangerous Animals, 80
Baz and Benz (McKinnon), 10
Be Brave, Little Penguin (Andreae), 40
Bear Came Along (Morris), 46
Beck, J.
    The Anzac Violin, 124
Becker, A.
    Journey, 95
    Quest, 95
    Return, 95
Beer, S.
    Alpha Pups! 23
beginning books
    alphabet books, 23–29, **26**, 132, 138
    colours, 31
    concept books, 29–31
    counting books, **26**, 27–29

importance of, **6**, 19–23, **21–22**, 31
Indigenous perspectives and illustrations in, 132
Bell, D.
   The Underwater Fancy-Dress Parade, 40
The Bell Rang (Ransome), 119
Belonging (Baker), 43
Ben-Barak, I.
   Argh! There's a Skeleton Inside You! 79
   Do Not Lick This Book, 79
Berger, S.
   The Sharey Godmother, 94–95
Berry, C.
   Chicken Break! A Counting Book, 29
Berube, K.
   Mae's First Day of School, 106
Beth: The Story of a Child Convict (Wilson), 120
Bev and Kev (Germein), 112
Big Bad Bushranger (Brown), 129
The Big Book of Antarctica (Hope), 81
Big Talk: Poems for Four Voices (Fleischman), 69
Big Tree (Selznick), 170
Billie and the Blue Bike (Kwaymullina), 133
Billie B. Brown series (Rippin), 56, 59
Bin Salleh, R.
   Alfred's War, 123, 139
Bindi (Saunders), 140
Bink and Gollie (DiCamillo and McGhee), 57
Binks, A.
   Night Walk, 111
Binti (Okorafor), 97
biography, 84–85
Bishop, R.S., 172
Blabey, A.
   Bad Guys series, 93, 169
   Don't Call Me Bear! 10
   Pig the Pug, 38, 156
Black Cockatoo (Merrison and Hustler), 140
Black is a Rainbow Color (Joy), 113
Blackall, S.
   Farmhouse, 121
   Hello Lighthouse, 48, 121
Blackbar (book app), 145
Blackwood, F., 67
Bland, N.
   The Fabulous Friend Machine, 50
   Three Billy Goats Gruff, 42, 90
   Trick Number Two, 94
   The Very Cranky Bear, 38, 49
Blue Flower (Hartnett), 112
Blumberg, F.C., 149
board books, 19–20, 23, 28, 29

A Boat of Stars: New Australian Children's Poems (Connolly and Prior), 71
Bobtail's Friend (Collard-Spratt and Ferro), 136
Boo Loves Books (Baillie), 108
book apps, 144, 145–146, 147. *See also* digital texts
The Book with No Pictures (Novak), 161
Boom! Bellow! Bleat! (Heard), 69
Boomerang and Bat (Greenwood), 139
Booth, C.
   The Anzac Tree, 123
Borando, S.
   Shake the Tree! 46
Born to Fly (McWilliams), 84
Bouncing Back: An Eastern Barred Bandicoot Story (Cleaver), 80
The Boy and the Gorilla (Azúa Kramer), 109
Boy (Cummings), 41
Boyle, J.W.
   The Shop Train, 122
Bradshaw, F.
   The Great Lizard Trek, 80
Brain Candy (National Geographic Kids), 83
Braun, D.
   Wild Animals of the North, 76
Brian, J.
   Where's Jessie? 122–123
Briggs, K., 133
Briggs, S.
   Can You See Me? (with Harvey), 132
Brim, W.
   ABC Dreaming, 138
Brooks, P.J., 149
Brooks, W.M., 55
Brother Moon (Yoelu), (138
Brown, B.
   Big Bad Bushranger, 129
Brown, D. [Dan]
   Wild Symphony, 69, 146
Brown, D. [Don]
   Older Than Dirt (with Perfit), 170
Brown, M.W., 36
Bunny the Brave War Horse (MacLeod), 124
Bunting, L.
   Another Book about Bears (with P. Bunting), 158
Bunting, P.
   as illustrator, 171
   Another Book about Bears (with L. Bunting), 158
   Not Cute, 160
   The Wonderful World of Ants, 171
The Bushfire Book (Marsden), 83–84
Butler, D.H.
   King & Kayla series, 59

Butt Out! (McKenzie), 161, 163
Button, J.
   Steve Goes to Carnival, 133
By the Billabong (Finn), 48

Caisley, R.
   Rocky and Louie (with Walleystack), 134
Campbell, R.
   Dear Zoo, 22
The Camping Trip (Mann), 112
Can I Touch Your Hair? (Latham and Waters), 70
Can You Find 12 Busy Bees? (Winch), 29
Can You Make a Scary Face? (Thomas), 11
Can You See Me? (Briggs and Harvey), 132
Canty, J.
   Shapes and Colours, 30
Caravette, L., 55
Cart, M., 154
Cassidy, S.
   Helen's Birds, 109
Castles, J.
   Say Yes, A Story of Friendship, Fairness and a Vote for Hope, 119
The Cat and the King series (Donaldson), 58
A Cat Called Trim (Flinders), 120
The Cat in the Hat (Dr. Seuss), 54
The Cat Man of Aleppo (Shamsi-Basha and Latham), 125–126
Ceremony (Goodes), 137
Charlie's Swim (Wright), 125
Charlotte's Web (White), 91
Chicken Break! A Counting Book (Berry), 29
children's literature
   current and future trends in, 167–173
   definition of, 5
   developmental sequence of, 5, **6**
   importance of, 6–7, 16–17
   literacy and, 1–7, **2**, *3*, 16–17
   theories of, 13–16, **14–15**
   See also reading aloud
Christmas Truce (Robinson), 125
The Chronicles of Prydain (Alexander), 92–93
Cianciolo, P.J., 55
Cicada (Tan), 44, 46
Circle (Baker), 43
civil rights, 119–120
Clancy & Millie and the Very Fine House (Gleeson), 40
Clark-Robinson, M.
   Let the Children March, 120

Cleaver, R.
   Bouncing Back: An Eastern Barred Bandicoot Story, 80
Cleo Stories series (Gleeson), 57, 60
A Climate in Chaos (Layton), 82
Cline-Ransome, L.
   Narrative of the Life of Frederick Douglass, 120
   Overground Railroad, 120
Coffin, L.
   Free Diving, 139
Cohen, S.
   My Dead Bunny, 158–159
Colderley, C., 72
Collard-Spratt, R.
   Bobtail's Friend (with Ferro), 136
   Grandfather Emu (with Ferro), 136
Collins, S.
   Hunger Games trilogy, 97
Colouroos (McGregor), 31
colours, 31, 132
Colours of Australia (Bancroft), 132
The Colours of History: How Colours Shaped the World (Gifford), 82, 83
Colton, N.
   Jasper and Scruff series, 58
Coming Home to Country (Bancroft), 136–137
community, 113–114
concept books, 29–31
concrete poems, 68–69
Connolly, M.
   A Boat of Stars: New Australian Children's Poems (with Prior), 71
Coombes, D.
   Going to the Footy, 133
Cooper, J., 42
Coote, M.
   Azaria, 140
Copus, J.
   My Bed is an Air Balloon, 69
Copycat Science (Barfield), 82
Cossins, J.
   The Ultimate Animal Counting Book, 83
counting books, **26**, 83, 132
Counting Our Country (Daniels), 28
Courage, M., 143, 144, 149
Court, M.
   Antarctica, 79
Crab: A Snappy Book of Colours (Hegarty), 31
Crabbing With Dad (Seden), 134
craft books, 83–84

Craft, J.
  New Kid, 170
Crawford, J.
  I Remember, 134–135
Creech, S.
  Hate that Cat, 71
  Love that Dog, 71
critical theory, **14**
The Crossover (Alexander), 172
crossover specialised books, 83
Cullinan, B., 29–30, 35, 37, 90, 118
cultural literacy, 7
Cummings, P.
  Boy, 41
Cunning Crow (Dreise), 135
A Curious Collection of Peculiar Creatures (Bayly), 80
Curse of the Vampire Robot (Base), 94
Cyclone (Frech), 41, 47, 123
Cyril and Pat (Gravett), 48, 49

D-Bot Squad series (Park), 57
Daddo, A.
  Old Friends, New Friends, 104
  Whatcha Building? 113
Dahl, R.
  Matilda, 157
Dahl, S.
  Madame Badobedah, 44
Daisy Gets Lost (Raschka), 43
Daley, M., 6, 7, 11, 78–79, 86, 118, 153
Dallimore, P.
  The Three Little Bush Pigs, 91, 129
Daniels, J.
  Counting Our Country, 28
The Dark (Snicket), 108
Dauvillier, L.
  Hidden: A Child's Story of the Holocaust, 125
Davies, J.
  Meet the Ancient Greeks, 58
Davies, N.
  The Day War Came, 109
Day Break (McQuire), 139
A Day in the Life of a Poo, a Gnu and You (Barfield), 76
The Day the Crayons Came Home (Daywalt), 47
The Day the Crayons Quit (Daywalt), 47
The Day War Came (Davies), 109
The Day We Built the Bridge (Tidy), 121–122
Daywalt, D.
  The Day the Crayons Came Home, 47
  The Day the Crayons Quit, 47
de la Peña, M.
  Last Stop on Market Street, 113, 170
  Milo Imagines the World, 113
Dear Substitute (Raschka), 106
Dear Zoo (Campbell), 22
death and dying, 108–109
Deeves, P.
  All Aboard! True Train Tales, 83
deGennaro, S.
  We're Stuck! 46
Del Rizzo, S.
  My Beautiful Birds, 41, 47, 109
Denton, T., 83, 93, 169
Device 6 (book app), 145
Diary of a Wombat series (Frech), 47
DiCamillo, K.
  Bink and Gollie (with McGhee), 57
diCamillo, K.
  Flora & Ulysses: The Illuminated Adventures, 169
Dickinson, M.
  The Kitchen Science Cookbook, 83–84
Dickson, J.
  M is for Mutiny! History by Alphabet, 26, 83
A Different Pond (Phi), 41, 110
digital texts, 143–148, **148**, 173
Dirt by Sea (Wagner), 130
Do Not Lick This Book (Ben-Barak), 79
Dog Breath (Pilkey), 163
Donaldson, J.
  The Cat and the King series, 58
Don't Call Me Bear! (Blabey), 10
Don't Forget (Godwin), 113–114
Don't Let the Pigeon Drive the Bus! (Willems), 36
Dorléans, M.
  The Night Walk, 111
Dorling Kindersley (DK), 80, 81, 82
Dr. Seuss
  ALA and, 59
  The Cat in the Hat, 54
  Green Eggs and Ham, 54
Dreaming (Dreamtime) stories, 130, 136
Dreaming of Australia A to Z (Racklyeft), 24–25, *25*
Dreiling, K.
  A Perfect Pig, 104
Dreise, G.
  Awesome Emu, 135
  Cunning Crow, 135
  Hello and Welcome, 131, 136
  Kookoo Kookaburra, 135

Mad Magpie, 135
My Culture and Me, 137
Silly Birds, 135
Dresang, E., 168
Drought (Frech), 41, 47, 123
Dry to Dry (Freeman), 79
Duck and Penguin are NOT Friends (Woolf), 9, 154–155
Duck, Duck, Moose (Bardhan-Quallen), 158
Duck, Duck, Moose (Gifford), 158
Ducks Away (Fox), 13, 28
Dufft, S.
  Paula Knows What To Do, 109
Dumbleton, M.
  Anisa's Alphabet, 26, *27*, 41, 45
Dust Echoes (internet text), 147

Eastman, P.D.
  Are You My Mother? 132
ebooks, 143–144, 173. *See also* digital texts
Ella and the Ocean (Tanner), 48
Ellie's Dragon (Graham), 103
Elliott, D.
  In the Past, 72
Elvgren, J.
  The Whispering Town, 125
Emmerichs, B., 83
Emmitt, M., 1
emotions, 106–107
Encyclopedia of Animals (Howard), 81
endpages, 36, *37*, 47
Epic! 147
equality, 119–120
Eragon (Paolini), 91, 96
Eric (Tan), 46
Escape! The Story of the Great Houdini (Fleischman), 86
Estela, L.
  Girl on Wire, 45
  Suri's Wall, 36
Eureka! A Story of the Goldfields (Wilson), 122
Evans, G.
  Norton and the Borrowing Bear, 104
experiment and activity books, 81–82
Explore Your World: Weird, Wild, Amazing! (Flannery), 78
Extraordinary! (Harrison), 49

The Fabulous Friend Machine (Bland), 50
fairy tales, 41–42, 89–91. *See also* fantasy literature
Falconer, I.
  Olivia series, 112

family, 104–106, 134–135
Family Forest (Kane), 105
Family (Muir and Lawson), 135–136
Family Tree (Pyke), 106
Fan Brothers
  The Barnabus Project, 95
  Lizzy and the Cloud, 95
The Fantastic Flying Books of Mr. Morris Lessmore (book app), 146
The Fantastic Flying Books of Mr. Morris Lessmore (Joyce), 146
Fantastic Football Poems (Foster), 72
fantasy literature
  evaluation criteria for, 98, **98**
  importance of, 89–92, 98–99
  picture books as, 41–42, 93–96
  science fiction and, 97
  themes in, 97–98
  traditional elements of, 92, **92**
  traditional vs. modern fantasy and, 92–93
Farmhouse (Blackall), 121
Farrell, A.
  The Hike, 112
fears, 40, 107–108
The Feather (Wild), 45
Feel the Beat (Singer), 72
feelings, 106–107
Fenton, C.
  To the Bridge, 36, 121–122
Ferro, J.
  Bobtail's Friend (with Collard-Spratt), 136
  Grandfather Emu (with Collard-Spratt), 136
Fienberg, A. and B.
  Alphabetical Tashi: A Story Told in ABC, 23
Finding François (Gordon), 104
Finding Winnie (Messier), 124
Finn, M.
  By the Billabong, 48
Fire (Frech), 41, 47, 123
Fiore, C., 55
First Field Guide to Australian Frogs & Reptiles (Slater), 80
The First Scientists (Tutt), 140
First World War, 67, 123–125
Fisher, A.
  'Snowy Benches,' 66
Flanagan, J.
  Ranger's Apprentice series, 91
Flannery, T.
  Explore Your World: Weird, Wild, Amazing! 78
Flapper, VC (Wilson), 125

Fleischman, P.
  Big Talk: Poems for Four Voices, 69
  I Am Phoenix, 69
  Joyful Noise, 69
  The Matchbook Diary, 120
Fleischman, S., 160
  Escape! The Story of the Great Houdini, 86
Fletcher, T.
  Space Band, 171
Flinders, M.
  A Cat Called Trim, 120
Flood (Frech), 41, 47, 123
Flora & Ulysses: The Illuminated Adventures (diCamillo), 169
Flora series (Idle), 43
Florette (Walker), 111
Flotsam (Wiesner), 43
Fly (McGeachin), 50
The Flying Light (Yang), 43
folk tales, 41–42, 89–91, 95. *See also* fantasy literature
Follow Follow (Singer), 69
Footpath Flowers (Lawson), 44
Foreman, M.
  Stubby: A True Story of Friendship, 124
Foster, J.
  Fantastic Football Poems, 72
  Loopy Limericks, 68
Found in Melbourne (O'Callaghan), 29
Found in Sydney: A Counting Adventure (O'Callaghan), 29
Found (Pascoe), 131, 135
Fox, D.
  How to Make a Friend in 6 Easy Steps, 103–104
Fox, M.
  on early literacy experiences, 2, 5, 7, 21
  on language, 49
  Ducks Away, 13, 28
  Hello Baby! 76
  Koala Lou, 9, 11, 38, 47, 129
  Possum Magic, 47, 49, 129
  on reading aloud, 10
  Ten Little Fingers and Ten Little Toes, 13
  The Tiny Star, 108
Franceschelli, C.
  Alphablock, 26
Franco, B.
  Messing Around on the Monkey Bars, 69
Frank's Red Hat (Avery), 159–160
Free Diving (Coffin), 139
free verse, 70–71
Freeman, E.B., 133, 172

Freeman, P.
  Amazing Australian Women, 84
  Dry to Dry, 79
Freewater (Luqman-Dawson), 172
French, J.
  historical fiction and, 118
  Cyclone, 41, 47, 123
  Diary of a Wombat series, 47
  Drought, 41, 47, 123
  Fire, 41, 47, 123
  Flood, 41, 47, 123
  Josephine Wants to Dance, 38
  Pandemic, 123
  When the War is Over, 123
The Friendly Games (Baillie), 109
friendship, 40, 103–104
Frost, A.
  The Awesome Book of Space, 82
Frost, J., 79
Fry, D., 138

Galda, L., 29–30, 35, 37, 90, 118
Garland, M.
  Miss Smith Reads Again! 91
  Miss Smith Under the Ocean, 91
  Miss Smith's Incredible Storybook, 91
Garrish, M., 144
The Gaskitts series (Ahlberg), 57
Gathering Blue (Lowry), 97
Gecko (Huber), 79
gender theory, **15**
Gerber, C.
  Seeds, Bees, Butterflies, and More! 69
Geringer, J., 168, 169, 172
Germein, K.
  Bev and Kev, 112
Ghost-o-Matic (app), 146
The Ghostkeeper's Journal and Field Guide (Asher), 146
Gibbes, L.
  Searching for Cicadas, 79
Gifford, C.
  The Colours of History: How Colours Shaped the World, 82, 83
Gifford, L.
  Duck, Duck, Moose, 158
Gill, M.
  Ice Breaker! An Epic Antarctic Adventure, 79, 83
Girl from the Sea (Wild), 10, 45
Girl on Wire (Estela), 45
Gittel's Journey (Newman), 120

The Giver (Lowry), 97
Gleeson, L.
   Clancy & Millie and the Very Fine House, 40
   The Cleo Stories series, 57, 60
Gleitzman, M., 118
Go Go and the Silver Shoes (Godwin), 104
Goade, M., 172
Godwin, J.
   on picture books, 36
   transitional novels and, 56
   Don't Forget, 113–114
   Go Go and the Silver Shoes, 104
   I'll Always be Older Than You, 105
   Little One, 112
   One Blue Shoe, 29
   Starting School, 40, 106
   Tilly, 48–49
   Watch This!: A Book about Making Shapes (with Orpin), 30
Going to the Footy (Coombes), 133
Gold! (Kerin), 122
Goldilocks and the Three Dinosaurs (Willems), 42
Goldilocks and the Three Koalas (Richards), 129
Goldstone, B.P., 173
Good Question: A Tale Told Backwards (Whiting), 42
The Good Son: A Story From the First World War (Ober), 123
Goodbye House, Hello House (Wild), 47, 111
Goodes, A.
   Back on Country, 137
   Ceremony, 137
   Somebody's Land, 137
Goodnight Already! (John), 157, 159
The Goozillas series (Green), 57–58
Gorbachev, V.
   No Swimming for Nelly, 40
Gordon, G.
   Finding François, 104
Grady, C.
   Write To Me: Letters from Japanese American Children to the Librarian They Left Behind, 125
Graham, B.
   Ellie's Dragon, 103
   Home in the Rain, 105
   The Underhills: A Tooth Fairy Story, 94
   Vanilla Ice Cream, 3, 4, 46
   Want to Play Trucks? 112–113
Graham, I.
   My Best Book of Spaceships, 82

grammar, 77
Grandfather Emu (Collard-Spratt and Ferro), 136
Grandma's Treasured Shoes (Vass), 110
graphic novels, 125, 140
Gravas, N.
   Noodle Bear, 49–50
Graves, B., 54, 59–60
Gravett, E.
   Cyril and Pat, 48, 49
Gray, K.
   Oi Dog! series, 38
   Oi Frog! series, 26
   You're Called What? 161
The Great Lizard Trek (Bradshaw), 80
Greder, A.
   The Island, 44–45
   The Mediterranean, 44–45
Green, D.
   The Goozillas series, 57–58
Green Eggs and Ham (Dr. Seuss), 54
Green on Green (White), 31
Green, P.
   'Which Jack?' 65
Greenwood, M.
   Boomerang and Bat, 139
   The Happiness Box, 83
   Our Country: Ancient Wonders, 130
Greig, L.
   Sweep, 107
Grey, M.
   Traction Man series, 94
Griffiths, A., 154
   The 13-Storey Treehouse, 93
   The Bad Book, 67
   Treehouse book series, 169
   The Very Bad Book, 67, 67
Griffiths, N.
   Ten Pound Pom, 120
Grimm Brothers, 90
Gryphon Award, 59
The Guardian (newspaper), 145
Guest, P.
   Windows, 41
Guillain, A.
   One Banana, Two Bananas (with C. Guillain), 29
Guillain, C.
   One Banana, Two Bananas (with A. Guillain), 29
   What Did the Tree See? 121
The Gum Family Finds Home (McCartney), 130
Guyku (Raczka), 68

H is for Haiku: A Treasury of Haiku from A to Z (Rosenberg), 68
Hachette Australia, 81
haikus, 68
Hallifax, C.
  Never Forget, 123
Halloween (Seinfeld), 48
Hammill, E.
  Over the Hills and Far Away, 66
The Happiness Box (Greenwood), 83
Harrison, P.
  Extraordinary! 49
  Wild Bush Days, 122
Harry Potter series (Rowling), 91, 93, 96
Hartley, D.
  Strangers on Country (with Murray), 139
Hartnett, S.
  Blue Flower, 112
Harvey, B.
  Can You See Me? (with Briggs), 132
Harvey, R.
  Off We Go Around Australia, 130
  In Our Bush, 130
  To the Top End, 130
Hate that Cat (Creech), 71
Hathorn, L.
  The ABC Book of Australian Poetry, 71
  Miss Franklin: How Miles Franklin's Brilliant Career Began, 121
  A Soldier, a Dog and a Boy, 124
Haughton, C.
  Maybe, 155
  Shhh! We Have a Plan, 155
Heard, G.
  Boom! Bellow! Bleat! 69
Hegarty, P.
  Crab: A Snappy Book of Colours, 31
  Koala: A Book of Counting, 28
  We are Family, 106
Helen's Birds (Cassidy), 109
Hello and Welcome (Dreise), 131, 136
Hello Baby! (Fox), 76
The Hello, Goodbye Window (Juster), 47
Hello, Jimmy! (Walker), 50, 105–106
Hello Lighthouse (Blackall), 48, 121
Hendrix, J.
  Shooting at the Stars, 124
Henkes, K.
  Lilly's Purple Plastic Purse, 38, 48
  Wemberly Worried, 40, 107
Henry and Bea (Bagley), 109

Henson, H.
  That Book Woman, 121
Heritage Heroes series, 85
Herrick, S.
  How to Repaint a Life, 70–71
  Zoe, Max, and the Bicycle Bus, 70–71
Hesse, K.
  Out of the Dust, 71
Hey Jack! series (Rippin), 56, 59
Hidden: A Child's Story of the Holocaust (Dauvillier), 125
Hidden Wonders (Lonely Planet Kids), 82
High Five to the Boys (Penguin), 84
Higuera, D.B.
  The Last Cuentista, 172
The Hike (Farrell), 112
Hike (Oswald), 112
A Hippy-Hoppy Toad (Archer), 11
Hirsh-Pasek, K., 149
historical fiction
  Australian history and, 120, 121–123
  equal rights and, 119–120
  evaluation criteria for, **119**
  general history and, 121
  immigration stories and, 120–121
  importance of, 117–118, 126
  Indigenous literature and, 119, 123, 125, 139
  war and, 123–126
The History of Little Goody Two-Shoes (Newbery), 38–39, *39*
The Hobbit (Tolkien), 92–93
Hobbs, L.
  Mr Chicken series, 12, 36, 160
  Mr Chicken All Over Australia, 129, 156
  Mr Chicken Goes to Paris, 36, 37
Hold On! Saving the Spotted Handfish (Newton), 80
Home in the Rain (Graham), 105
Hope, C.
  The Big Book of Antarctica, 81
Houston, B., 132
How I Learned to Fall out of Trees (Kirsch), 111
how-to books, 83–84
How to Make a Friend in 6 Easy Steps (Fox), 103–104
How to Repaint a Life (Herrick), 70–71
Howard, J.
  Encyclopedia of Animals, 81
Huber, R.
  Gecko, 79
Huck, C., 19, 35–36, 38
The Human Body Survival Guide (Ivanoff), 81–82

Humes, H.
  I Want to be a Superhero, 133
humour
  authority figures and, 155, 157–158
  evaluation criteria for, 162, **162**
  humorous characters and, 155, 156–157
  humorous discourse (language play) and, 155, 160–162, 163
  humorous verse and, 67, *67*
  importance and benefits of, 153–154, 163
  incongruity and, 155, 159–160
  physical humour and, 155, 158–159
The Hundred-Year Barn (MacLachlan), 121
Hunger Games trilogy (Collins), 97
Hunt, D.
  My Real Friend, 36, 40, 103
Hunter, R., 139
Hustler, H.
  Black Cockatoo (with Merrison), 140
Hutchings, M.
  Your Birthday was the Best! 159
  Your School is the Best, 159

I am Actually a Penguin (Taylor), 49
I am Not a Worm (Tulloch), 159
I Am Phoenix (Fleischman), 69
I Am the Seed that Grew the Tree (Waters), 72
I Can Only Draw Worms (Mabbitt), 159
I Just Ate My Friend (McKinnon), 103–104
I NEED a Parrot (McKimmie), 47
I Remember (Crawford), 134–135
I Say Boo, You Say Hoo (Kane), 161–162
I Want My Hat Back (Klassen), 156
I Want to be a Superhero (Humes), 133
I Was Only Nineteen (Schumann), 123
Ice Breaker! An Epic Antarctic Adventure (Gill), 79, 83
identification books, 80–81
identity, 112–113
Idle, M.
  Flora series, 43
I'll Always be Older Than You (Godwin), 105
The Illustrated Encyclopaedia Ugly Animals (Bayly), 76, 80
The Illustrated Encyclopaedia of Dangerous Animals (Bayly), 80
immigration stories, 120–121. *See also* refugees
In Our Bush (Harvey), 130
In the Past (Elliott), 72
Inanimate Alice (internet text), 146–147
incongruity, 155, 159–160

The Incredible Freedom Machines (Saunders), 95
Indigenous literature
  evaluation criteria for, 131–132, **131**
  family in, 134–135
  historical fiction as, 119, 123, 125, 139
  importance of, 130–131, 140–141
  morality and values in, 135–136
  nature in, 138
  for older readers, 140
  politics and, 139–140
  realistic themes in, 132–134
  strong connection to country in, 136–138
  for younger readers, 132
informational books, 75
internet texts, 146–147
Interrupting Chicken series (Stein), 91
intrinsic motivation, 153–154
The Invention of Hugo Cabret (Selznick), 169–170
The Island (Greder), 44–45
Ivanoff, G.
  The Australia Survival Guide, 81–82
  The Human Body Survival Guide, 81–82
Ivy and Bean series (Barrows), 60
Ivy Bird (McCartney), 111
Izzy and Frank (Lehman), 111

Jackson, R.
  The Three Billy Goats Gruff, 90
Jacobs, J., 63, 64, 93, 107
Janeczko, P.
  on poetry, 63, 66
  A Poke in the Eye, 69
  The Proper Way to Meet a Hedgehog, 72
Jasper and Scruff series (Colton), 58
Jay, A., 69
Jenkins, S.
  as illustrator, 76
  Life on Earth, 76
Jetty Jumping (Rowe), 107
Joey Counts to Ten (Morgan), 28, 132
John, J.
  Goodnight Already! 157, 159
Jolly, J.
  One Step at a Time, 44
  Radio Rescue! 122
  Tea and Sugar Christmas, 122
Jones, D.W.
  The Tough Guide to Fantasyland, 96, 98
Jones, R.
  A Natural History of Insects in 100 Limericks, 68
Josephine Wants to Dance (Frech), 38

Journey (Becker), 95
The Journey (Senna), 45
Joy, A.
   Black is a Rainbow Color, 113
Joyce, W.
   The Fantastic Flying Books of Mr. Morris Lessmore, 146
   The Numberlys, 146
Joyful Noise (Fleischman), 69
Julian at the Wedding (Love), 113
Julian is a Mermaid (Love), 113
Jurassic Pug Knows Shapes (Abey), 30
Juster, N.
   The Hello, Goodbye Window, 47

Kalani, S.
   Space on Earth, 82
Kane, J.
   I Say Boo, You Say Hoo, 161–162
Kane, K.
   Family Forest, 105
Kasten, W., 102, 117
Katz, D., 56
Kaufman, A.
   Aurora Cycle series, 97
Keep an Eye on this Kiwi (Tulloch), 157
Keller, L.
   Arnie the Doughnut, 96
   Potato Pants, 160
Kelly, D.
   Me and You, 106
Kelly, L., 132–133
Kennedy, L., 135–136, 136
Kerin, J.
   Gold! 122
Kick With My Left Foot (Seden), 133
Kickett-Tucker, C.
   Ninni Yabini, 138
Kids Who Did (Murray), 85
Kiefer, B.Z.
   on beginning books, 22
   on early literacy experiences, 20, 21
   on fantasy literature, 89, 90, 96
   on historical fiction, 117–118, 121, 123
   on love of reading, 16–17
   on multicultural literature, 172
   on non-fiction texts, 76
   on poetry, 63
   on reading aloud, 7, 13
   on realistic fiction, 101
   on transitional novels, 55

King & Kayla series (Butler), 59
King of the Outback (Weidenbach), 122
King, S.M., 56, 94
   Leaf, 43
   Three, 48
Kirsch, V.X.
   How I Learned to Fall out of Trees, 111
The Kitchen Science Cookbook (Dickinson), 83–84
Klassen, J.
   I Want My Hat Back, 156
   This is Not My Hat, 9, 38, 156, 162
   We Found a Hat, 156
Knowledge Encyclopedia Ocean! (DK), 80
Koala: A Book of Counting (Hegarty), 28
Koala Lou (Fox), 9, 11, 38, 47, 129
Kobald, I.
   My Two Blankets, 41, 109
Kookaburra (Saxby), 79, 80
Kookoo Kookaburra (Dreise), 135
Korchek, L.
   Adventures of Cow, 48
Korman, G., 154
Kotzwinkle, W.
   Walter the Farting Dog (with Murray), 163
Kraegel, K.
   This is a Book of Shapes, 30
Kuenzler, L.
   Not Yet, Zebra, 27
Kunhardt, D.
   Pat the Bunny, 22
Kwaymullina, A.
   as illustrator, 20, 132, 133
   Billie and the Blue Bike, 133
   The Lost Girl, 134
Kwaymullina, B.
   Little Koala Lost, 28

Landsberg, M., 153, 160
Landsberry, B.
   Anzac Ted, 124
language play (humorous discourse), 155, 160–162, 163
lap books, 19
LaRochelle, D.
   See the Cat: Three Stories About a Dog, 59
Larry, H. I.
   Zac Power series, 57, 59
The Last Cuentista (Higuera), 172
Last Stop on Market Street (de la Peña), 113, 170

Latham, I.
   Can I Touch Your Hair? (with Waters), 70
   The Cat Man of Aleppo (with Shamsi-Basha), 125–126
Laugh Lines (Mallan), 156
Lawson, J.
   Footpath Flowers, 44
Lawson, O.
   Let's Count Australian Animals, 28
Lawson, S.
   Family (with Muir), 135–136
   Respect (with Muir), 135–136
Layton, N.
   A Climate in Chaos, 82
Lazar, T.
   7 Ate 9, 160–161, 163
   The Upper Case, 161
Lea, E.
   Aussie Animal Opposites, 30
Leaf (King), 43
Leatherdale, M.B.
   Stormy Seas: Stories of Young Boat Refugees, 85
Ledden-Lewis, C., 135
Lee, J.
   Pool, 43
Leffler, D., 134, 139, 140
Lehman, B.
   Museum Trip, 43
   The Red Book, 43
   The Secret Box, 43
Lehman, B.A., 133, 172
Lehman, K.
   Izzy and Frank, 111
   Wren, 105
L'Engle, M.
   A Wrinkle in Time, 91
Lessac, F.
   A is for Australia, 26–27
Lester, A., 47
Lester, H., 159
Let the Children March (Clark-Robinson), 120
Let's Count Australian Animals (Lawson), 28
Lewis, C.S.
   The Lion, the Witch and the Wardrobe, 91
Lewis, H.
   Bad Apple (with Sanders), 161
Liang, L.A., 54, 59–60
life-cycle books, 81
Life Cycles: Everything From Start to Finish (DK), 81
Life on Earth (Jenkins), 76
Light's Out, Leonard (Pyke), 108

Lilly's Purple Plastic Purse (Henkes), 38, 48
limericks, 68
Lindstrom, C.
   We Are Water Protectors, 172
The Lion, the Witch and the Wardrobe (Lewis), 91
listening, 1–2, **2**, 4
literacy, 1–7, **2**, *3*, 16–17
Little Bird's Day (Morgan), 138
Little Golden Books series, 36
Little Koala Lost (Kwaymullina), 28
Little One (Godwin), 112
Little People, Big Dreams series, 85
A Little Pretty Pocket-book, Intended for the Instruction and Amusement of Little Master Tommy, and Pretty Miss Polly (Newbery), 39
Little Quack (Anderson), 28
The Little Red Fort (Maier), 95
Little Red the Inventor (AR story), 146
The Little Wooden Horse (Wilson), 120
Lizzy and the Cloud (Fan Brothers), 95
Lloyd, A.
   The Upside-down History of Down Under, 83
Lofts, P., 47
Lonely Planet Kids, 76, 82
Long, D.
   Survivors, 85
Looking After Country with Fire (Steffensen), 137
Loopy Limericks (Foster), 68
The Lord of the Rings (Tolkien), 92–93
The Lost Girl (Kwaymullina), 134
The Lost Thing (Tan), 44, 45
Lottie & Walter (Walker), 40, 107
Louise, Z.
   Mum for Sale, 157, 171
Love (Averiss), 106
Love, J.
   Julian at the Wedding, 113
   Julian is a Mermaid, 113
Love that Dog (Creech), 71
Lowry, L.
   Gathering Blue, 97
   The Giver, 97
   The Messenger, 97
Lunch at 10 Pomegranate Street (Sala), 83–84
Luqman-Dawson, A.
   Freewater, 172
lyrical poems, 68–69

M is for Mutiny! History by Alphabet (Dickson), 26, 83

Mabbitt, W.
   I Can Only Draw Worms, 159
Macinnis, P.
   Australian Backyard Earth Scientist, 81
   Australian Backyard Explorer, 81
MacLachlan, P.
   The Hundred-Year Barn, 121
MacLeod, E.
   Bunny the Brave War Horse, 124
Mad Magpie (Dreise), 135
Madame Badobedah (Dahl), 44
Mae's First Day of School (Berube), 106
Magerl, C.
   Maya & Cat, 40
Maier, B.
   The Little Red Fort, 95
Main Abija My Grandad (Rogers), 134
Malibirr, J.W.
   Thank You Rain! 138
Mallan, K., 156, 157
Mallery, S.
   A Most Unusual Day, 105
Mama Baby (Raschka), 31
'The Man from Snowy River' (Patterson), 65
Man from Snowy River (Patterson), 67
Mann, J.K.
   The Camping Trip, 112
Marsden, P.
   The Bushfire Book, 83–84
Martin, E.W.
   The Wonderful Things You Will Be, 68
The Marvels (Selznick), 170
Mason, K. and P.
   Amazing Australians in their Flying Machines, 84
The Matchbook Diary (Fleischman), 120
Matilda (Dahl), 157
Matteson, A., 147
Matthew Flinders: Adventures on Leaky Ships (Wilkinson), 85
Maya & Cat (Magerl), 40
Maybe (Haughton), 155
McCartney, T.
   as illustrator, 78
   on picture books, 36
   on realistic fiction, 102
   Australia Illustrated, 83
   The Gum Family Finds Home, 130
   Ivy Bird, 111
   This is Banjo Paterson, 84
   This is Captain Cook, 84

McCord, D.
   'Song of the Train,' 64
McDonald, L., 6, 118
McFarlane, S., 57
McGeachin, J.
   Fly, 50
McGhee, A.
   Bink and Gollie (with DiCamillo), 57
McGhee, P., 160
McGill-Franzen, A., 55–56
McGillis, R., 13
McGregor, A.
   Anemone is not the Enemy, 79
   Colouroos, 31
McInerney, A.
   Bad Crab, 156, 171
McKenna, B.E.
   Ubby's Underdogs, 140
McKenzie, H.
   Butt Out! 161, 163
McKimmie, C.
   I NEED a Parrot, 47
McKinley, A.
   Nine Lives Newton, 155
McKinnon, H.
   Baz and Benz, 10
   I Just Ate My Friend, 103–104
McNair, J.C., 55
McQuire, A.
   Day Break, 139
McWilliams, B.
   Born to Fly, 84
Me and My Fear (Sanna), 108
Me and You (Kelly), 106
Medina, M.
   Merci Suárez Changes Gears, 172
The Mediterranean (Greder), 44–45
Meet Millie (book app), 145
Meet series (Penguin), 84
Meet the Ancient Greeks (Davies), 58
Merci Suárez Changes Gears (Medina), 172
Merrison, C.
   Black Cockatoo (with Hustler), 140
   My Deadly Boots, 134
The Messenger (Lowry), 97
Messier, M.
   Finding Winnie, 124
   Sergeant Billy: The True Story of the Goat Who Went to War, 124
Messing Around on the Monkey Bars (Franco), 69

Metzenthen, D.
    One Runaway Rabbit, 48
Meyer, S.L.
    New Shoes, 120
Mia Moves Out (Paul), 105
Migrants (Watanbe), 110
Miller, P.Z.
    My Brother the Duck, 40, 105
Milo Imagines the World (de la Peña), 113
Milroy, H.
    Backyard Birds, 138
    Backyard Bugs, 138
Mineker, V., 70
Mirror (Baker), 42–43
Mirror Mirror (Singer), 69
Miss Franklin: How Miles Franklin's Brilliant Career Began (Hathorn), 121
Miss Smith Reads Again! (Garland), 91
Miss Smith Under the Ocean (Garland), 91
Miss Smith's Incredible Storybook (Garland), 91
Molly the Pirate (Teece), 133
Monson, D., 156
Moore, G.
    Rise Up: Ordinary Kids with Extraordinary Stories, 85
Mora, O.
    Thank you, Omu! 48
morality and values, 135–136
Morgan, S.
    Joey Counts to Ten, 28, 132
    Little Bird's Day, 138
    The River, 138
    Thank You Rain! 138
    An A to Z Story of Australian Animals, 24–25, 132
Morpurgo, M.
    Poppy Field, 124–125
Morris, R.T.
    Bear Came Along, 46
    This is a Moose, 46
Morris, S. [Sandra]
    North and South, 78, 82
Morris, S. [Suzanne]
    A Trapezoid is Not a Dinosaur! 30
Moses, A.
    Bat vs Poss, 38, 47
A Most Unusual Day (Mallery), 105
motivation, 153–154
Mould, S.
    The Bacteria Book, 79
moving, 40, 110–111
Moving Tales, 145

Mr Chicken series (Hobbs), 12, 36, 160
Mr Chicken All Over Australia (Hobbs), 129, 156
Mr Chicken Goes to Paris (Hobbs), 36, *37*
Mr Huff (Walker), 107
Muir, F.
    Family (with Lawson), 135–136
    Respect (with Lawson), 135–136
multicultural literature, 171–172
Mum for Sale (Louise), 157, 171
Mum's Elephant (O'Keefe), 135
Munde, G., 157
Murphy, J.
    Welcome to Country, 131, 136
    Wilam, 136
Murphy, S.
    Roses are Blue, 71
Murray, G.
    Walter the Farting Dog (with Kotzwinkle), 163
Murray, K.
    Kids Who Did, 85
    Strangers on Country (with Hartley), 139
    When Billy was a Dog, 49
Museum Trip (Lehman), 43
My Beautiful Birds (Del Rizzo), 41, 47, 109
My Bed is an Air Balloon (Copus), 69
My Best Book of Spaceships (Graham), 82
My Brother the Duck (Miller), 40, 105
My Culture and Me (Dreise), 137
My Dead Bunny (Cohen), 158–159
My Deadly Boots (Merrison), 134
My First Book of Haiku Poems (Ramirez-Christensen), 68
My Friend Fred (Watts), 12, 48, 104
My Lost Mob (Tyson), 132
My Name is Henry Fanshaw (Torckler), 124
My New Home (Altés), 111
My Real Friend (Hunt), 36, 40, 103
My Strange Shrinking Parents (Sworder), 44
My Two Blankets (Kobald), 41, 109
The Mysteries of the Universe (DK), 82

Narrative of the Life of Frederick Douglass (Cline-Ransome), 120
narrative poems, 67
National Geographic Kids, 83
A Natural History of Insects in 100 Limericks (Jones), 68
nature, 111–112, 138
Neale, M., 132–133
Never Forget (Hallifax), 123
Never Lose Hope (Wilson), 120

New Kid (Craft), 170
New Shoes (Meyer), 120
New Shoes (Raschka), 30
New Zealand's Backyard Beasts (Barraud), 81
Newbery, J.
    The History of Little Goody Two-Shoes, 38–39, *39*
    A Little Pretty Pocket-book, Intended for the Instruction and Amusement of Little Master Tommy, and Pretty Miss Polly, 39
Newman, L.
    Gittel's Journey, 120
Newton, G.M.
    Hold On! Saving the Spotted Handfish, 80
Nicky & Vera (Sis), 125
Night Walk (Binks), 111
The Night Walk (Dorléans), 111
Nilsen, A., 157
Nilsen, D., 157
Nine Lives Newton (McKinley), 155
Ninni Yabini (Kickett-Tucker), 138
Nix, G., 91
    Old Kingdom series, 96
    transitional novels and, 56
No Swimming for Nelly (Gorbachev), 40
Nodelman P., 16
non-fiction texts
    biography and autobiography, 84–85
    craft and how-to books and, 83–84
    crossover specialised books and, 83
    evaluation criteria for, **85**, 86
    experiment and activity books and, 81–82
    grammar and textual features in, 77–80
    identification books and, 80–81
    importance of, 75–76, 86
    life-cycle books and, 81
    survey books and, 82
Noodle Bear (Gravas), 49–50
North and South (Morris), 78, 82
Norton and the Borrowing Bear (Evans), 104
Norton, D., 37
Not Cute (Bunting), 160
Not Yet, Zebra (Kuenzler), 27
Novak, B.J.
    The Book with No Pictures, 161
novels, **6**
The Numberlys (book app), 146
The Numberlys (Joyce), 146

Ober, P.-J.
    The Good Son: A Story From the First World War, 123

O'Callaghan, J.
    Found in Melbourne, 29
    Found in Sydney: A Counting Adventure, 29
Off We Go Around Australia (Harvey), 130
Oi Dog! series (Gray), 38
Oi Frog! series (Gray), 26
O'Keefe, M.J.N.
    Mum's Elephant, 135
Okorafor, N.
    Binti, 97
Old Friends, New Friends (Daddo), 104
Old Kingdom series (Nix), 96
Older Than Dirt (Brown and Perfit), 170
Olive (Wyatt), 108
Olivia series (Falconer), 112
The One and Only Ivan (Applegate), 71
One Banana, Two Bananas (Guillain and Guillain), 29
One Blue Shoe (Godwin), 29
One Fox: A Counting Book Thriller (Read), 29
One Keen Koala (Wild), 28
One Photo (Watkins), 45, 108
One Runaway Rabbit (Metzenthen), 48
One Step at a Time (Jolly), 44
onomatopoeia, 65
Open Your Heart to Country (Seymour), 137
Opitz, M.F., 4, 55, 153
oral language (speaking), 1–2, **2**, 4
Orpin, B.
    Watch This!: A Book about Making Shapes (with Godwin), 30
Oscar's American Dream (Wittenstein), 121
Oswald, P.
    Hike, 112
Ottley, M., 36, 95
Our Country: Ancient Wonders (Greenwood), 130
Our Place series
    (Muir and Lawson), 135–136
Out of the Dust (Hesse), 71
Out of Wonder (Alexander et al.), 72
Over the Hills and Far Away (Hammill), 66
Overground Railroad (Cline-Ransome), 120
Owl Moon (Yolen), (111

Page, R.
    The Shark Book, 76
    What Do You Do if You Work at the Zoo? 76
Palatini, M.
    The Web Files, 12–13
The Panda Problem (Underwood), 158
Pandemic (Frech), 123

Paolini, C.
    Eragon, 91, 96
A Parade of Animals (Priddy), 28
Park, L., 57
Park, M.
    D-Bot Squad series, 57
Parker, A.
    Twig, 106
Parker, D.
    Sarah and the Steep Slope, 107
Parr, T., 20
Pascoe, B.
    Found, 131, 135
    Young Dark Emu: A Truer History, 172
Pat the Bunny (Kunhardt), 22
Patterson, B.
    'The Man from Snowy River,' 65
    Man from Snowy River, 67
    Waltzing Matilda, 67
    We're All Australians Now, 67
Paul, M.
    Mia Moves Out, 105
Paula Knows What To Do (Dufft), 109
The Pedlar Lady of Gushing Cross (book app), 145
Penny and Penelope (Richards), 95
Percival, T.
    Ruby's Worry, 107
Percy Jackson and the Lightning Thief (Riordan), 93
Percy Jackson series (Riordan), 91
A Perfect Pig (Dreiling), 104
Perfit, M.
    Older Than Dirt (with Brown), 170
Perkins, G.
    A Walk in the Bush, 111
Phi, B.
    A Different Pond, 41, 110
physical humour, 155, 158–159
picture books
    audience and, 48–49
    digital texts as, 145, 146, 149
    evaluation criteria for, 45, **46**, 50, 162–163
    fantasy literature and, 41–42, 93–96
    format and, 46–47
    humour in, 154–155, 156, 158–159, 160–161, 162
    importance and benefits of, 4, **6**, 35–37, 50
    language in, 49–50
    lessons in, 38–39
    non-fiction texts as, 79–80
    for older readers, 44–45
    poetry and, 70

reading aloud and, 11–12
realistic themes in, 40
refugees in, 41, 44–45
role of animals in, 38, 102
role of illustrations in, 11–12, 47–48
social issues in, 40–41
type and font in, 47
as wordless, 42–44
Pig the Pug (Blabey), 38, 156
Pilkey, D.
    Dog Breath, 163
Playing with Collage (Baker), 77, 83–84
Poetree (Reynolds), 70
poetry
    compilations and, 71–72
    creative versions and, 69
    evaluation criteria for, **72**
    free verse and, 70–71
    importance of, 63–64, 72–73
    lyrical poems and, 68–69
    picture books and, 70
    rhythm and, 64–68, *67*
A Poke in the Eye (Janeczko), 69
Polacco, P.
    Tucky Jo and Little Heart, 125
politics, 139–140
polygenesis, 90
Pool (Lee), 43
pop-up books, 22
Poppy Field (Morpurgo), 124–125
Possum Magic (Fox), 47, 49, 129
post-colonial theory, **15**
post-structuralism, **14**
postmodernism, **14**
Potato Pants (Keller), 160
Press Here (Tullet), 23, 161
Preston-Gannon, F., 72
Priddy, R.
    A Parade of Animals, 28
Prior, N.J.
    A Boat of Stars: New Australian Children's Poems (with Connolly), 71
The Proper Way to Meet a Hedgehog (Janeczko), 72
Pryor, B.M.
    Story Doctors, 137–138
Purdie, S.
    Shirley Purdie, 134
Pyke, J.
    Family Tree, 106
    Light's Out, Leonard, 108

Quest (Becker), 95

Racklyeft, J.
   Dreaming of Australia A to Z, 24–25, *25*
Raczka, B.
   Guyku, 68
   Wet Cement: A Mix of Concrete Poems, 69
Radio Rescue! (Jolly), 122
Ramirez-Christensen, E.
   My First Book of Haiku Poems, 68
Ranger's Apprentice series (Flanagan), 91
Ransome, J.E.
   The Bell Rang, 119
Raschka, C.
   as illustrator, 47, 69
   A Ball for Daisy, 43
   Daisy Gets Lost, 43
   Dear Substitute, 106
   Mama Baby, 31
   New Shoes, 30
   A Song About Myself, 70
The Read-Aloud Handbook (Trelease), 7
Read, K.
   One Fox: A Counting Book Thriller, 29
reading, 1–2, **2**, 5
reading aloud
   digital texts and, 148–149
   humour and, 161–162
   importance of, 7–13, **8**, *8*, 16
   picture books and, 35, 42
   poetry and, 64, 69
   See also beginning books
Ready Rabbit? (Roberton), 40
realistic fiction
   community in, 113–114
   death and dying in, 108–109
   evaluation criteria for, 102–103, **103**
   family in, 104–106
   fears in, 107–108
   feelings and emotions in, 106–107
   friendship in, 103–104
   identity in, 112–113
   importance and benefits of, 101–102, 114
   moving in, 110–111
   nature in, 111–112
   refugees in, 109–110
   school in, 106
   See also historical fiction
realistic themes, 40, 132–134
The Red Book (Lehman), 43
The Red Tree (Tan), 44

Reeder, S.O.
   Australia's Wild Weird Wonderful Weather, 78
   Will the Wonderkid: Treasure Hunter of the Australian Outback, 85
refugees, 41, 44–45, 85, 109–110
Reibstein, M.
   Wabi Sabi, 68
   Yugen, 68
Reimer, M., 16
Respect (Muir and Lawson), 135–136
Return (Becker), 95
Rex, A.
   Ava's Spectacular Spectacles, 90–91
Reynolds, S.L.
   Poetree, 70
rhyme patterns, 65, 68
rhythm, 49, 64–68, *67*
Richards, D.
   Penny and Penelope, 95
   Watch Me, 120–121
Richards, K.
   Goldilocks and the Three Koalas, 129
Riddle, T.
   Yahoo Creek: An Australian Mystery, 76
RIF (Reading is Fundamental), 147
Riordan, R.
   Percy Jackson and the Lightning Thief, 93
   Percy Jackson series, 91
Rippen, S., 54
Rippin, S.
   Billie B. Brown series, 56, 59
   Hey Jack! series, 56, 59
Rise Up: Ordinary Kids with Extraordinary Stories (Moore), 85
The River (Morgan), 138
Roach, A.
   Took the Children Away, 139
Roberton, F.
   Ready Rabbit? 40
Robinson, H.
   Christmas Truce, 125
   Where the Poppies Now Grow, 125
Robobaby (Wiesner), 95
Rockford's Rock Opera (book app), 146
Rockhopping and Landing with Wings (Balla), 112
Rockpools: A Guide for Kiwi Kids (Barraud), 81
Rocky and Louie (Walleystack and Caisley), 134
Rodda, E.
   Rondo series, 91, 93
Rodney Loses It! (Bauer), 13, 156

Rogers, K.
  Main Abija My Grandad, 134
Rondo series (Rodda), 91, 93
Roo Knows Blue (Treml), 31
Room on our Rock (Temple and Temple), 45
Rosen, M.
  Uncle Gobb series, 58
Rosenberg, S.
  H is for Haiku: A Treasury of Haiku from A to Z, 68
Roser, N., 54
Roses are Blue (Murphy), 71
Ross Johnston, R., 130, 131, 135, 137–138
Rowe, A.
  Jetty Jumping, 107
Rowling, J.K.
  Harry Potter series, 91, 93, 96
Ruby's Worry (Percival), 107

Sabuda, R., 22
Sala, F.
  Lunch at 10 Pomegranate Street, 83–84
Sanders, B.
  Bad Apple (with Lewis), 161
Sanna, F.
  Me and My Fear, 108
Sarah and the Steep Slope (Parker), 107
Sargeant, B., 144, 149
Sarzin, L.
  Stories for Simon, 119
Saturday is Swimming Day (Yum), (107
Saunders, K.
  Bindi, 140
  The Incredible Freedom Machines, 95
Savage, S.
  Where's Walrus? 43
Saxby, C.
  The ANZAC Billy, 124
  Kookaburra, 79, 80
Say Yes, A Story of Friendship, Fairness and a Vote for Hope (Castles), 119
school, 40, 69, 106
School of Monsters series (Rippen), 54
Schumann, J.
  I Was Only Nineteen, 123
science fiction, 97
Scieszka, J., 154
  Battle Bunny (with Barnett), 170–171
  The Stinky Cheese Man and Other Fairly Stupid Tales, 42, 90
  The True Story of the Three Little Pigs, 42, 90, 91
Scott, H.
  Teacup House series, 58

Searching for Cicadas (Gibbes), 79
Second World War, 125–126
The Secret Box (Lehman), 43
Seden, P., 133
  Crabbing With Dad, 134
  Kick With My Left Foot, 133
See the Cat: Three Stories About a Dog (LaRochelle), 59
Seeds, Bees, Butterflies, and More! (Gerber), 69
Seinfeld, J.
  Halloween, 48
Selznick, B.
  Big Tree, 170
  The Invention of Hugo Cabret, 169–170
  The Marvels, 170
  Wonderstruck, 170
Sendak, M.
  Where the Wild Things Are, 94
Senna, F.
  The Journey, 45
Sergeant Billy: The True Story of the Goat Who Went to War (Messier), 124
Seymour, J.
  Baby Business, 137, 172
  Open Your Heart to Country, 137
Shake the Tree! (Borando), 46
Shamsi-Basha, K.
  The Cat Man of Aleppo (with Latham), 125–126
Shapes and Colours (Canty), 30
The Sharey Godmother (Berger), 94–95
The Shark Book (Page), 76
Sharratt, N., 58
She'll Be Coming Round the Mountain (Topp Twins), 42
Shhh! We Have a Plan (Haughton), 155
Shirley Purdie (Purdie), 134
Shooting at the Stars (Hendrix), 124
The Shop Train (Boyle), 122
Sibberson, F., 53–54
'Sick' (Silverstein), 65
Silly Birds (Dreise), 135
Silverstein, S.
  'Sick,' 65
Singer, M.
  Feel the Beat, 72
  Follow Follow, 69
  Mirror Mirror, 69
  Wild in the Streets: 20 Poems of City Animals, 72
Sipe, L.R., 168, 169, 170, 171
Sis, P.
  Nicky & Vera, 125

Skybrary, 147
Slater, P.
   First Field Guide to Australian Frogs & Reptiles, 80
slavery, 119–120
Smith, J., 90, 158
Smith, L., 42
Snicket, L.
   The Dark, 108
'Snowy Benches' (Fisher), 66
social issues, 40–41
social justice, 109–110
A Soldier, a Dog and a Boy (Hathorn), 124
Somebody's Land (Goodes), 137
A Song About Myself (Raschka), 70
'Song of the Train' (McCord), 64
Sorry Day (Vass), 119, 140, 172
Space Band (Fletcher), 171
Space on Earth (Kalani), 82
The Space Race (Yalda), 79
speaking (oral language), 1–2, **2**, 4
Speechley, M.
   The All New Must Have Orange 430, 45
Stanford, S.
   The Amazing Recycling Project Book, 83–84
Starting School (Godwin), 40, 106
Steffensen, V.
   Looking After Country with Fire, 137
Stein, D.E.
   Interrupting Chicken series, 91
Steve Goes to Carnival (Button), 133
Stewart, S.
   What's Out There? Amazing Plants, Rocks, Creatures, and Cultures that Make Australia Extraordinary, 82
The Stinky Cheese Man and Other Fairly Stupid Tales (Scieszka), 42, 90
Stolen Generation, 119
Stories for Simon (Sarzin), 119
Stormy Seas: Stories of Young Boat Refugees (Leatherdale), 85
Story Doctors (Pryor), 137–138
Storybox, 147
Strangers on Country (Hartley and Murray), 139
Stubby: A True Story of Friendship (Foreman), 124
Suri's Wall (Estela), 36
survey books, 82
Survivors (Long), 85
Sweep (Greig), 107
Sworder, Z.
   My Strange Shrinking Parents, 44
Szymusiak, K., 53–54

Tacky the Penguin series (Lester), 159
Takei, G.
   They Called Us Enemy, 125
Tales From Outer Suburbia (Tan), 44
Tan, S.
   The Arrival, 43, 44, 45, 170
   Cicada, 44, 46
   Eric, 46
   The Lost Thing, 44, 45
   The Red Tree, 44
   Tales From Outer Suburbia, 44
Tanner, L.
   Ella and the Ocean, 48
Tap, Tap, Tap: Dance, Dance, Dance (Tullet), 23
Tarakson, S
   Aliens, Ghosts and Vanishings, 76
Taylor, M.
   100 Ways to Fly, 71
Taylor, S.
   I am Actually a Penguin, 49
Tea and Sugar Christmas (Jolly), 122
Teacup House series (Scott), 58
Teece, L.
   Molly the Pirate, 133
Temple, C., 64, 89, 94, 102
Temple, J. and K.
   Room on our Rock, 45
Ten Little Fingers and Ten Little Toes (Fox), 13
Ten Pound Pom (Griffiths), 120
Ten Sleepy Sheep (Treml), 29
Thank you, Omu! (Mora), 48
Thank You Rain! (Morgan), 138
That Book Woman (Henson), 121
That's Not My . . . series (Watt), 22
Theodor Seuss Geisel Award, 59
They Called Us Enemy (Takei), 125
This Book is Gray (Ward), 31
This is a Book of Shapes (Kraegel), 30
This is a Moose (Morris), 46
This is Banjo Paterson (McCartney), 84
This is Captain Cook (McCartney), 84
This is Not My Hat (Klassen), 9, 38, 156, 162
This is Where I Stand (Werry), 123
Thomas, J.
   Can You Make a Scary Face? 11
Thomas, K.
   Allergic Alpaca, 27
Three Billy Goats Gruff (Bland), 42, 90
The Three Billy Goats Gruff (Jackson), 90

Three (King), 48
The Three Little Bush Pigs (Dallimore), 91, 129
The Three Pigs (Wiesner), 91
Tidy, S.
   The Day We Built the Bridge, 121–122
Tiger, Tiger, Burning Bright! (Waters), 72
Tilly (Godwin), 48–49
Tilly (Walker), 105
The Tiny Star (Fox), 108
To the Bridge (Fenton), 36, 121–122
To the Top End (Harvey), 130
Tolkien, J.R.R.
   The Hobbit, 92–93
   The Lord of the Rings, 92–93
Tolman, M.
   The Treehouse, 43–44
Tomsic, M., 172
Took the Children Away (Roach), 139
Topp Twins
   She'll Be Coming Round the Mountain, 42
Torckler, G.
   My Name is Henry Fanshaw, 124
The Tough Guide to Fantasyland (Jones), 96, 98
toy books, 22
Traction Man series (Grey), 94
transitional novels, **6**, 53–60, **60**
A Trapezoid is Not a Dinosaur! (Morris), 30
Treehouse book series (Griffiths), 169
The Treehouse (Tolman), 43–44
Trelease, J., 7
Treml, R.
   Roo Knows Blue, 31
   Ten Sleepy Sheep, 29
Trick Number Two (Bland), 94
The True Story of the Three Little Pigs (Scieszka), 42, 90, 91
Tucky Jo and Little Heart (Polacco), 125
Tullet, H.
   Press Here, 23, 161
   Tap, Tap, Tap: Dance, Dance, Dance, 23
Tulloch, S.
   I am Not a Worm, 159
   Keep an Eye on this Kiwi, 157
Tunnell, M., 63, 64, 93, 107
Turner, R.
   Whose Nose Do You Suppose? 80
Tutt, C.
   The First Scientists, 140
Twig (Parker), 106
Tyson, V.
   My Lost Mob, 132

Ubby's Underdogs (McKenna), 140
The Ultimate Animal Counting Book (Cossins), 83
Uncle Gobb series (Rosen), 58
The Underhills: A Tooth Fairy Story (Graham), 94
The Underwater Fancy-Dress Parade (Bell), 40
Underwood, D.
   The Panda Problem, 158
The Upper Case (Lazar), 161
The Upside-down History of Down Under (Lloyd), 83
Urban, L.
   Weekends with Max and His Dad, 59

Vanilla Ice Cream (Graham), *3*, 4, 46
Vass, C.
   Grandma's Treasured Shoes, 110
   Sorry Day, 119, 140, 172
The Very Bad Book (Griffiths), 67, *67*
The Very Cranky Bear (Bland), 38, 49
viewing and visual literacy, 1–4, **2**, *3*, 167–170. *See also* picture books
visualisation, 12
Vooks, 147

Wabi Sabi (Reibstein), 68
Wagner, M.
   Dirt by Sea, 130
A Walk in the Bush (Perkins), 111
Walker, A.
   as illustrator, 113–114
   Florette, 111
   Hello, Jimmy! 50, 105–106
   Lottie & Walter, 40, 107
   Mr Huff, 107
   Tilly, 105
Walleystack, P.
   Rocky and Louie (with Caisley), **134**
Walsh, M., 148, 168
Walter the Farting Dog (Kotzwinkle and Murray), 163
Waltzing Matilda (Patterson), 67
Wang, A.
   Watercress, 41, 110
Want to Play Trucks? (Graham), 112–113
war, 67, 123–126
Ward, L.
   This Book is Gray, 31
Ward, N., 55–56
Watanbe, I.
   Migrants, 110
Watch Me (Richards), 120–121
Watch This!: A Book about Making Shapes (Godwin and Orpin), 30

Watercress (Wang), 41, 110
Waters, C.
　Can I Touch Your Hair? (with Latham), 70
Waters, F.
　I Am the Seed that Grew the Tree, 72
　Tiger, Tiger, Burning Bright! 72
Watkins, R.
　One Photo, 45, 108
Watt, F.
　That's Not My . . . series, 22
Watts, F.
　My Friend Fred, 12, 48, 104
We are Family (Hegarty), 106
We Are Water Protectors (Lindstrom), 172
We Found a Hat (Klassen), 156
The Web Files (Palatini), 12–13
Weekends with Max and His Dad (Urban), 59
Weidenbach, K.
　King of the Outback, 122
Weirdwood Manor series (book app), 145–146
Welcome to Country, 136
Welcome to Country (Murphy), 131, 136
Wemberly Worried (Henkes), 40, 107
Wentworth, M., 72
We're All Australians Now (Patterson), 67
We're Stuck! (deGennaro), 46
Werry, P.
　This is Where I Stand, 123
Wet Cement: A Mix of Concrete Poems (Raczka), 69
What Did the Tree See? (Guillain), 121
What Do You Do if You Work at the Zoo? (Page), 76
Whatcha Building? (Daddo), 113
Whatley, B., 28, 41, 47
What's Out There? Amazing Plants, Rocks, Creatures, and Cultures that Make Australia Extraordinary (Stewart), 82
When Billy was a Dog (Murray), 49
When Numbers Met Letters (Barr), 29
When the War is Over (Frech), 123
Where Do They Go? (Alvarez), 68
Where the Poppies Now Grow (Robinson), 125
Where the Wild Things Are (Sendak), 94
Where's Jessie? (Brian), 122–123
Where's Walrus? (Savage), 43
'Which Jack?' (Green), 65
The Whispering Town (Elvgren), 125
White, D.
　Green on Green, 31
White, E.B.
　Charlotte's Web, 91
Whiting, S.
　Good Question: A Tale Told Backwards, 42
Who Sank the Boat? (Allen), 38
Whose Nose Do You Suppose? (Turner), 80
Wiesner, D.
　Flotsam, 43
　Robobaby, 95
　The Three Pigs, 91
Wilam (Murphy), 136
Wild Animals of the North (Braun), 76
Wild Bush Days (Harrison), 122
Wild in the Streets: 20 Poems of City Animals (Singer), 72
Wild, M.
　The Feather, 45
　Girl from the Sea, 10, 45
　Goodbye House, Hello House, 47, 111
　One Keen Koala, 28
Wild Symphony (Brown), 69, 146
Wilhelm, J., 3, 12
Wilkinson, C.
　Matthew Flinders: Adventures on Leaky Ships, 85
Will the Wonderkid: Treasure Hunter of the Australian Outback (Reeder), 85
Willems, M., 54
　Don't Let the Pigeon Drive the Bus! 36
　Goldilocks and the Three Dinosaurs, 42
Williams, G., 36
Wilsdorf, A., 11
Wilson, M.
　as illustrator, 67
　Beth: The Story of a Child Convict, 120
　Eureka! A Story of the Goldfields, 122
　Flapper, VC, 125
　The Little Wooden Horse, 120
　Never Lose Hope, 120
Winch, G.
　on literacy, 1, 4, 5, 6, 7, 42, 77
　on multicultural literature, 171–172
　Can You Find 12 Busy Bees? 29
Window (Baker), 43
Windows (Guest), 41
A Wise Use of Time (book app), 145
Wittenstein, B.
　Oscar's American Dream, 121
Wolfie: An Unlikely Hero (Abela), 42
The Wonderful Things You Will Be (Martin), 68
The Wonderful World of Ants (Bunting), 171
Wonderscope (app), 146
Wonderstruck (Selznick), 170

Woodson, J., 172
Woolf, J.
   Duck and Penguin Are NOT Friends, 9, 154–155
wordless picture books, 42–44
Wren (Lehman), 105
Wright, E.
   Charlie's Swim, 125
A Wrinkle in Time (L'Engle), 91
Write To Me: Letters from Japanese American Children to the Librarian They Left Behind (Grady), 125
writing, 1–2, **2**, 5
Wyatt, E.
   Olive, 108

Yahoo Creek: An Australian Mystery (Riddle), 76
Yalda, A.
   The Space Race, 79
Yang, Y.
   The Flying Light, 43

Yoelu, M.
   Brother Moon, 138
Yolen, J.
   on fantasy literature, 96
   Owl Moon, 111
young adult literature, 5, **6**
Young, D., 19, 35–36
Young Dark Emu: A Truer History (Pascoe), 172
Young, E., 68
Your Birthday was the Best! (Hutchings), 159
Your School is the Best (Hutchings), 159
You're Called What? (Gray), 161
Yugen (Reibstein), 68
Yum, H.
   Saturday is Swimming Day, 107

Zac Power series (Larry), 57, 59
Zbaracki, M.D., 4, 5, 153, 163, 168, 169, 172
Zoe, Max, and the Bicycle Bus (Herrick), 70–71